GROWTH OF REAL SECTOR IN INDIAN ECONOMY

GROWTH OF REAL SECTOR IN INDIAN ECONOMY

Editors

ANIL KUMAR THAKUR

and

DALIP KUMAR

Published on behalf of
THE INDIAN ECONOMIC ASSOCIATION

DEEP & DEEP PUBLICATIONS PVT. LTD.
F-159, Rajouri Garden, New Delhi - 110 027

GROWTH OF REAL SECTOR IN INDIAN ECONOMY

ISBN 978-81-8450-064-6

Typeset by RAHUL COMPOSERS
358, Pocket-B, Phase-II, Sector 16-B, Dwarka, New Delhi - 110 075

Printed in India at NEW ELEGANT PRINTERS
A-49/1, Mayapuri, Phase-I, New Delhi - 110 064

Published by DEEP & DEEP PUBLICATIONS PVT. LTD.,
F-159, Rajouri Garden, New Delhi - 110 027 • Phone : 25435369, 25440916
E-mail : ddpubs@gmail.com • ddpbooks@yahoo.co.in
Showroom :
2/13, Ansari Road, Daryaganj, New Delhi - 110 002 • Telefax : 23245122

Contents

Foreword

Indian economy has undergone a rapid structural tıansformation in the past few decades. While the share of primary sector in Gross Domestic Product (GDP) declined from 59.2 per cent in 1950-51 to about 21.1 per cent in 2005-06, that of tertiary sector increased from 27.5 per cent in 1950-51 to 54.1 per cent in 2005-06 and the share of secondary sector increased from 13.3 per cent in 1950-51 to 24.8 per cent in 2005-06. However, one needs to analyse whether such a structural change in the economy affects the social inclusion in the process of growth. In the past few years, the GDP at factor cost has increased at the rate of about 8 to 9 per cent per year, while the annual growth rate of agricultural GDP was less than 2 per cent. The declining share of agriculture in GDP has not been associated with proportionate decline in agricultural workforce. Even the overall increase in GDP growth rate has not been associated with proportionate increase in employment. Also the performance of different regions have varied widely. As a result, inter-sectoral and inter-regional disparities in growth are on the increase. The book entitled, 'Growth of Real Sector in Indian Economy', edited by Anil Kumar Thakur and Dalip Kumar merits close reading by all concerned, as various papers included in the book analyse the growth patterns from various angles. The growth patterns of income, employment, savings and investment in various sectors and regions have been analysed and presented in a lucid and interesting manner. I am sure, the book will be of great value and interest to planners, policy-makers, teachers, students and all those concerned about rapid, albeit inclusive growth of Indian economy.

T. HAQUE
Chairman
Commission for Agricultural Costs and Prices
Government of India, New Delhi

List of Contributors

A.K. Choudhary, Department of Agricultural Economics, Rajendra Agricultural University, Pusa, Bihar.

Amalendu Kumar, Research Officer, Agro-Economic Research Centre for Bihar & Jharkhand, T.M. Bhagalpur University, Bhagalpur.

Anjani Kumari Jha, Chairman, Development of Indian Society and Culture, Delhi.

Ashwini Kant Jha, Professor of Economics, BNM University (W.C.), P.G. Centre, Saharsa, Bihar.

Bal Krishna Jha, University Professor, Department of Rural Economics and Co-operation, S.K.M. University, Dumka.

Bhavna Jha, Lecturer in IRPM, MAM College, Naugachhia, T.M. Bhagalpur University, Bihar.

Birendra Kumar, Department of Ancient History, Kisori Sinha College, Aurangabad, Bihar.

D.K. Sinha, Department of Agricultural Economics, Rajendra Agricultural University, Pusa, Bihar.

Dalip Kumar, Manager (Projects), National Council of Applied Economic Research, New Delhi.

Dhananjay Kumar, Department of Geography, S.G.G.S. College, Patna City, Patna (Bihar).

K.B. Padmadeo, Department of Applied Economics & Commerce, S.B.A.N. College Darheta Lari, Arwal (Bihar).

Krishna Nand Yadav, Department of Economics, R.L.S.Y. College, Aurangabad (Bihar).

Kumar Ratnesh, Lecturer, Department of P.G. Studies and Research in Economics, Pt. J.N.P.G. College, Banda (U.P.).

Md. Masood Alam, Research Scholar, Department of Rural Economics & Co-operation, T.M. Bhagalpur University, Bhagalpur.

Md. Tarique, University Department of Economics, B.R.A. Bihar University, Muzaffarpur.

Meera Ranjan Lal, Department of Economics, J.D. Womens College, Patna, Bihar.

N.K. Thakur, Marketing Manager, GNFC Limited, Lucknow.

Narendra Prasad, Department of Economics, Magadh University, Bodh Gaya.

Niranjan Kumar Jha, Coordinator, Development of Indian Society and Culture, Delhi.

P.N. Sharma, Prof. (Rtd.), P.G. Department of Economics, Nalanda College, Biharsharif.

R.K.P. Singh, Department of Agricultural Economics, Rajendra Agricultural University, Pusa, Bihar.

Reeta Sinha, Lecturer in Economics, T.N.B. Law College, Bhagalpur.

Ruddar Datt, Visiting Professor, Institute for Human Development, New Delhi, Formerly, University of Delhi, Delhi.

Shambhu Deo Mishra, Research Associate, Agro-Economic Research Centre for Bihar & Jharkhand, Bhagalpur.

Sita Ram Singh, Principal & Professor of Economics, A.N. College, Patna, Bihar.

Sri Niwas Pandey, Department of Applied Economics & Commerce, S.B.A.N. College, Darheta Lari, Arwal (Bihar).

Vinod Kumar, Department of Agricultural Economics, Rajendra Agricultural University, Pusa, Bihar.

Abbreviations

AMS - Agricultural Marketing Service
CDS - Current Daily Status
COMFED - Co-operative Milk Producers' Federation Limited
CSO - Central Statistical Organisation
CWS - Current Weekly Status
DES - Directorate of Economic and Statistics
DGET - Director General of Employment and Training
EPIP - European Policy for Intellectual Property
EPZ - Export Promoting Zone
ESB - Employment on Salary Basis
EXIM - Export Import Policy
FCI - Food Corporation of India
FYM - Farm Yard Manure
GATT - General Agreement on Tariff and Trade
GCA - Gross Cropped Area
GDCF - Gross Domestic Capital Formation
GDP - Gross Domestic Product
GDS - Gross Domestic Saving
HYV - High Yield Variety
IADP - Integrated Agricultural/Rural Development Project
IIP - Index for Industrial Production
IMF - International Monetary Fund

IPR	-	Intellectual Property Rights
ISID	-	Institute for Studies in Industrial Development
IT	-	Information Technology
KVIC	-	Khadi and Village Industries Corporation
LPG	-	Liberalisation, Privatisation and Globalisation
MCP	-	Microsoft Certified Professional
MPCE	-	Monthly Per Capita Expenditure
MSP	-	Minimum Support Price
MT	-	Metric Tonne
NIC	-	National Industry Code
NRI	-	Non-residence of India
NS	-	Non-significant
NSSO	-	National Sample Survey Organisation
PMGSY	-	Pradhan Mantri Gram Sadak Yojana
PMGY	-	Pradhan Mantri Grammoday Yojana
PPP	-	Purchasing Power Parity
QR	-	Quantitative Restriction
RBI	-	Reserve Bank of India
SAP	-	Structural Adjustment Programme
SDP	-	State Domestic Product
SE	-	Self Employment
SGSY	-	Swaranjayanti Gram Sawarojgar Yojana
SMEs	-	Small and Medium Enterprises
SRGY	-	Sampoorna Gramin Rojgar Yojana
SSI	-	Small Scale Industry
TRIPs	-	Trade Related Intellectual Property's
TFR	-	Total Factor Productivity
TII	-	Total Input Index
TOI	-	Total Output Index
UPA	-	United Progressive Alliance
UPS	-	Usual Principal Status
UPSS	-	Usual Principal and Subsidiary Status
UR	-	Uruguay Round
WE	-	Wage Paid Employment

Introduction

Real sector refers to the sector in which productions of goods and services are carried through combined utilization of raw materials and other production factors such as labour force, land and capital or by means of production process. The Indian economy is the third largest in the world as measured by Purchasing Power Parity (PPP). When measured in USD exchange-rate terms, it is the twelfth largest in the world, with a GDP of US $ 1.0 trillion (2007). India is the second fastest growing economy in the world, with a GDP growth rate of 9.4 per cent for the fiscal year 2006-07. However, India's huge population results in a per capita income of $ 4,031 at PPP and $ 885 at nominal (2007 estimate). The World Bank classifies India as a low-income economy. Two-thirds of the Indian workforce still earn their livelihood directly or indirectly through agriculture. Services are the growing sector and are playing an increasingly important role in India's economy. Primary sector was dominant sector of the economy up to 1980s. But the whole scenario changed by 1980s. In 1980s, the service sector output increased the rate of 6.63 per cent per annum in 1990s to 7.71 per cent. In 2006-07. This sector has maintained 11.1 per cent per annum growth (*Economic Survey*, 2006-07). The real estate sector comprises of a collection of both industrial and service sectors. The year 2006 saw real estate boom and is to gather further momentum in year 2007. The Prime Minister's Economic Advisory Council too has projected the growth of 9.0 per cent for Indian economy in 2007-08. The

Council's forecast is higher than the RBI's estimate of 8.5 per cent growth for 2007-08. However, according to 'Economist' (May 21, 2007), India's real GDP growth is likely to moderate slightly to 8.5 per cent in 2007-08.

TRENDS OF EMPLOYMENT IN REAL SECTOR

India is fifteenth in services output. It provides employment to 23 per cent of work force, and it is growing fast at the growth rate of 7.5 per cent in 1991-2000 which is up from 4.5 per cent in 1951-80. It has the largest share in the GDP, accounting for 53.8 per cent in 2005 up from 15 per cent in 1950. The growth in the (Information Technology) IT sector is attributed to increased specialisation, availability of a large pool of low cost, but highly skilled, educated and fluent English-speaking workers on the supply side and on the demand side, increased demand from foreign consumers interested in India's service experts or those looking to outsource their operations. Unemployment in India is characterised by chronic underemployment or disguised employment. Government schemes that target eradication of both poverty and unemployment, (which in recent decades has sent millions of poor and unskilled people into urban areas in search of livelihoods) attempt to solve the problem, by providing financial assistance for setting up businesses, skill honing, setting up public sector enterprises, reservations in governments, etc. The decreased role of the public sector after liberalisation has further underlined the need for focusing on better education and has also put political pressure on further reforms. In August 2005, the Indian parliament passed the *Rural Employment Guarantee Bill*, the largest programme of this type in terms of cost and coverage, which promises 100 days of minimum wage employment to every rural household in 2007 in India's 600 districts. Animal husbandry and dairying are vital sectors of India's economy, more particularly the rural economy. It provides a significant proportion of self-employment opportunity in the employment generated in the agriculture livestock sector.

Eminent economist Ruddar Datt presents a lucid picture of 'Employment and Unemployment in India'. The regime of controls and licenses had resulted into corruption and formation of nexus between the politicians and bureaucrats, which was acting as a shackle on the growth process. Hence, economic liberalisation was hailed in the same manner as socialism was considered to be the only method of achieving growth with social justice during the first four decades of planned development in the 20th century. The period between 1977-78 to 1993-94 witnessed the declining trend in all the four categories of unemployment. The chapter peeps through the unemployment scenario highlighting the rural-urban disparities, male-female ratio, regional differences, organised-unorganised dichotomy, differences in self-employment, salaried and casual employment, etc. On the basis of available data and investigative analysis, the author has presented some pragmatic future strategies. The only answer to the grim situation is to increase the productivity and quality of the unorganised sector by removing the growth constraints and ensuring a level playing field for this sector. To increase the labour productivity, more emphasis should be given on the growth of the organised sector than on substituting labour by capital. To improve the job, quality and its security, legislative changes are needed with regard to basic social security measures, working condition, minimum wages and protection of labour interests.

Owing to the momentous changes in the world economy in the last decade of the 20th century, and subsequent liberalisation policy adopted by most of the countries, India also responded by introducing wide economic reforms. The basic objective was to lay the foundation of sustained growth of output and employment in the context of increasing global competition. The increase of the GDP growth rate during last 16 years of reform was not accompanied by a commensurate increase in employment. The reason was near stagnation of employment in public sector due to its withdrawal from several areas, down-sizing of labour forces in this sector and shedding off excess labour as well as introduction of new and modern technology by private sector in the wake of fierce global competition due to rapid liberalisation. Analysing various data, the author P.N. Sharma has touched upon various aspects of employment and unemployment dimensions like trends in employment in terms of GDP growth, and sectoral changes in the employment rate in the organised sector. The author discussed the findings and recommendations by Special Task force of employment and unemployment by the Planning Commission and hints at the future strategies to face the challenges of reduction in unemployment.

'Growth and Employment in Indian Economy: An Analysis of Sectoral Composition, Trends and Gender Issues', written by Dalip Kumar, is an attempt to explore the employment growth in the public and private sectors during 1990s. Depending mainly on the secondary data, this paper investigates the employment and unemployment structure through various angles. It explains the trends of employment growth both in public and private sectors, changes in the employment pattern by industry division, inter-state disparities in employment. The paper focuses on various aspects of women's employment like changing pattern in the organised and unorganised sector, comparative estimate of women employment in major states, women employment by status, female employment in agricultural sector, etc. Referring to the various theories, the author opines that the Demand-management Policies based on the Keynesian theory is more relevant in the present Indian context. Lamenting at the slackening employment opportunities due to lack of invisible resources in the state of Bihar, despite considerable potential, the author suggests that the state should encourage financial institutions and private sectors to establish and maintain industrial growth and various infrastructure projects.

India's growth performance in the period 1950-51 to 1980-81 witnessed economic growth average close to 3.5 per cent but it is the same period the growth of per capita GDP was hardly 1.5 per cent. There was a dismal rise in the living standard of the masses. Economic growth accelerated to 5.6 per cent in 1980, and per capita growth average to 3.5 per cent. The last decade witnessed the fastest growth in India's recorded history. India assumed the rank among the 10 fastest growing countries of the world. In the chapter 'Uneven Growth Trend: Some Policy Concerns'. Kumar Ratnesh analyses some data to find the sectoral variations in the GDP growth, Saving and Investment, and uneven growth in different regions in terms of per capita income. The sustainable economic growth hinges on the availability of infrastructures. In absence of strongly enabling environment and transparent regulatory mechanism, there has been no adequate investment in private sector to compensate for the decline in the public spending in infrastructure.

GROWTH IN AGRICULTURAL SECTOR

The agriculture sector, which has been so long the mainstay of the Indian Economy, now accounts for only about 18.5 per cent of GDP in 2006-07, yet employs over 50 per cent of the population. For some years after independence, India depended on foreign aid to meet its food needs, but in the last 35 years, food production has risen steadily, mainly due to the increase in irrigated areas and widespread use of high-yield varieties of seeds, fertilizers, and pesticides. The country has large grain stockpiles (around 45 million tons) and is a net exporter of food grains. Agriculture has faced stagnation in growth; services have seen a steady growth. Of the total workforce, 8 per cent is in the organised sector, two-thirds of which are in the public sector.

Agriculture and allied sectors like forestry, logging and fishing accounted for 18.5 per cent of the GDP in 2005, employed 60 per cent of the total workforce and despite a steady decline of its share in the GDP, is still the largest economic sector and plays a significant role in the overall socio-economic development of India. With a creditable showing by the agricultural sector, except in 2002-03, the growth in the Gross Domestic Product (GDP) has been quite impressive and the peak of 8.5 per cent was reached in 2003-04, aided by bumper food and cash crops, sustained rise in industrial output and impressive performance of the services sector.

The production of total foodgrains has increased from 50.8 million tonnes in 1950-51,108.4 million tonnes in 1970-71, 176.4 million tonnes in 1990-91 to 208.60 million tonnes in 2005-06. The major food grains have higher growth rates than the minor food grains. The productivity of food grains has jumped from 552 kg/ha in 1950-51 to 1715 kg/ha in 2005-06. Against this remarkable achievement, production of pulses remains stagnant at 14.91 million tonnes except for a few years. The oil seed technology mission has improved the oil seed production in recent years reaching 27.98 million tonnes in 2005-06. During last fifty years wheat has shown maximum improvement in the productivity followed by rice in the major food grains. Minor food grains production and productivity did not show much improvement.

The production of rice has increased from 20.6 million tonnes in 1950-51, to 74.29 million tonnes in year 1990-91, 84.98 million tonnes in the year 2000-01 to 91.79 million tonnes in the year 2005-06. Rice reached from 668 kg/ha in year 1950-51 to 2102 kg/ha in year 2005-06. After Independence wheat has shown tremendous improvement in the productivity. It was 6.46 million tonnes in year 1950-51, 36.31 million tonnes in year 1980-81, 55.14 million tonnes in year 1990-91, 69.68 million tonnes in year 2000-01 and 69.35 million tonnes in year 2005-06. The productivity of wheat at 663 kg/ha in 1950-51 has increase to 2619 kg/ha in year 2005-06. The production of pulses remained stagnant. India is the world's largest producer, consumer and importer (over 2 million tonnes) of a variety of pulses. Total pulse production has increased from 8.41 million tonnes in year 1950-51 to 11.82 million tonnes in year 1970-71, 14.26 million tonnes in year 1990-91 and 13.39 million tonnes in year 2005-06.

Cash crops, especially tea and coffee, are the major export earners. India is the world's largest producer of tea, with annual production of around 470 million tons, of which 200 million tonnes is exported. India also holds around 30 per cent of the world spice market, with exports around 120,000 tonnes per year. The Centre for Monitoring Indian Economy (CMIE) expects crop production to rise by a higher 2.6 per cent in 2007-08 as against 0.9 per cent increase in 2006-07. This higher growth estimate largely reflects recovery in oilseeds production during the year 2007-08. (*Bank of Baroda Quarterly Economic Review*, April-June 2007).

The consumption of total fertilizer nutrients in the state, increased by 7.5 per cent from 1.050 Mt during 2004-05 to 1.129 Mt during 2005-06. All the three nutrients recorded positive growth during the period. The consumption of N and P_2O_5 at 0.847 and 0.253 Mt recorded increase of 7.4 per cent and 4.8 per cent, respectively, during 2005-06 over 2004-05. The consumption of K_2O at 28.7 thousand tonnes, represented a growth of 46.4 per cent during the period. NPK use ratio narrowed from 40.3:12.3:1 during 2004-05 to 29.6:8.8:1 during 2005-06. Kharif:Rabi shares in total fertiliser consumption changed from 37:63 during 2004-05 to 38:62 during 2005-06. The per hectare consumption of total fertilizer nutrients increased from 166.2 kg during 2004-05 to 178.6 kg. during 2005-06.

Bal Krishan Jha and Amalendu Kumar make "An Analytical Study on Growth, Trends and Stability of Major Kharif Crops in various Agro-Climatic Zones of Jharkhand". Beginning from the consequences of division of Bihar, the chapter elaborates the present state of affairs in Jharkhand. Writer's main focus into study the cropping pattern during pre- and post-green revolution, to measure growth rate in agricultural production and productivity. Special emphasis is on two major kharif crops of Rice and Maize. The area under rice cultivation has declined but its productivity has increased. Data related to area under rice cultivation and productivity have been analysed for different agro-climatic zones in four different periods. Statistical methods of Standard Deviations as well as Co-efficient of variation have been adopted to gauge the magnitude of variation in absolute as well as average in terms of area, production and productivity in rice.

WTO and its impact upon Indian Agriculture has been a subject matter of heated debates, frayed tempers, extreme views and eventually more confusion. The impacts of WTO on our agriculture emanate mainly due to the basic premises, which are wrongly conceived, and the vital issues, which are demoted to auxiliary position under WTO. The impacts will be discernible if farmers instead of farming are taken into account. In the chapter 'WTO and Indian Agriculture', Sita Ram Singh makes scholarly efforts to discuss the role of WTO and its impacts on the growth of Indian agriculture. As a successor of GATT, WTO has been playing a crucial role and making concerted efforts in bringing redical shift in the development paradigm at national and global levels. The liberalization of the world trade in agriculture, under the present circumstance, is going to benefit more to developed countries rather than the developing countries.

The chapter 'Agricultural Growth and Indian Economy' is written by Krishna Nand Yadav. Despite industrialisation, agriculture continues to be the main stay of Indian Economy. In 1990's the growth in agricultural output was 2.26 per cent per annum as against 3.17 per cent during 1980's. Agricultural exports increased from $ 3.2 billion in year 1991-90 to $ 6.86 billion in 1996-97 but thereafter declined to $ 5.5 billion by year 2000. The increase in exports was due to devaluation of the Indian rupee and opening of economy. The author analyses sets of data related to areas under irrigation in different states, capital formation in agriculture, flow of institutional credit in agriculture, share of agriculture in State Domestic Product, per capita net availability of food grains, and state-wise index of infrastructure development and food grain productivity in Indian States. The author opines that in order to make Indian agriculture globally competitive, there is need of investment in rural infrastructure, research and development and effective institutions which can promote efficiency by reducing transaction costs. There are some issues, which need to be addressed like improving the productivity, healthy credit system, proper marketing network, and promotion of value addition and removal of trade barriers.

"Economic Growth and Agricultural Development in 20th Century: Some Reflections" penned by authors-duo Ashwini Kant Jha and Bhawna Jha is an attempt to elaborate accelerated growth rate in GDP and per capita income after independence. The period 1950-51 to 1999-2000 witnessed GDP growth rate at 4:16 per cent and per capita income at 1.77 per cent. The Indian economy faced some crises in 1965-66 and 1966-67 due to successive droughts. The crises of 1980s was the result of mismatch between revenue receipts (16.6%) and revenue expenditure (17.1%). Though the export increased by 10 per cent during 1985-90 but it was not adequate to finance mounting expenditure on import of machinery. It led to inflate India's external borrowings. The situation was further aggravated by rise in oil prices as a result of gulf war and political in stability in India.

In the wake of severe economic crises reforms began to be introduced after 1991. The new policy succeeded in restoring the confidence of investors and accelerating the GDP as well as per capita income. But there is deceleration in agriculture. The situation is alarming as the liberalisation policy is inclined towards rich farmers. There is reason to fear that the bias may endanger the socio-economic structure of rural economy.

"Indian Agriculture: Growth Yield and Output" is written by K.B. Padmadeo and Sri Niwas Pandey. The liberalisation of economy in 1990s brought some rays of hope for Indian agriculture. The signing of GATT accord was expected to be instrumental in promoting multilateralism and in increasing international trade in agricultural and other commodities as well as services. But in recent years there has been declaration in Indian agriculture due to decline in investment, cutting down of duty on edible oil and increased prices. Hence, there is need of giving high priority to public sector investment in rural infrastructure, land reforms, consolidation of land holdings, creation of infrastructure and creation of institutions like trading houses, market intelligence and creation of network of information on national and international prices.

'Agricultural Economy of Bihar: Potential, Compulsion and Options' jointly written by Anjani Kumar Jha and Niranjan Kumar Jha is reflection of Agricultural economy of Bihar in comparison to that of India and a few better performing states. Despite the vast tract of fertile land, abundance of water resources and hard working workforce, Bihar's economy is passing through the gloomy phase of its development. This gloomy picture can be seen within the frame of per-capita income, per capita agricultural income, per hectare productivity, fertilizer consumption, use of modern implements, R&D infrastructure and public investment, etc. Bihar finds no place on the industrial map and hence dependence on agriculture is a matter of compulsion also. But there is complete failure in the task of water-management without which nothing positive can be expected.

The chapter on "Role of Fertilizer in Indian Agriculture: An Analysis' by Birendra Kumar and Meera Ranjan Lal, is an attempt to analyse the fertilizer consumption ratio in some developed countries and its impacts on the per hectare yield. It also refers to fertilizer consumption and its impacts on per hectare yield. To bring second green revolution, the role of balanced dozes of fertilizers is necessary.

'Role of Fertilizers on Indian Agriculture' is written by N.K. Thakur. The chapter elaborates the importance of agriculture and the role of fertilizers in increasing the agricultural productivity. In 50 years of planned development, there has been significant increase in the nutrient consumption per annum, and per hectare consumption of NPK per hectare and its consequent total food grain production. The per capita land has reduced to 0-12 hectare but the rapid increase in population will lead to create food-scarcity. Hence the increasing trend in fertilizer consumption is an essential requirement to ensure nutritional security in the second most populous country of the world.

'Trend in Total Factor Productivity of Crop Sector in Bihar during Green Revolution Period' is written jointly by R.K.P. Singh, A.K. Chaudhary and Vinod Kumar. Over the past three decades the staple foodgrains production has increased dramatically and contributed substantially to the food security. The indiscriminate exploitation of natural resources has raised concern about the long-term sustainability of the agricultural production system and environment. There is concern for declining soil health and other related environmental problems. If the sustainability issue of crop sector is not addressed, it may adversely affect the economic growth and household food security. To enhance the level of investment, there is need to take decisions considering the future prospects, investors have to be assured of dynamism and efficiency in overall governance, and the rates of taxation and tariffs should be stabilised.

The chapter "Rice Production Trend in Bihar during Last Two Decades: A Regional Analysis" written jointly by D.K. Sinha, A.K. Chaudhary and R.K.P. Singh gives focus on various aspects of rice-production in Bihar. The overall annual compound growth rate increased from 0.02 per cent in 1981-82 to 2.87 per cent in 2001-02. The chapter analyses the zonal as well as seasonal variations in rice production. Production and productivity of various season rice crop has got stabilised in Bihar during 1990s. It could be possible because the adoption level of rice production technology seems to be getting matured.

The theme of the chapter "Trends in Growth of Pulse Production: An Analytical Study of Tal Region of Bihar", is discussed by author duo Shambhu Deo Mishra and Md. Masood Alam. Both in terms of quality and quantity, India is the largest producer of pulses, which are the richest, and the best sources of protein. Predominantly being the vegetarian country, pulses are the main sources of protein, calcium and vitamins. Share of Bihar in the pulse production is about 6.50 per cent to the country's Pulse production. There are several constraints in the pulse production, which need to be removed. There is need of improving infrastructure and providing needful facilities so that Bihar continues to have its significant share in the total pulse production in the country.

INDUSTRIAL SECTOR GROWTH

The industrial sector registered an annual growth of 11.1 per cent in May 2007 as against 11.7 per cent in May 2006. This marginal slowdown in industrial growth was primarily contributed by the manufacturing sector, which reported a growth of 11.9 per cent in May 2007 as against 13.3 per cent in May 2006. However, the performance of mining and power sectors improved to 3.7 per cent and 9.4 per cent respectively in May 2007 (from 2.9% and 5.0% respectively in May 2006). The reported slowdown is not a serious concern as cumulative industrial growth is still at 11.7 per cent in April-May 2007 as against 10.8 per cent in April-May 2006 despite a rapid appreciation of rupee against the U.S. dollar and substantial hardening of interest rates during the year 2007 so far. In 2006-07, GDP grew at the rate of 9.2 per cent in spite of agriculture making a contribution of only 2.7 per cent. The 10 per cent growth in industrial output raised their production with the export demand also for steel, textiles, non-ferrous metals, gem and jewelry and other products being brisk. World prices for the related items too were higher than domestic prices. The main thrust of industrial growth has come from the services sector. Services contribute to 55.1 per cent of the GDP in year 2006-07 along with 11.2 per cent annual grow. Rapidly, the quality and complexity of the type of services being marketed is on the rise to match world standards.

The industry group "Wood & Wood Products" and "Furniture & Fixtures" have shown the highest growth of 132.8

per cent, followed by 40.4 per cent in "Jute and other Vegetable Fibre Textiles (except cotton)" and 24.8 per cent in "Food Products". On the other hand, the industry group "Transport Equipment & Parts" have shown a negative growth of 0.1 per cent, followed by five per cent in "Other Manufacturing Industries". As per Use-based classification, the sectoral growth rates in May 2007 over May 2006 are 10.2 per cent in basic goods, 22.9 per cent in capital goods and 9.1 per cent in intermediate goods. Continued buoyancy in capital goods reflects the sustainable momentum in investment sentiment in the economy. (*Bank of Baroda Quarterly Economic Review*, April-June).

India is fast becoming a major force in the Information Technology sector. According to the National Association of Software and Service Companies (NASSCOM), over 185 Fortune and 500 companies use Indian software services. Indian software and services exports are expected to earn about $ 40 billion in 2007-08 (according to NASSCOM, July, 07 Report) as demand for outsourcing remain very strong. The world's software giants such as Microsoft, Hughes and Computer Associates, which have made substantial investments in India, are increasingly tapping this potential. A number of multi-nationals have leveraged the relative cost advantage and highly skilled manpower base available in India, and have established shared services and call centers in India to cater to their worldwide needs.

The software industry was one of the fastest growing sectors in the last decade with a compound annual growth rate exceeding 50 per cent. India's success in the software sector can be largely attributed to the industry's ability to cultivate superior knowledge through intensive R&D efforts and the expertise in applying the knowledge in commercially viable technologies.

The chapter on 'Industrial Development in India: Reflections on Growth and Deceleration' is prepared by Narendra Prasad. The author analyses the pattern, growth and declaration of industrial production in India after independence. In the beginning of the plan period, Nehru-

Mahalanobis strategy of industrial development was adopted. The strategy gave emphasis on the heavy industry under the public sector keeping in view the goal of establishing the socialistic pattern of society. During the initial period, industrial growth witnessed steady growth rate of 8 per cent but the later phase witnessed the deceleration.

'Disturbing Trends in Sectoral Composition of India's National Income' is written by Reeta Sinha. It is an attempt to take note of the changing contours of sectoral composition of India's National income in the post-1991 period and to find out the disturbing trends in the sectoral composition. Agriculture has improved enough to bring self-sufficiency in food-supply but rural economy is still replanted with unemployed labour. Due to low employment generating potential of secondary and tertiary sectors, there has been concentration of work force in agriculture and hence the incidence of rural poverty has been on the rise. Bright picture of shining India on Tertiary front and suicides by farmers on agricultural front are the reasons far distortions. There is earnest need to bridge the gulf between various sectors of economy.

The chapter of the book 'Reflections on Linkages of Real Sectors in India' is written by Dhananjay Kumar. In the first three decades of planned economic development; India's main strategy was import-substitution. There has been structural shift in Indian economy, which is reflected by the changes in the shares of agriculture, industry and service sector in the GDP. The author stresses the need for a proper balancing of the "inward looking" and "outward looking" strategies by promoting agriculture and export-oriented endeavors. Policy measures in the agenda of second-generation reforms should focus on stimulating demand in the agricultural sector in rural areas by diversifying economic activities.

Md. Tarique paper titles 'Growth of Agriculture in the Post-Liberalisation Era' analysing agricultural performance during the post reform era. While analysing the agricultural data showing a very dismal figure in its growth in the post liberalisation era. Yield growth decelerated throughout the 1990s to only about 1 per cent per annum from 3 per cent during the 1980s, indicating a potentially serious exhaustion of technological progress. The data for growth rates in area, production and yield shows overall dismal figures for Indian economy in the post liberalisation era. Rice and pulses have shown negative growth rates in terms of area sown. Though the figure for wheat is positive, data for all the commodities taken together gives a negative trend. This paper also cover a comparative study of some of the other countries in the world with that of India. It is clearly explain how much India lags behind with respect to the variables like crop production index, food production index, livestock production index, cereal yield and agricultural productivity in both pre-and post-liberalisation era. China was below India in terms of crop production index, food production index and livestock production index in the pre-reform era. But after making a spectacular performance in the post-liberalisation era, it is not only far ahead of India but also even in a better position than many developed countries in terms of these indices. India has done well in terms of the growth rates of various indices (except productivity index), the country lags far behind if given a look at the absolute figures. Some of the reasons for these lower absolute values and a dismal compound rate of increase in the overall productivity.

The assessment of India's achievement in Real Sector in the last 60 years after independence gives both the satisfying and the disturbing feelings. Beginnings the journey from almost 'nowhere', in the 60th year of independence India occupies front seat among the comity of nations in terms of Purchasing Power Parity, Gross Domestic Product and other economic indicators. India's real GDP growth rose to marginally in 2007-08. The policy of economic liberalisation has freed the Indian Economy from the shackles of quota-permit Raj, corruption and nexus between politicians and bureaucrats. In the first three decades of Plan period the GDP growth rate stood at 1.5 per cent and there was dismal rise in the living standard. But 1990s, witnessed the fastest growth rate. Despite the decline in its share to GDP, Agriculture is still the largest sector employing 60 per cent of the total workforce and contributing immensely to the socio-economic development of India. Despite remarkable achievements, the Indian economy is still facing the twin problems of poverty and unemployment.

This book contains 19 chapters contributed by authors who have sincerely attempted to investigate and peep through the achievements, problems and future prospects. This book will be of great interest and help to all those who are anyhow concerned with Indian economy whether as students, researchers, planners, policy-makers and all.

ANIL KUMAR THAKUR
DALIP KUMAR

CHAPTER

1

Employment and Unemployment in India

RUDDAR DATT

Economic liberalisation was introduced with a gusto in 1991 and the main argument given was that the regime of controls and licences has put fetters on the development process. Unless controls and licences regime is not dismantled, the economy would not be able to expand. Investment was stifled, the regime had resulted in the growth of corruption and established a nexus between the politicians and the bureaucrats, which was acting as a shackle on the growth process. It was hoped that once the economy is freed from the regime of controls, quotas and licences, it shall result in a much higher growth rate of Gross Domestic Product (GDP) and a significant expansion of employment. Economic liberalisation was hailed as a panacea in the same manner as socialism was considered to be the only method of achieving growth with social justice during the first four decades of development.

It would be of interest to understand as to what happened to the process of employment growth in the post-liberalisation period. Although the reform process resulted in an acceleration of GDP growth, it was not accompanied by a commensurate increase in employment. As facts stand today, public sector employment was halted because the public sector began to withdraw from several areas. Moreover, in its effort to shed extra fat, the public sector units started the process of downsizing by getting rid of redundant labour. It was expected that since organised private sector was expected to be the torchbearer of economic reforms, employment in the organised sector would grow at a much faster rate. But this did not happen even in the private sector. Faced with the process of internal liberalisation and of globalisation, even in the private sector, industrial units started shedding excess labour and to compete with foreign players, new technology was increasingly introduced resulting in loss of jobs. Thus, the growth rate of employment in the economy, which was of the order of 2.0 per cent per year during the 10-year period 1983 to 1993-94 as per NSS data, sharply declined to less than 1 per cent in the period 1993-94 to 1999-2000. As a result, the critics of economic reforms described the process of economic liberalisation as that of 'jobless growth'.

It would be, therefore, appropriate to review the dimensions of the problem of unemployment and employment during the last two decades.

Changing Dimensions of Unemployment and Employment

From data provided in Table 1.1, certain disturbing trends in the unemployment rates become evident in the post-reform period. Although the reforms were introduced in 1991, yet the year 1991-92 was particularly a depressed year and the reform process really got a going by 1993-94. Thus, 1993-94 to 1999-2000—the 6 year period can be considered as the period of liberalisation. It may be noted that all the four categories of unemployment showed a declining trend during the period 1977-78 to 1993-94, but the trend got reversed during 1993-94 and 1999-2000. Open employment as measured by UPS criterion

TABLE 1.1
Unemployment Rates : Alternative Measures

(Percentage of Labour Force)

	Usual principal status (UPS)	*Usual principal and subsidiary status (UPSS)*	*Current weekly status (CWS)*	*Current daily status (CDS)*
Rural				
1977-78	3.26	1.54	3.74	7.70
1983	1.91	1.13	3.88	7.94
1987-88	3.07	1.98	4.19	5.25
1 993-94	1.80	1.20	3.00	5.63
1999-2000	1.96	1.43	3.91	7.21
Urban				
1977-78	8.77	7.01	7.86	10.34
1983	6.04	5.02	6.81	9.52
1987-88	6.56	5.32	7.12	9.36
1993-94	5.21	4.52	5.83	7.43
1999-2000	5.23	4.63	5.89	7.65
All-India				
1977-78	4.23	2.47	4.48	8.18
1983	2.77	1.90	4.51	8.28
1987-88	3.77	2.62	4.80	6.09
1993-94	2.56	1.90	3.63	6.03
1999-2000	2.81	2.23	4.41	7.32

Note : These estimates are based on NSS data combined with Census data.
Source : Planning Commission, (2001) Report of Task Force on Employment Opportunities, Table 2.1.

declined from 4.23 per cent in 1977-78 to 2.56 per cent in 1993-94, but indicated an increase to 2.81 per cent in 1999-2000.

The Current Weekly Status (CWS) unemployment rate which was 4.48 per cent in 1977-78 declined to 3.63 per cent in 1993-94, but rose to 4.41 per cent in 1999-2000.

Even the most comprehensive measure of unemployment, viz., Current Daily Status (CDS) unemployment rate declined form 8.18 per cent in 1977-78 to 6.03 per cent in 1993-94, but the declining trend reversed to 7.32 per cent in 1999-2000.

The same situation can be observed with respect to both urban and rural areas. However, it may be noted that whereas CDS rate for urban areas increased very slightly from 7.43 per cent in 1993-94 to 7.65 per cent in 1999-2000, this very rate increased much faster from 5.63 per cent in 1993-94 in the rural areas to 7.21 per cent in 1999-00. The same phenomenon could be observed in all the four measures of unemployment both in the rural and the urban areas. This underlines the relative neglect of the rural economy in the first phase of economic reforms.

Usual Principal Status (UPS) measures open unemployment throughout the year, but Current Daily Status (CDS) besides taking into account open unemployment also measures under-employment. From the data given in Table 1.4, it becomes obvious that whereas the UPS rates are modest, the CDS rates are quite high. In other words, the major problem of the Indian economy is not open unemployment but under-employment.

Growth Rates of Employment

The growth rates of unemployment and labour force derived from NSS data are given in Table 1.2. From this data, the following points emerge:

1. The growth rate of employment declined sharply from 2.04 per cent per annum during the 10-year period 1983 to 1993-94 to barely 0.98 per annum during the period 1993-94 to 1999-2000. The Task Force on Employment Opportunities admitting deceleration in employment growth mentions: "This sharp deceleration in the growth of employment has naturally been the focus of much attention and comment, raising fears that economic growth in 1990s has been of a 'jobless' variety. This implies that the growth rate in employment is less than the growth rate in labour force and this has resulted in an increase in the unemployment rate.
2. In agriculture, the growth rate of employment observed during 1983 to 1993-94 was 1.51 per cent, but

TABLE 1.2
Growth of Employment by Sectors

	Employed workers (million)			*Annual growth rate (%)*	
Industry	*1983*	*1993-94*	*1999-2000*	*1983-94*	*1994-2000*
PRIMARY	208.99 (69.0)	245.16 (65.5)	239.83 (60.4)	1.60	-0.34
1. Agriculture	207.23 (68.4)	242.46 (64.8)	237.56 (59.8)	1.51	-0.34
2. Mining and quarrying	1.76 (0.6)	2.70 (0.7)	2.27 (0.6)	4.16	-2.85
SECONDARY	41.66 (13.8)	55.53 (14.8)	66.91 (16.8)	2.90	3.14
3. Manufacturing	34.03 (11.2)	42.50 (11.3)	48.01 (12.1)	2.14	2.05
4. Electricity, gas and water supply	0.85 (0.3)	1.35 (0.4)	1.28 (0.3)	4.50	-0.88
.5. Construction	6.78 (2.2)	11.68 (3.1)	17.62 (4.4)	5.32	7.09
TERTIARY	52.11 (17.2)	73.76 (19.7)	90.26 (22.7)	3.53	2.42
6. Trade	19.22 (6.3)	27.78 (7.4)	37.32 (9.4)	3.57	5.04
7. Transport, Storage and Communications	7.39 (2.4)	10.33 (2.8)	14.69 (3.7)	3.24	6.04
8. Financial Services	1.70 (0.6)	3.52 (0.9)	5.08 (1.3)	7.18	6.20
9. Community, social and personal	23.80 (7.9)	32.13 (8.6)	33.20 (8.4)	2.90	0.55
Services Total employment	302.76 (100.0)	374.45 (100.0)	397.00 (100.0)	2.04	0.98

Notes : 1. Growth rates for the primary sector have been worked on the basis of data by the Task Force on Employment Opportunities.

2. Figures in parenthesis give the percentage of the sector in the total employment during the respective year.

Source : Compiled and computed from the data provided by the Planning Commission (2001), *Report of Task Force on Employment Opportunities*, Table 3.2.

during the period of liberalisation, the growth rate of employment became negative (–0.34%) during 1993-94 and 1999-2000.

3. In the manufacturing sector, employment growth rate was 2.14 per cent during 1983 to 1993-94, but declined marginally to 2.05 per cent during 1993-94 to 1999-2000.
4. Construction sector witnessed an employment growth of 5.32 per cent during 1983 to 1993-94, and this growth rate further increased to 7.09 per cent during 1999-2000.
5. In trade, employment growth rate was of the order of 3.57 per cent during 1983 and 1993-94 and it improved further to 5.04 per cent during 1993-94 to 1999-2000.
6. In transport, storage and communications, employment growth rate increased sharply from 3.24 per cent during 1983 to 1993-94 to 6.04 per cent during 1993-94 and 1999-2000.
7. Financial services witnesses a marginal decline in growth rate from 7.18 per cent during 1983 to 1993-94 to 6.20 per cent during 1993-94 and 1999-2000, though the growth rate was sufficiently high.
8. Community, social and personal services witnessed a sharp deceleration in employment growth from 2.90 per cent during 1983 to 1993-94 to merely 0.55 per cent during 1993-94 and 1999-2000. This was largely the consequence of shedding the load of excess employment in the public sector by imposing a continuous ban on recruitment and not filling up even the positions vacated by retirement of public sector employees.

We have grouped the data into primary, secondary and tertiary sectors. In the primary sector, there is a deceleration of growth rate of employment during post liberalisation period (1994-2000). In the secondary sector, the combined effect of manufacturing and construction resulted in a modest improvement in the growth rate from 2.90 per cent in the pre-liberalisation decade to 3.14 per cent in the post liberalisation period. However, in the tertiary (or service) sector, there is a deceleration in growth rate of employment to 2.42 per cent in the post-liberalisation period as against 3.53 per cent in the pre-liberalisation decade. This was mainly the consequence of a sharp deceleration in employment growth in the community, social and personal services to 0.55 per cent in the post-liberalisation period as against 2.90 per cent in the pre-liberalisation decade.

From Table 1.3, two patterns in employment generation may be noticed—the first pattern pertains to the period 1983 to 1993-94. In this pattern, nearly 51 per cent of additional employment came from the primary sector, 19 per cent from the secondary sector and 30 per cent from the tertiary sector. In the second pattern that developed during 1993-94 and 1999-2000, nearly 50 per cent of the additional employment was generated in the secondary sector and 73 per cent in the tertiary sector; however, in the agricultural sector, there was a fall in employment by nearly 23 per cent. The post-liberalisation period thus appears to be one, which neglected agriculture. The virtual stagnation of the agricultural sector in terms of output

TABLE 1.3

Share of Different Sectors in Increase of Employment

(million)

Period I	*1983 (1)*	*1993-94 (2)*	*Increase during during (1983-93)*	*Share in Increase (%)*
Primary	208.99	245.16	36.17	50.5
Secondary	41.66	55.53	13.87	19.3
Tertiary	52.11	73.76	21.65	30.2
Total	302.76	374.45	71.69	100.0
Period II	*1993-94*	*1999-2000*	*Increase During 1 994-00*	*Share in Increase (%)*
Primary	245.16	239.83	–5.33	–23.6
Secondary	55.53	66.91	11.38	50.4
Tertiary	73.76	90.26	16.50	73.2
Total	374.45	397.00	22.55	100.0

Source : Compiled and computed from the data given in Table 1.2.

and deceleration in terms of employment appears to be the distinguishing feature of this pattern.

Unemployment Rates—Urban and Rural Differences

Data provided in Table 1.4 reveal that unemployment rates are traditionally higher in urban areas than in rural areas. As against an unemployment rate of 10.3 per cent in 1977-78 in urban areas, the rural unemployment rate was 7.7 per cent (CDS basis). There was a significant fall in the rural unemployment rate in 1987-88 to 5.3 per cent, but the urban unemployment rate was of the order of 9.4 per cent, significantly higher. After 1993-94, the period of liberalisation rural unemployment rate again increased to 7.2 per cent while urban unemployment also marginally increased to 7.7 per cent during 1993-94 to 1999-2000. Higher levels of unemployment in the urban areas could be explained by

Table 1.4
Unemployment* among Urban and Rural Areas

(As percent of labour force)

	Rural Areas			*Urban Areas*		
Survey Period	*Male*	*Female*	*Persons*	*Male*	*Female*	*Persons*
1977-78	7.1	9.2	7.7	9.4	14.5	10.3
1983	7.5	9.0	7.9	9.2	11.0	9.5
1987-88	4.6	6.7	5.3	8.8	12.0	9.4
1993-94	5.6	5.6	5.6	6.7	10.5	7.4
1999-2000	7.2	7.3	7.2	7.2	9.8	7.7

Note : *Unemployment Rate on Current Daily Status Basis.

Source : National Sample Survey Organisation.

a larger proportion of organised sector unemployment which forces people to either remain employed or unemployed, since the chances for getting engaged in low productive activities are relatively fewer. As against this, the rural areas indicate higher levels of disguised unemployment. Gradual and continuous decline of urban unemployment rates till 1993-94 and even a very marginal increase in 1999-2000 may be due to greater attention being given to urban areas in the development process, but the increase in unemployment rates in rural areas may be due to the neglect of rural areas in the post-reform period. It may be also be due to a shift in the composition of employment from self-employment to casual labour.

Male-Female Differences

Table 1.4 also brings out the stark reality that female unemployment rates are significantly higher in urban areas at 9.8 per cent as compared to male unemployment rate at 7.2 per cent in 1999-00. Over the last-two decades, however, female unemployment rates have come down from 14.5 per cent in 1977-78 to 9.8 per cent in 1999-2000, but the male unemployment rates declined form 9.4 per cent to 7.2 per cent during this period. This only underlines the fact that there is a greater absorption of female labour in urban areas and this trend needs to be strengthened so as to completely eliminate male-female differences in unemployment rates.

In the rural areas, male-female unemployment rates showed divergence during 1977-78 and 1987-88, but thereafter the difference in male-female unemployment rates seems to have narrowed down during 1993-94 and 1999-2000.

Unemployment Rate Across Household Monthly Per Capita Expenditure

Table 1.5 provides information according to Household Monthly Per Capita Expenditure (MPCE) Classes for the year 1999-2000 on the UPSS and CDS criteria basis separately. A close perusal of the data reveal that both in the rural and the urban areas, the lower consumption groups show much lower UPSS rates of unemployment on the basis of the UPSS criterion, but this pattern gets reversed on the basis of CDS criterion. But as the expenditure levels improve, there is an increase in unemployment rate on the basis of UPSS criterion and a fall on the basis of CDS criterion. In other words, the difference between UPSS and CDS rates indicates a decline with increase of MPCE of the class. This only highlights the stark reality that the poor cannot afford to remain unemployed since their

TABLE 1.5
Unemployment Rates by Household Monthly Per Capita Expenditure (MPCE) 1999-2000

(As % of labour force)

	Rural			Urban			
MPCE	*UPSS*	*CDS*	*Difference*	*MPCE*	*UPSS*	*CDS*	*Difference*
0-225	1.06	11.31	10.25	0-300	2.91	9.61	6.70
225-255	1.02	9.62	8.60	300-350	5.21	9.67	4.46
255-300	1.27	8.12	6.85	350-425	4.08	8.20	4.12
300-340	0.98	7.46	6.48	425-500	5.43	9.20	3.77
340-380	1.20	6.56	5.36	500-575	5.81	9.20	3.39
380-420	1.43	6.18	4.75	575-665	8.12	8.63	0.51
420-470	1.59	6.48	4.89	665-775	5.85	8.19	2.34
470-525	1.79	6.14	4.35	775-915	4.95	7.18	2.23
525-615	1.78	5.60	3.82	915-1120	5.08	6.65	1.57
615-775	2.21	6.06	3.85	1120-1500	4.21	5.68	1.47
775-950	2.44	5.57	3.13	1500-1925	3.49	4.67	1.18
950 and above	2.54	5.25	2.71	1925 and above	2.99	4.10	1.11
All	1.43	7.21	5.78	All	4.63	7.65	3.02

Source : NSSO Survey, 55th Round (1999-2000).

waiting power is very weak and take up any work-low paid or high paid, full time or part timet continuous or intermittent to make both ends meet. The high degree of CDS unemployment rate is a reflection of the high degree of under-employment among the poor.

Unemployment Rates and Regional Differences

Data about 17 major states of the country pertaining to unemployment rates has been presented in Table 1.6. Although during 1999-2000, the All-India unemployment rate was 7.29 per cent, states show very wide variations from about 3 per cent in Himachal Pradesh and Rajasthan to about 12 per cent in Tamil Nadu, about 15 per cent in West Bengal and about 21 per

TABLE 1.6
Unemployment Rates *and Regional Differences

	State	*Unemployment Rate* 1987-88	1993-94	1999-2000
1.	Kerala	21.19	15.50	20.77
2.	West Bengal	8.13	9.87	14.95
3.	Tamil Nadu	10.36	11.44	12.05
4.	Assam	50.9	7.96	8.00
5.	Andhra Pradesh	7.35	6.67	7.94
6.	Orissa	6.44	7.28	7.38
7.	Bihar	4.04	6.25	7.35
8.	Maharashtra	4.67	4.97	7.09
9.	Haryana	7.59	6.59	4.67
10.	Gujarat	5.79	5.73	4.63
11.	Karnataka	5.06	4.89	4.61
12.	Madhya Pradesh	2.86	3.42	4.60
13.	Delhi	4.77	1.91	4.58
14.	Uttar Pradesh	3.44	3.45	4.27
15.	Punjab	5.07	3.08	4.15
16.	Rajasthan	5.74	1.33	3.06
17.	Himachal Pradesh	3.12	1.82	2.93
	All-India	6.09	6.03	7.29

Note : *Current Daily Status Basis. States have been arranged in the descending order of unemployment rates for 1999-2000.

Source : National Sample Survey organisation.

cent in Kerala. It is rather intriguing that a state like Kerala, which has shown the sharpest decline in poverty, should also show the highest rate of unemployment. The Planning Commission Task Force suggests the following tentative hypothesis to explain variations: "States where wages are kept higher than the neighbouring regions either by strengthening the bargaining power of labour or by provision of social security (Kerala, West Bengal and Tamil Nadu) have a higher incidence of unemployment." But the question which the Task Force does not answer is: Should these states weaken the bargaining power of labour or not take social security measures in view of the fact that neighbouring states do not realise their social responsibility? It would be more desirable to examine in depth the social and economic conditions in different states so as to understand more fully the inter-state variations.

Structure of Employment in India

The structure of employment may be studied by recognising the following characteristics: (i) Distinction between organised and unorganised sector, and (ii) the relative share of self-employment, regular salaried employment and casual labour. It would be of interest to examine the structure from these two points of view.

Organised *vs.* Unorganised Sector Employment

The organised sector usually refers to employment in the public sector and in private sector establishments employing 10 or more persons. It is commonly believed that wages in the organised sector are much higher than in the unorganised sector. Moreover, the organised sector being regulated also provides greater job security and other benefits. Within the organised sector, jobs in the public sector receive relatively higher wages and accompanying benefits than those in the private sector for similar skills. Besides this, public sector offers greater job security.

Data given in Table 1.7 reveal that the share of organised sector employment in total employment, which was of the order of 7.93 per cent in 1983 as well as 1988 declined to 7.08 per cent in 1999-2000. The organised sector employment, which was 24 million in 1983, increased to 27.37 million in 1994 indicating a growth rate of 1.20 per cent per annum during 1983-94. However, during the post reform period (1994-2000), organised sectored employment crept up slowly from 27.37 million in 1994 to 28.22 million in 1999-2000, indicating a growth rate of merely 0.53 per cent per annum. This was largely the consequence of virtual stagnation of employment in the public sector during 1994-2000 and growth rate was (-) 0.03 per cent per annum, but the private sector employment grew from 7.93 million in 1994 to

Table 1.7
Total Employment and Organised Sector Employment

Sector	Employment (million)			Growth rate (% per annum)		
	1983	1988	1994	1999-2000	1983-94	1994-2000
(1)	(2)	(3)	(4)	(5)	(6)	(7)
1. Total population	718.21	790.00	895.05	1004..10	2.12	1.93
2. Total labour force	308.64	333.49	381 .94	406.05	2.05	1.03
3. Total employment	302.75	324.29	374.45	397.00	2.04	0.98
4. Organised sector employment	24.01 (100.0)	25.71 (100.0)	27.37 (100.0)	28.11 (100.0)	1.20	0.53
5. Public sector	1 6.46 (68.6)	18.32 (71.3)	1 9.44 (71.0)	19.41 (69.1)	1.52	-0.03
6. Private sector	7.55 (31.4)	7.39 (28.7)	7.93 (29.0)	8.70 (30.9)	0.45	1.87
7. 4 as % of 3	7.93	7.93	7.30	7.08		
8. 2 as % of 1	43.0	42.2	42.7	40.4		

Notes : 1. Total employment figures are on Usual Status (UPSS) basis.

2. The organised sector employment figures are as reported in the Employment Market Information System of Ministry of Labour and pertain to 31st March of 1983,1994 and 1999.
3. Figures in brackets indicate the percentage of employment in the public sector and private sector to total organised sector employment.

Source : Compiled and computed from Planning Commission (2001), Report of the Task Force on Employment Opportunities, p. 2.25.

8.70 million in 1999-2000 indicating a growth rate of 1.87 per cent per annum. Bus since the public sector accounted for over 69 per cent of total employment in the organised sector, enlargement of private sector employment was not able to effectively offset the deceleration experienced in the public sector employment.

It may be noted from Table 1.8 that in agriculture, organised sector employment is negligible. Even in a major sector like manufacturing, organised sector employment is only of the order of 14 per cent and as much as 86 per-cent of employment is generated through the unorganised sector viz.,

TABLE 1.8

Organised Sector Employment by Industry

	1993-94		*1999-2000*		*Share of Organised Sector (per cent)*	
	Total[3]	*Organised Sector*[1]	*Total*[4]	*Organised Sector*[2]	*1993-94*	*1999-2000*
Agriculture	242.46	1.48	237.56	1.39	0.61	0.58
Mining and	2.70	1.09	2.27	1.01	40.37	44.49
Quarrying manufacturing	42.50	6.40	48.01	6.75	15.05	14.06
Electricity, gas and water supply	1.35	0.97	1.28	1.00	71.85	78.12
Construction	11.68	1.23	17.62	1.18	10.53	6.70
Trade	27.78	0.45	37.32	0.49	1.62	1.31
Transport, storage and comm.	10.33	3.11	14.69	3.15	30.11	21.44
Financial services	3.52	1.53	5.05	1.65	43.46	32.67
Community, social and personal services	32.13	10.93	33.20	11.49	34.02	34.61
Total	374.45	27.18	397.00	28.11	7.26	7.08

Notes : 1 and 2 as on 31.3.1993 and 31.3.1999. 3 and 4 as on 1.1.94 and 1.1.2000.

Sources: 1. DGET for employment in organised sector.

2. NSSO, 55th *Round of Employment and Unemployment in India* (1999-2000).

hand looms and powerlooms and other village and small scale industries, i.e., tiny sector in the SSI sector. There is deceleration in organised sector employment in financial services, transport, storage and communications. There is virtual stagnation in organised sector employment in community, social and personal services. In trade, organised sector employment is negligible at 1.31 per cent. Deceleration of growth in organised sector employment has led to the shift towards unorganised sector, which implies a shift from better quality and secure employment to inferior and insecure employment.

Self-employed, Regular Salaried and Casual Labour

Data on the basis of category of employment is given in Table 1.9 separately for rural and urban areas. In rural areas, in 1999-2000, 56 per cent of the workers were self-employed, about 7 per cent were regular salaried workers and 37 per cent were casual labourers. The proportion of self-employment in rural areas was around 63 per cent in 1977-78 and it has shown a decline over the last two decades. The share of regular salaried workers has slightly declined from 7.7 per cent in 1977-78 to 6.7 per cent in 1999-2000. But there has been an increase in casual labour from 29.7 per cent in 1977-78 to 37.3 per cent in 1999-2000. The increase in casual labour is a reflection of the conversion of marginal cultivators into agricultural labourers.

The situation is very different in urban areas. The share of self-employment, though significant, has remained more or less about 42 per cent during the entire period 1977-78 to 1999-2000. Similarly, the regular salaried workers have been around 40 per cent and only 18 per cent of urban workers are casual labourers. The scenario, by category of employment, was more or less stable in the urban areas during 1977-78 to 1999-2000.

Taking the country as a whole, whereas in 1977-78, about 59 per cent were self-employed, 14 per cent were regular salaried workers and 27 per cent were casual labour, the situation changed by the year 1999-2000 and 53 per cent were self-employed, 14 per cent were regular salaried workers and 33 per cent were casual labourers. In other words, the regular salaried workers proportion has remained constant during the last two decades and the decline witnessed in self-employment was converted into

TABLE 1.9
Distribution of Workers (Usual Status) by Category of Employment

(% of total workers)

	Year	Category of employment		
		Self-employment	*Regular salaried*	*Casual*
1.	Rural areas			
	1977-78	62.6	7.7	29.7
	1983	61.0	7.5	31.5
	1987-88	59.4	7.7	32.9
	1993-94	58.0	6.4	35.6
	1999-2000	56.0	6.7	37.3
2.	Urban areas			
	1977-78	42.4	41.8	15.8
	1983	41.8	40.0	18.2
	1987-88	42.8	40.3	16.9
	1993-94	42.3	39.4	18.3
	1999-2000	42.1	40.1	17.8
3.	Rural and Urban combined			
	1977-78	58.9	13.9	27.2
	1983	57.4	13.9	28.7
	1987-88	56.0	14.4	29.6
	1993-94	54.8	13.2	32.0
	1999-2000	52.9	13.9	33.2

Source : NSSO Surveys.

higher proportion of casual labour. Since casual labour is not associated with job security and other associated benefits, increase in the proportion of casual labour is generally treated as an index of deterioration in the quality of employment.

Employment Policies and the Unorganised Sector

The *Task Force on Employment Opportunities* headed Dr. Montek Singh Ahluwalia submitted its report to the Planning Commission on 1st July 2001. The Report was sharply criticised by economists, sociologists, policy-makers and trade union leaders. The Task Force suggested measures like boosting private sector investment in agriculture, development of integrated agricultural complexes and food parks by the corporate sector, to give contracts to agro-companies to develop degraded and waste lands, to involve large industrial units, including MNCs to develop food processing industries, to

Table 1.10

Profile of Employment and Unemployment

	1983	*1999-2000 (Million persons)*	*1993-94*	*Employment growth rate (% per annum)*	
				1983-1993-94	*1993-94 to 1999-2000*
All India					
1. Population	718.20	894.01	1003.97	2.0	1.95
2. Labour force	261.33	335.97	363.33	2.43	1.31
3. Work force	239.57	315.84	336.75	2.7	1.07
4. No. of un-employed (2-3)	21.76	20.13	26.58	-0.08	4.74
5. Unemployment rate (%) (4+2x100)	8.33	5.99	7.32		
		Rural			
Population	546.61	658.83	727.50	1.79	1.67
Labour force	204.18	255.38	270.39	2.15	0.96
Workforce	187.92	241.04	250.89	2.40	0.96
No. of unemployed	16.26	14.34	19.50	-1.19	5.26
Unemployment rate (%)	7.96	5.61	7.21		
		Urban			
Population	171.59	234.98	27.47	3.04	2.74
Labour force	57.15	80.60	92.95	3.33	2.40
Workforce	51.64	74.80	85.84	3.59	2.32
No. of unemployed	5.51	5.80	7.11	0.49	3.45
Unemployment rate (%)	9.64	7.19	7.65		

Source : Planning Commission (2002), Report of Special Group on Targeting Ten Million Employment Opportunities per year.

involve large firms in construction, retail trade, road transport etc. In other words, the total responsibility for employment generation was to be given to the corporate sector. To facilitate this process, the report suggested total dereservation of small industries in the next four years and reform of the labour laws by deleting chapter VB of the Industrial Disputes Act so as to give the employers an unbridled right to hire and fire labour. It was felt by the policy makers that such failed strategy, if followed, would create greater resistance because it was anti-labour and pinned exclusive faith on GDP growth via corporation of the economy. It was largely believed that most of the recommendations were employment restricting, rather than employment generating. It was also believed that with this strategy to achieve the goal of creating 10 million jobs per year as directed by the Prime Minister, was well-nigh impossible.

Although the Planning Commission did not formally reject the Report of the Task Force, but it gave burial to this Report by appointing S.P. Gupta Special Group on Targeting 10 Million Employment Opportunities on 5th September 2001.

Estimate of Employment and Unemployment

The Special Group on the basis of the NSS data has estimated the number of unemployed to be of the order of 26.58 million in 1999-2000, as against 20.13 million in 1993-94 (current daily status basis). The growth rate of unemployed works out to be 4.74 per cent per annum for 1993-94 to 1999-00, as against a decline in the number of unemployed during 1983 to 1993-94. This only underlines the fact that unemployment rate which was 8.33 per cent in 1983 declined to 5.99 per cent by 1993-94, but increased to 7.32 per cent in 1999-2000. The Special Group Report mentions: The present rising unemployment is primarily an outcome of a declining job creating capacity of growth, observed since 1993-94. The employment growth fell to 1.07 per cent per annum (between 1993-94 and 1999-2000) from 2.7 per cent per annum in the past (between 1983 and 1993-94) in spite of acceleration in GDP growth from 5.2 per cent between 1983 and 1993-94 to 6.7 per cent between 1993-94 and 1999-2000". "Explaining the situation, the Special Group Report mentions: The employment elasticity of the 80s and early 90s of 0.52 went down to 0.16 in the late nineties. The organised sector's employment generating capacity (measured in terms of employment elasticity) came down to near zero and in the public sector has been negative in most cases. This is primarily because of:

(i) The present policy of shedding excess labour that this sector is carrying in order to meet the growing market competition, often known as right-sizing;

(ii) the trend towards increasing capital intensity per unit of output; and

(iii) the pattern of growth moving in favour of capital intensive sectors."

Organised *vs.* Unorganised Sector Employment and Unemployment Scenario

Employment in the organised sector has been hardly 8.34 per cent, of which public sector accounts for 5.77 per cent and private sector only 2.57 per cent in the total employment generated in 1999-2000.

The organised sector is dominated by public sector which contributed 70 per cent of the total employment in this sector. This is mainly in (i) mining, (ii) electricity and water, and (iii) community and social services. These three constitute nearly 60 per cent of public sector employment and unfortunately, all of them are showing negative employment elasticity. This only underlines the fact that the public sector contributed to a very small extent in total employment generation during 1993-94 to 1999-2000. It implies that the public sector has shown almost a jobless growth, when its employment elasticity was 0.015. Further, in future a large part of this sector's potential may be negated by the impending downsizing policy (often called as right-sizing) of the government, which affects this sector significantly.

The main source of employment generation is the unorganised sector of economy including self-employment and small business where the present contribution is as high as 92 per cent of the total employed labour force. Its main employment generating activities are: (a) agriculture and allied,

(b) trade, restaurants and hotels including tourism, (c) some of the social sectors like education and health, (d) small and medium enterprises mainly in rural non-farm sector, (e) transport and construction. It may be noted that small and medium enterprises contribute to nearly 80 per cent of manufacturing employment and its employment elasticity is relatively 3.8 times more than that of the organised sector. Thus, to achieve a more favourable effect on employment, what is needed is a shift in the percentage composition of manufacturing in favour of small and medium enterprises (SMEs).

Agriculture is another source of employment generation as it accounts for 57 per cent of India's total employment in 1999-00. Between 1983 and 1993-94, its employment elasticity was as high as 0.70, but in the post-reform period (1993-94 to 1999-2000), its employment elasticity has declined to 0.01. "But given an appropriate policy, this sector can still be a gold mine for generating faster employment by changes in the sectoral composition of agriculture in favour of labour intensive high value areas like horticulture, floriculture, agro-forestry, minor irrigation, watersheds etc.

The other employment generating areas in the unorganised sector that have been identified are trade, restaurants and tourism, and information technology (IT). They are all witnessing a high growth of above 9.0 per cent per annum and are having very high employment elasticities. The transport, construction and the other service sectors are also equally equipped for high growth and employment intensiveness.

The special Group Report concluded its analysis of employment situation in the following manner: "To sum up, with some changes in the inter and intra sectoral composition and adopting appropriate labour intensive technology, growth in the unorganised sector can be significantly raised. The appropriate organised sector, especially its public sector component, has a rather low employment generating potential, being handicapped by a negative employment elasticity with the exception of the financial sectors and potentiality in certain parts of social sector like education, health etc. But these two have as a low weightage as 3.3 per cent to the total employment. The community and social services need a major change in the composition in favour of health, education etc. and only then can it substantially contribute to the growth. Already a significant increase in the weightage of this sector in this group is in sight. It was 25.8 per cent in 1993-94 and 33.3 per cent now. These two sub-sectors together are showing a growth rate of around 4.5 per cent per annum compared to this sector's growth of 0.2 per cent per annum between 1993-94 and 1999-2000. Given the Tenth Plan target on education, literacy and health standard, the scope of its growth and potential employment generation is very high."

As the absorption capacity for high skill jobs has its own limit in the organised sector, the future plan for education and training should keep in mind the type of skills needed for many newly emerging activity sectors like IT, tourism, financial services and the vast unorganised SSI and services sector including the new areas in agriculture and the non-farm rural activities.

The Future Strategy

On the basis of the data collected and analysed by the special Group, it was found that in the unorganised sector, the employment elasticity was as high as 0.213 in 1999-2000 whereas in the organised sector, it was as low as 0.066, i.e. almost a jobless growth. Moreover, in the year 1999-2000, the total contribution to employment by the organised sector was only 8 per cent of which private sector segment's contribution was hardly 2.5 per cent. Rest 92 per cent came from the unorganised sector. The Special Group, therefore, opined: "On this basis, one can see even if the organised sector grows at 20 per cent per annum and the private organised sector at 30 per cent per annum, their contribution to total employment will increase hardly by 1.5 to 2 per cent of the total over the Tenth Plan. This proposition however remains hypothetical since given the capital intensity in this sector as of today (above 5.5), this high growth will not be sustainable because of the saving investment constraint of the economy. On the basis of this ground reality, the Group concluded that exclusively for generating the desirable high level of employment, we have to target the unorganised sector, including small and medium enterprises, which also cover a large part of the services sector of the economy.

TABLE 1.11
Present Employment Scenario in India (1983 to 1999-2000)

	Current daily status			*Employment growth rate*		*GDP growth rate (% per annum)*		*Employment elasticity*	
	1983	*1993-94*	*1999-2000*	*1983-1993-94*	*1993-94-1999-00*	*1983-1993-94*	*1993-94-99-00*	*1983-84-1993-94*	*1993-94-1999-00*
	1	2	3	4	5	6	7	8=4/6	9=5/7
1. Agriculture	151.35 (63.18)	190.72 (60.38)	190.94 (56.70)	2.03	0.02	2.9	3.1	0.70	0.01
2. Mining and quarrying	1.74 (0.73)	2.54 (0.80)	2.26 (0.67)	3.66	-1.91	6.2	4.7	0.59	-0.41
3. Manufacturing	27.69 (11.56)	35.00 (11.08)	40.79 (12.11)	2.28	2.58	6.0	7.8	0.38	0.33
4. Electricity, gas and water supply	0.83 (0.34)	1.43 (0.45)	1.15 (0.34)	5.29	-3.55	8.4	6.8	0.63	-0.52
5. Construction	7.17 (2.99)	11.02 (3.99)	14.95 (4.44)	4.21	5.21	4.9	6.3	0.86	0.82
6. Trade, hotels and restaurants	18.17 (7.58)	26.88 (8.51)	37.54 (11.15)	3.81	5.72	5.6	9.2	0.68	0.62
7 Transport, storage and communications	6.99 (2.92)	9.88 (3.13)	13.65 (4.05)	3.36	5.53	6.1	8.7	0.55	0.63

8. Finance, insurance, real estate and Business services	2.10 (0.88)	3.37 (1.07)	4.62 (1.38)	4.54	5.40	10.1	8.4	0.45	0.64
9. Commity, social and personal services	23.52 (9.82)	34.98 (11.08)	30.84 (9.16)	3.88	-2.08	5.7	8.4	0.68	-0.25
All	239.57 (100.0)	315.84 (100.0)	336.75 (100.0)	2.70	1.07	5.2	6.7	0.52	0.16

Note : Figures in brackets are percentages of total employment in respective column.
Source : Compiled and computed from the Report of the Special Group on Targeting Ten Million Employment Opportunities per year (2002)

Data provided in Table 1.16 reveals that in 1999-2000, the unorganised sector contributed nearly 59 per cent to GDP, but its contribution to employment was of the order of 92 per cent. Besides this, it contribution to exports was also substantial. But of late, because of the opening-up of the economy with deregulation and market orientation including withdrawal of several key subsidies, the unorganised sector in general and especially some of its components are meeting with growing sickness and slowing down of activities. During 1993-94 and 1999-2000, as a consequence of the policies of liberalisation, the flow of bank credit of scheduled Commercial Banks increased significantly towards the organised sector from 46.2 per cent in 1993-94 to 62.9 per cent in 1999-2000, whereas in the unorganised sector, it fell from 53.8 per cent in 1993-94 to 37.1 per cent in 1999-2000. This was despite the fact that the unorganised sector continued to provide employment to 92 per cent workforce in the economy. This affects the growth rate and efficiency of the unorganised sector. This trend has to be reversed. Special Group, therefore, recommended:

To sum up, the employment strategy for future, to meet the plan's employment goals is to encourage the use of labour intensive and capital saving technology, in general and to rejuvenate the growth of the unorganised sector in particular, which at present contributes 92 per cent to the country's employment and enjoys more than seven times labour intensity per unit of production, as compared to the organised sector. However, the unorganised sector needs to be made more productive to sustain itself against the domestic and international competition by proper choice of programmes and policies compatible with India's economic reforms and the WTO rules."

Drawing lessons from international experience, the Special Group Report repudiates the view of some economists, more especially that of the chairman of the Taskforce of the Planning Commission on Employment Opportunities Dr. Montek Singh Ahluwalia that the organised sector with its better productivity and high job quality is going to replace unorganised small business totally to provide higher growth, better quality of life and employment in the economy. But facts, pertaining to most developed and newly industrialised economies, reveal that

TABLE 1.12

Employment Scenario (1999-2000) in India

	Total*	Organisation Sector			% of organised sector to total sectoral employment	% of public sector to total employment	% of public sector to organised sector	% of private sector to total organised sector
		Public sector	Private sector	Total				
	1	2	3	4=2+3	5=4/1	6=2/1	7=2/4	8=3/4
1. Agriculture	190.94	0.52	0.87	1.39	0.73	0.27	37.16	62.84
2. Mining and quarrying	2.26	0.93	0.09	1.02	44.69	41.15	91.41	8.59
3. Manufacturing	40.79	1.57	5.18	6.75	16.55	3.95	23.25	76.75
4. Electricity, gas and water supply	1.15	0.96	0.04	1.00	96.96	83.48	95.91	4.09
5. Construction	14.95	1.11	0.07	1.18	7.90	7.42	93.97	6.03
6. Trade, hotels and restaurants	37.54	0.16	0.32	0.49	1.31	0.43	23.54	66.46
7. Transport, storage and communications	13.65	3.08	0.07	3.15	23.08	22.56	97.81	2.19
8. Finance, insurance, real estate and business Services	4.62	1.30	0.36	1.65	35.71	29.14	78.34	21.66
9. Community, social and personal services	30.84	9.79	1.70	11.49	37.26	31.74	85.21	14.79
Total	336.75	19.42	8.70	28.11	8.34	5.77	69.06	30.94

Note : *On Current Daily Status basis.

TABLE 1.13
Output, Employment and Productivity of Organised and Unorganised Sectors of the Economy

	Total	*Organised Sector*		*Unorgansed sector*	*Grand total*
		Public sector	*Private sector*		
	(1)	*(2)*	*(3)*	*(4)*	*5=1+4*
Value added GDP (Rs. crores at 1993-94 prices)	2,56849	1,80,843	76,006	4,41,143	6,97,992
1993-94	(36.8)	(25.9)	(10.9)	(63.2)	(100.0)
1999-2000	4,18,920 (41.1)	2,66,519 (26.1)	1,52,401 (15.0)	6,00,425 (58.9)	1,019,345 (100.0)
Growth rate (%)	8.50	6.68	12.30	5.27	6.52
Bank credit (Rs. 000 crores)					
1993-94	80.8 (46.0)	28.1 (16.0)	52.7 (30.0)	94.9 (54.0)	175.7 (100.0)
1999-2000	247.4 (62.9)	66.8 (17.0)	180.6 (45.9)	145.9 (37.1)	393.3 (100.0)
Growth rate (%)	20.5	15.5	22.8	7.4	14.4

Employment (million)					
1993-94	27.18 (8.6)	19.30 (6.1)	7.88 (2.5)	288.66 (91.4)	315.84 (100.0
1999-2000	28.11 (8.35)	19.42 (5.77)	8.69 (2.58)	308.64 (61.65)	336.75 (100.0)
Growth Rate (%)	0.56	0.10	1.64	1.12	1.07
Employment elasticity	0.066	0.015	0.133	0.213	0.165
Labour productivity growth (%)	7.88	6.67	8.38	4.10	5.38
Relative Labour Intensity (Organised/Unorganised) 1999-2000	0.1345				

Notes : 1. Figures in brackets are percentages of grand total in the row.
2. Outstanding bank credit refers to all Scheduled Commercial Banks.

Source : Compiled and computed from Planning Commission (2002), Report of the Special Group on Targeting Ten Million Employment Opportunities per Year.

small business is providing major employment opportunities and also surviving alongside with the highly organised large sector. For example, in the US all firms under the small Business Act contribute nearly 50 per cent of the private workforce along with more than half of GDP. Similarly, in Japan, of the total 54.16 million people engaged nationwide (excluding those in primary industries), 42.27 million, i.e. 78 per cent employment is in small and medium enterprises and the total value in manufacturing from SMEs is 51 per cent, in wholesale trade 64 per cent and in retail 78 per cent. Similarly, in China, SMEs provide 75 per cent of urban job opportunities and their number of units exceeded 8 million, being 99 per cent of total enterprises in China. Therefore, the question of easing out the SMEs by large organised sector in India in foreseeable future is ruled out. The organised and unorganised sectors are to co-exist satisfying the different needs of development and growth, as has happened in most of the developed and newly industrialised economies.

The Special Group Report, therefore, Categorically Mentions

"The case for encouraging the growth of the organised sector is certainly supported by its capacity to invest in major infrastructure (in most cases, they are capital intensive) to give support systems to the rest of the economy, but for generation of employment, their growth cannot be regarded as the answer."

The total employment generation by the private organised sector is barely of the order of 2.58 per cent of the total. On account of its low employment base and low employment elasticity, even if it grows at the rate of 30 per cent per annum over the Tenth Plan period, its contribution to total employment will increase from 2.58 per cent to 3.5 per cent of the total employment by end of the Tenth Plan.

It has been argued by the Task Force on Employment Opportunities that the present Industrial Disputes Act (1956) should be amended to enable the employers to have complete freedom to hire and fire. Such a change in legal conditions will make the organised sector more employment-friendly and the employment generation in this sector can be improved. The

Special Group examined this question, but it held the view: "With considerable excess labour being carried by the public sector in the organised segment and a jobless nature of growth in the organised sector as a whole, the immediate effect may turn out to be net labour shedding. This should be assessed against the present high level of unemployment.

In this context, one should also remember that the social security support in India is much below the standard provided in developed countries, because of which their tolerance level of unemployment is very high. One should remember that the contribution of total employment by the organised private sector is hardly 3.5 per cent and, therefore the potential of generating sizeable employment in this sector, even by changing the law will be insignificant over the Tenth Plan period." But given the fact that the organised sector (especially the public sector) is already carrying excess labour, the immediate effect will be more firing than hiring. The Special Group, thus, stated: "Therefore, purely on the ground of employment generation, the favourable effect of any change in this legislation is marginal, at least in the short-term. Gradual withdrawal of the Act could be considered, observing the net impact on employment at every phase. Along with it, the social security coverage may be increased and care should be taken of the retrenched labour."

The Special Group did not deem it as a correct policy to seek the answer to the question of increasing productivity and job quality in the organised sector, as has been suggested by Ahluwalia Task Force on Employment Opportunity, but is of the strong view:

"The only answer to this situation is to increase productivity and job quality of the unorganised sector. It means that all attempts should be made to implement those policies, which will release the basic growth constraints and by ensuring a level playing field for this sector. . . . In the attempt to increase the labour productivity, more emphasis should be on the growth of this sector rather than for substituting labour by capital. Further, to improve the job quality and its security, major changes in legislation will be needed regarding basic social security measures working conditions, minimum wages and protection of labour interests."

To sum up, S.P. Gupta Special Group Report on Employment was unique in many ways:

- It rejected the reform process as a panacea for all ills of economy, especially referring to unemployment.
- It rejected the thesis of the reformists that the organised sector, more especially the corporate sector, could usher an era of zero unemployment and removal of poverty in the near future.
- It focused attention on the unorganised sector, which provides employment to 92 per cent of labour force and has remained neglected so far.
- It repudiated the theory that amendment of the Industrial Disputes Act to give power to the employers to hire and fire shall lead to enlargement of employment. Rather it would result in more firing than hiring.
- It underlined the need for improving productivity and job quality of the unorganised sector. For this purpose, it highlighted the need for major changes in legislation regarding basic social security measures, working conditions, minimum wages and protection of labour interests, rather than throwing the workers at the mercy of the market forces.
- It laid down a policy prescription for providing 50 million jobs during the Tenth Plan-30 million based on 8 per cent growth of GOP and 20 million based on Special programmes.
- It rejected the view that elasticity of employment in agriculture is zero. Rather it stressed the need to diversify and strengthen agriculture so that by 2011-12, about 51 per cent of employment is generated through agriculture.
- On the basis of international experience and the imperative need of our country, the Report brought out the fact that small and medium industries are not only to co-exist with large industries, but should also become the principal contributors to industrial growth and employment.

- The employment issue has to placed on a high priority and not treated as *"business as usual."* It, thus, sought active state intervention to resolve the issue.
- It underlined the need for a change in the credit policy of the banking system to stop the decline in the share of bank credit from 54 per cent to 37 per cent for the unorganised sector in the short-span of 6 years (1993-94 to 1999-2000).
- It highlighted the fact that the employment elasticity of the unorganised vis-a-vis the organised sector is 3.23 times and thus the State must protect and strengthen this sector.
- It warned the state that unless civil administration in the urban areas and the panchayats in the rural areas do not work hand in hand along with the state to reduce unemployment in the new environment, unemployment at the end of the Tenth Plan will reach 40 million i.e., nearly ten per cent of labour force—a very grim prospect indeed.
- If one studies carefully many of the policy changes suggested in Common Minimum Programme of the United Progressive Alliance Government led by the Congress in 2004, the conclusion is inescapable that S.P. Gupta's Special Group recommendations could be considered as the precursors of the new policy, though it may be noted that the NDA government did not seriously implement them.

Economic Reforms and Employment in India : Trends, Issues and Future Strategy

P.N. SHARMA

INTRODUCTION

The last decade of 20th century has witnessed marked and momentous changes in the world economy. In response to these changes, most of the countries have adopted the policy of liberalising their economies. India has also responded to these changes by introducing a wide ranging programme of economic reforms. Major reforms have been undertaken in industrial policy, foreign trade and exchange rates policies, taxation policies and financial sector. The basic medium-term objective of these policy reforms is to lay the foundation of sustained growth of output and employment in the context of increasing global competition (Singh, Manmohan, 1993). It was hoped that these reform measures would lead to higher growth of GDP and a significant expansion of employment and that growth would trickle down to the poorest sections of population. The new competitive economic scene will help to add both higher GDP growth rate and employment resulting into reduction in unemployment rate and thus, social justice would be met with. It is contended that structural adjustment would remove the rigidities and the factor price distortions in the economy and that it would change the industry-mix and the factor-mix in favour of labour (Bhagwati and Srinivasan, 1993; Joshi and Little, 1996).

Post-reform measures might help to increase employment as a result of greater labour market flexibility and increased trade-orientation leading to change in the industries in favour of labour intensive industries and techn iques of production (Singh, M., 1993; Papola, T.S., 1994). But some other experts maintain that the new economic policy measures have had adverse effects on employment. Some of the studies in this direction show that Structural Adjustment Policy has promoted only rise in unemployment rate in the country. According to Papola, this strend is likely to accelerate with liberalisation and opening-up of the economy, as the compulsions of international competiion are likely to further reduce the unemployment intensity partially because of the need for cost reduction but mostly for the reasons for improving the quality of the product (Papola, T.S., 1991). On balance more studies are pessimistic about prospects of employment growth in the post-reform period.

GDP GROWTH AND TRENDS IN EMPLOYMENT

The reform process has completed about thirteen years and this period is long enough to assess the impact of economic reforms on GDP and employment growth. It is beyond doubt that economic reforms have been able to promote a comparatively higher rate of growth as would be evident from Table 2.1.

Table 2.1 reveals that after the economic crisis of two years i.e. 1991-92 and 1992-93, GDP growth rate averaged to more than 6.7 per cent during the period 1993-94 to 1997-98. Thus, there is a definite indication that the as a result of the reform

TABLE 2.1
GDP Growth at Factor Cost (at 1993-94 Prices)

Year	GDP Growth Rate	Year	GDP Growth Rate
1980-81	7.3	1991-92	1.1
1981-82	5.8	1992-93	5.1
1982-83	2.7	1993-94	5.9
1983-84	7.5	1994-95	7.2
1984-85	4.2	1995-96	7.5
1985-86	4.5	1996-97	8.2
1986-87	4.1	1997-98	4.9
1988-89	3.6	1998-99	6.4
1989-90	10.1	1991-00	6.2
1990-91	6.7	2000-01	4.4
		2001-02	6.1
	Annual Average GDP Growth Rate		
1980-81to 1990-91		5.6	
1991-92 to 2001-02		5.7	

Source : Compiled from, Government of India, Economic Survey, 2003-2004, p. 5.4.

measures the growth momentum has been maintained after 1991-92 and the growth rate reachd an average level of 7 per cent during the four-year period (1994-95 to 1997-98). But, thereafter, the growth rate showed signs of deceleration. However, it is interesting to note that annual average growth rate during the pre-reform period (1980-81 to 1990-91) was about 5.6 per cent but the post-reform period (1990-91 to 2001-02) also indicates about the same annual average growth rate of the order of about 5.7 per cent. It is, therefore, obvious that the reform process has not shown better performance in comparison to the pre-reform period. This underlines the need to reorient the content of economic reforms in order to accelerate the rate of growth to such a high level as to make a definite dent on poverty and employment.

Now it would be interesting to assess the impact of reform measures on employment growth. The change in employment scenario before and after the economic reforms has been shown in Table 2.2.

TABLE 2.2
Change in Employment 1983-2000 (in lakhs)

Year	*Total*	*Organised Sector*	*Unorganised Sector*
1983	3,027.5	240.1	2787.4
1993-94	3,744.5	273.7	3470.8
1999-2000	3,970.0	281.1	3688.9
Annual Average Growth Rate of Employment (%)			
1983 to 1994	2.04	1.20	2.05
1994 to 1999-2000	0.98	0.53	1.00

Source : Compiled from data of Planning Commission (2001), Report of the Task Force on Employment Opportunities, p. 2.25.

Table 2.2 shows that total employment increased from 3027.5 lakhs in 1983 to 3744.5 lakhs in 1993-94 and further to 3,970 lakhs in 1979-2000. The rate of growth of employment during the period 1983 to 1993-94 was of the order of 2.04 per cent per annum which was just equal to the rate of growth of labour force during this period. It was hoped that if this rate of growth of employment is sustained in the next decade, the country would be able to bring about a significant reduction in the backlog of unemployment. But unfortunately, the overall growth rate of employment during the reform period turned out to be of the order of 0.98 per cent per annum only. Since the reform process is limited to the organised sector, more so to the corporate sector, the growth rate of employment in the organised sector also declined to 0.53 per cent per annum during 1993-94 to 1999-2000 as against 1.20 per cent per annum obtained during the pre-reform period (1993 to 1993-94). This was less than half of the growth rate of employment witnessed earlier.

There was also a substantial slow down in employment growth rate of the unorganised sector from 2.04 per cent during the pre-reform period (1983 to 1993-94) to merely 1.0 per cent during the reform period 1993-94 to 1999-2000. This clearly proves that the trickle down effects of growth process did not percolate to the poorest sections of population. All these trends make one rethink the utility of an exclusive policy on 'GDP Growth' in resolving poverty or employment (Gupta, S.P., 1999).

Thus, an increase of GDP growth rate during the reform period was not accompanied by a commensurate increase in employment. The reason is that there was near stagnation of employment in the public sector as it began to withdraw from several areas and public sector units started the process of downsizing by getting rid of abundant labour. It was expected that the organised private sector, which was the kingpin of economic reforms, would be able to provide higher level of employment. But this did not materialise. Faced with the prospect of global competition in the wake of liberalisation, even private sector industrial units started shedding excess labour and introducing new technology. All these measures resulted in loss of jobs even in the private sector. As most of the technological advances are of such nature that mannual work is being eliminated, the elasticities of job creation to economic growth is declining (Hashim, 1999). It is because of these reasons that the growth during the reform period has been decribed as "jobless growth".

Dimensions of Unemployment and Employment

Certain disturbing trends in the unemployment rates have been observed during the reform period as is evident from Table 2.3 which provides alternative measures of unemployment.

Table 2.3 reveals that all the four categories of unemployment showed a declining trend during the period 1977-78 to 1993-94, but the trend was reversed during the period 1993-94 to 1999-2000.

(i) Open unemployment as measured by UPS criterion, declined from 4.23 per cent in 1977-78 to 2.56 per cent in 1993-94 but increased to 2.81 per cent in 1999-2000.

(ii) Usual Principal and Subsidiary Status (UPPS) unemployment rate declined from 2.47 per cent in

TABLE 2.3
Alternative Measures of Unemployment

Percentage of Labour Force

	Usual Principal Status UPS	*Usual Principal and Subsidiary Status UPSS*	*Current Weekly Status CWS*	*Current Daily Status CDS*
Rural				
1977-98	3.26	1.64	3.74	7.70
1983	1.91	1.13	3.88	7.94
1987-88	3.07	1.98	4.19	5.25
1993-94	1.80	1.20	3.00	5.63
1999-00	1.96	1.43	3.91	7.21
Urban				
1977-78	8.77	7.01	7.86	10.34
1983	6.04	5.02	6.81	9.52
1987-88	6.56	5.32	7.12	9.36
1993-94	5.21	4.52	5.83	7.43
1999-2000	5.23	4.63	5.89	7.65
All India				
1977-78	4.23	2.47	4.48	8.18
1983	2.77	1.90	4.51	8.28
1987-88	3.77	2.62	4.81	6.09
1993-94	2.56	1.92	3.63	6.03
1999-2000	2.81	2.23	4.41	7.32

Note : Estimates are based on NSS data combind with Census data.
Source : Planning Commission, Report of Task Force on Employment Opportunities, Table 2.1.

1977-78 to 1.90 per cent in 1993-94 but again rose to 2.23 per cent in 1999-2000.

(iii) The Current Weekly Status (CWS) unemployment rate decreased from 4.48 per cent in 1977-78 to 3.63 per cent in 1993-94 but rose to 4.41 per cent in 1999-2000.

(v) The Current Daily Status (CDS) unemployment rate which is the most comprehensive measure of unemployment (as it, besides taking into account open unemployment also measures underemployment), declined from 8.18 per cent in 1977-78 to 6.09 per cent in 1993-94 but rose to 7.32 per cent in 1999-2000.

The same trend can be observed with respect to both urban and rural areas in all the four measures of unemployment. Another fact that emerges from the data is that while the Usual Principal Status (UPS) rates are modest, the CDS rates are quite high, indicating that the major problem of Indian economy is not open unemployment but under-employment.

A notable point in this regard is that the unemployment rates are traditionaly higher in urban areas than in rural areas. It would be evident from Table 2.3 that as against the unemployment rate of 10.3 per cent in 1977-78 in urban area, the rural unemployment rate was 7.7 per cent (CDS basis). There was a marked decline in the rural unemployment rate to 5.3 per cent in 1987-88, while the urban unemployment rate was significantly higher 9.4 per cent. During the liberalisation period 1993-94 to 1999-2000, rural unemployment rate again increased to 7.2 per cent while urban unemployment also marginally increased to 7.7 per cent. Higher levels of unemployment in the urban areas could be explained by a larger proportion of organised sector unemployment, while rural areas indicate higher levels of disguised unemployment. Gradual and continuous decline of urban unemployment rates till 1993-94 and even a very marginal increase in 1999-2000 may be due to greater attention being given to urban areas in development process, but increase in unemployment rate in rural areas may be due to neglect of rural areas in post-reform period. (Datt, Ruddar, 2003).

Sector-wise Growth Rates of Employment

It would be of interest to analyse the rate of growth of employment in different sectors of the economy. Table 2.4 provides an account of the growth rates of employment by sectors.

It can be seen from the table that the growth rate of total employment decreased sharply from 2.04 per cent per annum during the period 1983 to 1993-94 to 0.98 per cent per annum during the reform period (1993-94 to 1999-2000). The growth

TABLE 2.4

Sector-wise Growth Rate of Employment

Industry	*Employed Workers (Million)* 1983	1993-94	1999-00	*Annual Growth Rate (%)* 1983-94	1993-94 to 1999-2000
A. Primary Sector	208.99 (69.0)	245.16 (69.5)	239.83 (60.4)	0.60	-0.34
(i) Agriculture	207.23 (68.4)	242.46 (64.8)	237.56 (59.8)	1.51	-0.34
(ii) Mining and quarrying	1.76 (0.6)	2.70 (0.7)	2.27 (0.6)	4.16	-2.85
B. Secondary sector	41.66 (13.8)	55.53 (14.8)	66.91 (16.8)	2.90	3.14
(iii) Manufacturing	34.03 (11.2)	42.50 (11.3)	48.01 (12.1)	2.14	2.05
(iv) Electricity, gas and water supply	0.85 (0.3)	1.35 (0.4)	1.28 (0.3)	4.50	-0.88
(v) Construction	6.78 (2.2)	11.68 (3.1)	17.62 (4.4)	5.32	7.09
C. Tertiary sector	52.11 (17.2)	73.76 (19.7)	90.26 (22.7)	3.53	2.42
(vi) Trade	19.22 (6.3)	27.78 (7.4)	37.32 (9.4)	3.57	5.04
(vii) Transport, storage and Communications	7.39 (2.4)	10.33 (2.8)	14.69 (3.7)	3.24	6.04
(viii) Final services	1.70 (0.6)	3.52 (0.9)	5.08 (1.3)	7.18	6.20
(ix) Community, social and personal services	23.80 (7.9)	32.13 (8.6)	33.20 (8.4)	2.90	0.55
Total Employment	302.76 (100.0)	374.45 (100.0)	397.00 (100.0)	2.04	0.98

Notes : 1. Growth rates derived from NSS data.

2. Growth rates for primary sector calculated on the basis of data given by the Task Force on Employment Opportunities.

Source : Compiled from Planning Commission (2001), Report of Task Force on Employment Opportunities, Table 3-2.

rate of employment in agriculture was 1.60 per cent during the pre-reform period (1983 to 1993-94) but this rate declined sharply during the reform period (1993-94 to 1999-2000) and became negative (-0.34%). The employment growth rate in the manufacturing sector declined marginally from 2.14 per cent during the period 1983 to1993-94 to 2.05 per cent during the period 1993-94 to 1999-2000.

The sectors which have witnessed rise in the rate of employment growth are construction, trade, transport and communications. The unemployment growth rate in construction sector rose from 5.32 per cent during the period 1983 to 1993-94 to 7.09 per cent in during 1993-94 to 1999-2000, while in trade it improved from 3.57 per cent to 5.04 per cent during the same period. In transport, storage and communications, employment growth rate rose sharply from 3.24 per cent during 1983-1993-94 to 6.04 per cent during 1993-94 to 1999-2000. There was a marginal decline in the employment growth rate in financial services from 7.18 per cent during 1983 to 1993-94 to 6.20 per cent during 1993-94 to 1999-2000 while the community, social and personal services also witnessed a sharp decline in the rate of employment growth from 2.90 per cent during 1983 to 1993-94 to 0.55 per cent during 1993-94 to 1999-2000.

It becomes, therefore, evident that during the post-liberalisation period (1993-94 to 1999-2000), there has been a deceleration in the growth rate of employment in the primary sector. In the secondary sector, though manufacturing and electricity, gas and water supply witnessed a decline in the growth rate, the combined effect of manufacturing in a modest improvement in the growth rate from 2.90 per cent in the pre-reform period to 3.14 per cent in the post-reform perid. But the tertiary (Services) sector registered a decrease in growth rate of employment to 2.42 per cent during the post reform period as against 3.53 per cent in the pre-reform period. This was the result of a sharp fall in the employment growth rate in community, personal and social services from 2.90 per cent in the pre-reform period to 0.53 per cent in the post-reform period.

Data in Table 2.4 also indicate that during the pre-reform period (1983-84 to 1993-94), the proportion of workers employed in primary sector declined from 69.0 per cent to 65.5

per cent, the proportion workers employed in secondary sector increased slightly from 13.8 per cent to 14.8 per cent and that of workers employed in tertiary sector also increased from 17.2 per cent to 19.2 per cent. The same trend is discernible during the post-reform period (1993-94 to 1999-2000) the proportion of workers employed in primary sector declined further to 60.4 per cent while there was increase in the proportion of workers employed in secondary sector to 16.8 per cent and in tertiary sector to 22.7 per cent.

Two different patterns of employment generation emerge during the pre-reform period and post-reform period as shown in Table 2.5.

TABLE 2.5

Sector-wise Share in Increase of Employment

(Million)

Pre-reform period	*1983*	*1993-94*	*Increase during 1983 to 1993-94*	*Share in Increase (%)*
Primary sector	208.99	245.16	36.17	50.5
Secondary sector	41.66	55.53	13.87	19.3
Tertiary sector	52.11	73.76	21.65	30.2
Total	302.76	374.45	71.69	100.0
Post-reform period	*1993-94*	*1999-2000*	*Increase during 1994-2000*	*Share in Increase (%)*
Primary sector	245.16	239.83	-5.33	-23.6
Secondary sector	55.53	66.91	11.38	50.4
Tertiary sector	73.76	90.26	16.50	73.2
Total	374.45	397.00	22.55	100.0

Source : Compiled and computed from Table 2.4.

Agriculture Sector has some limitations. It is seasonal in nature and its dependent on climatic conditions and has a lower growth rate. As a result of globalisation, more exportable crops would be produced leading to a shift from low profit labour intensive consumption crops to high profit capital intensive crops. Export of foodgrains is likely to reduce further the food availability for the poorest and the most vulnerable groups in the population (Nath, 1995).

Employment in Organised Sector

The organised sector has also witnessed a decline in the rate of employment growth during the post-reform period. Organised sector usually refers to employment in the public and in the private sector establishments. It has been observed that wages in the organised sector are higher than in the organised sector. As the organised sector is regulated, it provides greater job security and other benefits. Within the organised sector; public sector provides more secure jobs, higher wages and other benefits in comparison to the private sector.

So far as the organised sector is concerned, the employment growth has been very slow. Table 2.6 provides the share of organised sector in total employment.

Data in Table 2.6 show that the share of organised sector employment in total employment was of the order of 7.93 per cent in 1983 as well as 1988, but it declined to 7.08 per cent in 1999-2000. The organised sector employment increased from 24.1 million in 1983 to 25.71 million in 1988 and further to 27.37 million in 1993-94. Thus, the rate of growth of organised sector employment was 1.20 per cent per annum during the pre-reform period. The organised sector employment increased from 27.37 million in 1993-94 to 28.11 million in 1999-2000, indicating a growth rate of only 0.53 per cent per annum. This was the result of stagnation of employment in the public sector which indicated a negative growth rate of -0.03 per cent per annum during the period 1994-2000. Though the employment growth rate of private sector was 1.87 per cent during this period, it could not offset the decline in public sector employment due to large share of the public sector in (69%) total employment.

It may be further added that in the organised sector, the major contribution of employment has been from the public sector (about 69%). But during the post-reform period, the rate of growth of employment in the public sector has kept on

TABLE 2.6

Employment in Organised Sector

Sector	Employment (million)				Growth Rate (% per annum)	
	1983	1988	1994	1999-2000	1983 to 94	1994-2000
(1)	(2)	(3)	(4)	(5)	(6)	(7)
1. Total population	718.21	790.00	895.05	1004.10	2.12	1.93
2. Total labour force	308.64	333.49	381.94	406.05	2.05	1.03
3. Total employment	302.75	324.29	374.45	397.00	2.04	0.98
4. Organised sector employment	24.01 (100.0)	25.71 (100.0)	27.37 (100.0)	028.11 (100.0)	1.20	0.53
5. Public sector	16.46 (68.6)	18.32 (71.3)	19.44 (71.0)	19.41 (69.1)	1.52	-0.03
6. Private sector	7.55 (31.4)	7.39 (28.7)	7.93 (29.0)	8.70 (30.9)	0.45	1.87
Per centage of public sector employment total employment	7.93	7.93	7.30	7.08		
7. Per centage of labour force to Total population	43.0	42.2	42.7	40.4		

Notes : 1. Figures of Total Employment are based on Usual Status (UPSS) basis.

2. Figures of organised sector employment pertain to 31st March of 1983, 1984, 1999 as reported by Ministry of Labour (in Employment Marker Information System).

3. Figures in brackets indicate percentage of employment in public sector and private sector to total employment.

Source : Compiled from—Planning Commission (2001) Report of the Task Force on Employment Opportunities, p. 2.25.

declining and from 1997 onward the growth rate of employment has to become negative. The private sector has witnessed a higher employment growth rate but from 1999 onward the employment has become negative in this sector also (Table 2.7).

TABLE 2.7
Growth Rate of Employment in Organised Sector

(Per cent)

Year	*Public Sector*	*Private Sector*	*Total Organised sector*
1991	1.52	1.24	1.44
1992	0.82	2.21	1.21
1993	0.60	0.06	0.44
1994	0.62	1.01	0.73
1995	0.11	1.63	0.53
1996	-0.19	5.62	1.51
1997	0.67	2.04	1.09
1998	-0.72	0.71	-0.27
1999	-0.15	-0.57	-0.17
2000	-0.52	-0.59	-0.75
2001	-0.91	0.06	-1.15
2002	-1.90	-2.54	-2.09

Source : Compiled from—Government of India, Economic Survey, 1998-99 (Table 10.8, p. 187) and Economic Survey, 2003-04 (Table 3.3, p. 550).

The hope that private section would create employment opportunities too has not materialised. The rising clamour in the private sector for computerisation, automation, robotisation, bio-technology development and revolution in information technology etc. has had the impact of replacing human hands and minds forcing millions of blue and white collar workers to be unemployed. Besides, in the post-reform period, the employers in India are clamouring for flexible labour market which implies their freedom in deciding wage employment and labour processes free from institutional and legal restrictions. All this is likely to lead to the closure of industries, retrenchment of workers etc. which will go against the interest of workers.

Task Force on Employment Opportunities

The perusal of the trend in employment growth and the pattern and structure of employment reveal that although the reform process resulted in an acceleration of GDP growth, it was not accompanied by commensurate increase in employment. As such the Planning Commission constituted a Task Force on Employment opportunities under the Chairmanship of Mr. Montek Singh Ahluwalia, Member, Planning Commission to examine the existing employment and unemployment situation in the country and to suggest strategies for employment generation for achieving the target of providing employment opportunities for ten crore people over the next 10 years—on an average and one crore people every year.

But despite dismal failure on employment front, the Task Force has opted to pursue the above failed strategy even for the next 12 years as given in the projections. As per the projections of the Task Force, 6.5 GDP growth will provide 71 million additional employment, (annual 5.9 million), while with 8 per cent and 9 per cent GDP growth rates, employment is expected to increase by 84 million (annual average of 7 million) and 98 million (annual average of 8.2 million) respectively. Thus, the Task Force failed to suggest an employment or growth strategy that could provide an annual average growth rate of 10 million jobs.

Thus, the Task Force recommended almost complete handing over of the economy to the corporate sector. But the policy-makers realised that this failed strategy, if followed, would create greater resistance because it was anti-labour and pinned exclusive faith in GDP growth via corporatisation of the economy. It was also realised that most of the recommendations were employment restricting rather employment generating (Datt, Rudder, 2003). It was also believed that with this strategy it was impossible to achieve goal of creating 10 million jobs per year as directed by the Prime Minister.

Future Strategy

The Task Force of the Planning Commission which was entrusted with the task of providing a suitable strategy of employment growth, opted to pursue the failed strategy on employment front even for the next 12 years. Its report was severely criticised by economists, sociologists, policy makers and trade union leaders. It was felt by most of the people that there was a need to evolve a new model of growth reconciling GDP growth and employment growth. Hence, the Planning Commission, instead of implementing the recommendations of the Task Force, appointed S.P. Gupta Special Group on Targeting Ten million Employment to suggest strategies and programmes in Tenth Plan for creating gainful employment of 10 million persons per year.

The Special Group, on the basis of NSS data found that the rising unemployment was the result of wrong strategy of growth pursued during the period of economic reforms.

In this Connection the Special Group Maintains

"The present rising unemployment is primarily the outcome of a declining job creating capacity of growth, observed since 1993-94. The employment growth rate fell to 1.07 per cent per annum (between 1993-94 and 1999-2000) from 2.7 per cent per annum in the past (between 1983 and 1993-94) in spite of acceleration of GDP growth rate from 5.2 per cent between 1983 and 1993-94 to 6.7 per cent between 1993-94 and 1999-2000. (Special Group, 2002). The Special Group further mentions : the employment elasticity of 80's and early 90's of 0.52 per cent went down to 0.16 per cent in late nineties. The organised sector's employment generating capacity (measured in terms of employment elasticity) came down to near zero and in the public sector has been negative in most cases. This is primarily because of:

(i) the present policy of shedding excess labour that this sector is carrying in order to meet the growing market competition often known as rightsizing.

(ii) the trend towards increasing capital intensity per unit of output.

(iii) the pattern of growth moving in favour of capital intensive sectors. (Special Group, 2020).

'To sum up, the employment strategy for the future, to meet the plan's employment goals is to encourage the use of labour intensive and capital saving technology, in general and to rejuvenate the growth of the unorganised sector in particular, which at present contributes 92 per cent to the country's employment and enjoys more than seven times labour intensity per unit of production, as compared to the organised sector. However, the unorganised sector needs to be made more productive to sustain itself against the domestic and international competition by proper choice of programmes and policies compatible with India's economic reforms and the WTO rules (Special Group, 2002, p. 7).

Drawing lesson from international experience, the Special Group Report repudiates the view that the organised sector with its better productivity and high job quality is going to replace unorganised small business totally to provide higher growth and employment in the country. The experience relating to several developed and newly industrialised economies, reveals that small business is providing major employment opportunities and also surviving along side with the highly organised large sector. In US all firms under Small Business Act contribute nearly 50 per cent of the private work force along with more than half of the GDP. Similarly, in Japan, of the total 54.16 million people engaged nation wide (excluding those in primary industries), 42.27 million (78%) employment is in small and medium enterprises. Thus, both the organised and unorganised sectors are to co-exist satisfying the different needs of growth and employment (Datt, Ruddar, 2003).

The Special Group has laid down a policy prescription for providing 50 million jobs during the Tenth Plan–30 million based on 8 per cent growth of GDP and 20 million based on Special Employment Programmes. It has underlined the need for improving productivity and job quality of the unorganised sector as also the need for major changes in legislation regarding basic social security measures, working conditions etc. The Group has underlined the need for complete coordination between the punchayats in rural areas, civil administration in urban areas and the State to reduce unemployment.

Conclusion

The economic reform measures were undertaken during the 90's with the hope that the growth strategy adopted during this period would lead to higher growth rate of GDP and to significant expansion of employment opportunities and that growth would trickle down to the poorest sections of population. But the experience of the post-reform period indicates that the trickle down effects of growth process did not percolate to the poorest sections of population. It would be a gross mistake to pursue the failed strategy of growth adopted during the post-liberalisation period which had a focus on only 7 per cent of labour force. The need of the hour is to evolve schemes for 93 per cent of the labour force of the unorganised sector. The objective of Tenth Five Year Plan warrants complete reversal of the trends observed during the post-liberalisation period. If this growth strategy is followed there is every possibility of jobless growth as there is no simple or unique correlation in the short run either in theory or Indian experience between the rate of growth of output and the rate of growth of employment. The statistics about several countries also indicate the lack of correlation between output and employment growth. In fact, the rate of investment and choice of technology determine the growth of employment.

In the new growth stragegy efforts should be made for restructuring the sectoral composition of output in favour of sectors and sub-sectors having higher employment strategy-especially in areas having higher rates of unemployment and under employment. Use of labour-intensive techniques should be encouraged in the maximum possible lines of production, far more effective use of macro-economic policies should be made for influencing private investment decisions in favour of the sectors and technologies with higher employment growth potential.

Higher emphasis should be placed on the development of agriculture and small scale industries and on creation of self-employment opportunities. In agriculture, more emphasis should be laid on extension of irrigation, especially minor irrigation works and watershed development with people's participation. Changes in crop pattern and development of allied agricultural activities like fishery and animal husbandry, dairy, poultry etc. which are highly employment generating, should be encouraged Degraded and waste lands should be developed through participatory efforts of panchayats. A vigorous programme of rural industrialisation should be launched and more emphasis should be laid on processing of agricultural produce, fruit and vegetable processing, village handicrafts, cottage industries etc. Agricultural cooperatives should be strengthened to undertake food processing activities and KVIC (Khadi and Village Industries Corporation) should be assigned the task of marketing. All kinds of supportive financial, technical and administrative measures should be provided for the programmes of rural industrialisation.

In the manufacturing sector, growth of small and cottage industries should be promoted in maximum lines of production and maximum use of labour intensive techniques should be encouraged in these industries as also in large scale industries as far as possible. Further dereservation of small scale industries products should be stopped and SSI sector should be helped on the lines suggested by S.P. Gupta Special Group.

In the services sector, two major areas of high employment potential are road construction and housing. In the field of road construction, besides national and state highways, priority should be given to rural road construction. Greater emphasis should be given on housing for the poor and on a programme of expansion of social infrastructive. There is also a need to promote the informal sector which is the major source of self-employment and casual labour. Information Technology Sector should be encouraged to spread its outreach to rural and remote areas. IT education should be made available to the economically weaker sections by a system of subsidies and differential fees.

It is such a model of development that can reconcile GDP growth and employment growth and provide growth in the social justice.

References

Banaji, Jairus (1994), "Globalisation, Restructuring and the Union", International Union of Food Workers Seminar Report, No. 8, quoted in Janardan, V. (1997), *EPW*, Vol. 32, No. 35, Aug.

Datt, Ruddar (2004), *Indian Economy*, S. Chand & Company, New Delhi.

Datt, Ruddar (2003), *Economic Reforms, Labour and Employment*, Deep and Deep Publications Pvt. Ltd., New Delhi.

Hajela, P.D. and Goswami, M.P. (2000), *Economic Reforms and Employment (ed.)*, Deep and Deep Publications Pvt. Ltd., New Delhi.

Rao, C.H.H. (1994), Reforming Agriculture in the New Context, *EPW* 16-17 April.

———, *Indian Agriculture : Emerging Perspective and Policy Issues, Economic and Political Weekly*, No. 53, Dec. 31.

Singh, Manmohan (1994), "India's Economic Reforms–Resolve for a New Dawn" *Economic Growth and Social Change*, New Delhi., Vol. IV, No. 1, March 1994.

Nath, G.R. (1995), 'Human Dimension of Structural Adjustment in India—Problems and Possibilities, the LTLE, Vol. 38, No. 4.

Planning Commission, Government of India, 'Highlights of Ninth Five Year Plan, 1997-2000', *Yojana*, May, 1999.

Planning Commission, (2001), Report of the Task Force on Employment Opportunities.

Planning Commission, Report of Special Group on Targeting Ten Million Employment Opportunities.

Hashim, H.R. (2000), Employment-unemployment in a Society of Transition, *Indian Journal of Labour Economics*, Vol. 43, No. 1, 2000.

Bhagwati, J. and T.N. Sriniwasan, (1993), 'India's Economic Reforms', Ministry of Finance, Government of India.

Joshi, Vijay and I.M.D. Little, (1996), 'India's Economic Reforms 1991-200', Oxford University Press, New Delhi.

Singh, M. (1993), New Economic Policy and Challenges before the Labour Economics, *Indian Journal of Labour Economics*, Vol. 36, No. 1.

Papola, T.S. (1991), Industry and Empoyment: Recent Indian Experience, ISID Foundation Day Lecture, New Delhi.

Papola, T.S. (1994), Employment Growth and Social Protection of Labour in India, *Journal of International Relations.*

Dave, B.D. (2001), Effects of Economic Reforms on Employment in Ruddar Datt's *Second Generation of Economic Reforms*, Deep & Deep Publications (P) Ltd., New Delhi.

CHAPTER

3

Growth and Employment in Indian Economy : An Analysis of Sectoral Composition, Trends and Gender Issues

DALIP KUMAR

INTRODUCTION

This paper is attempted to explore the employment growth in public and private sectors particularly during 1990s. The analysis basically relies on secondary data sources provided by Director General of Employment and Training (DGET), Ministry of Labour, Government of India and various NSS Rounds conducted by National Sample Survey Organisation (NSSO). This paper is divided into three parts. The first part deals with the employment trends in public and private sectors. This data National as well as State level for undivided Bihar. Inter state variations would also be analysed in the text. Employment trends for public for and private sector by Industry group will be discussed. The employment contribution of Bihar by industrial division will be discussed in this section. Employment's inter state disparities in major states will also be discussed. The second part of the paper deals with women employment in India and inter-state variations among males and females. Sectoral analysis of employment in organised sector from 1990 to 2002 will also be discussed. Women employment in organised sector by major Industry group will be discussed. The trends alongwith of female agricultural labour. The last part attempts to combine the main features and trends of employment followed by policy implication.

A little over 40 million persons are registered in the employment exchanges across the country. Employment exchanges are established by the states as a funnel through which a job seeker has to pass in order to ensure fairness and non-discrimination in appointments to various jobs. Employment exchanges do not create jobs; in fact, most of them have placed not more than a few hundred for many years. (Chidambaram, 2003). There is no accurate information of unemployment or on job creation. Government cannot create employment through fiat but has to depend on the market. (Mohan, 2004).

The rate of growth of the economy has been much slower than what would have been ideally required to find new job opportunities for additional labour force. Till 1970, the Indian economy grew at a rate of about 3.5 per cent per annum, employment grew at a rate of over 2 per cent , during the 1970s, growth rate was about 4 per cent was accompanied by employment growth of about 2 per cent and 5.5 per cent average growth of the GDP during the 1980s generated an employment of about 1.8 per cent per annum.The employment elasticities, measured as the ratio of employment growth to the growth of value added have declined. Employment elasticities are computed at sectoral level with data on sectoral output growth and employment growth during a certain period of time. These employment elasticities are then used for computing overall employment elasticities. The declining employment elasticity of growth, observed during 1994-2002, the special group has recommended that over and above the employment generated in the process of present structure of growth, there is a need to

TABLE 3.1
Level and Trends of Employment Growth in Public Sector by Industry Divisions in India

Sectors	1971	1976	1981	1986	1991	1996	2001	2002
(1)	(2)	(3)	(4)	(5)	(6)	(7)	(8)	(9)
0	2.52	2.70	2.97	3.00	2.94	2.78	2.61	2.56
		(5.92)	(5.02)	(2.87)	(1.11)	(-0.72)	(-1.53)	
1	1.68	5.40	5.29	5.49	5.24	5.10	4.55	4.58
		(31.95)	(2.64)	(3.42)	(0.61)	(-0.20)	(-2.55)	
2 & 3	7.48	8.33	9.68	10.24	9.70	8.96	7.48	7.20
		(6.77)	(6.21)	(3.83)	(0.44)	(-1.22)	(-3.85)	
4	8.22	4.05	4.39	4.41	4.77	4.89	4.91	4.90
		(-9.31)	(4.72)	(2.78)	(3.13)	(0.86)	-(0.21)	
5	4.02	7.43	7.04	6.67	6.03	5.97	5.65	5.49
		(18.15)	(1.94)	(1.60)	(-0.51)	(0.17)	(-1.42)	
6	2.99	0.45	0.77	0.74	0.79	0.82	0.84	0.80
		(-28.45)	(14.87)	(1.61)	(2.90)	(1.30)	(0.00)	
7	20.75	18.15	17.50	16.57	15.89	15.90	15.89	16.04
		(1.74)	(2.29)	(1.57)	(0.67)	(0.39)	(-0.33)	

(Contd.)

TABLE 3.1 (*Contd.*)

(1)	*(2)*	*(3)*	*(4)*	*(5)*	*(6)*	*(7)*	*(8)*	*(9)*
8	52.34	3.68 (-38.57)	4.84 (8.89)	5.83 (6.55)	6.24 (2.93)	6.59 (1.47)	6.69 (0.00)	6.56
9	0.00	49.81 (46.03)	47.51 (2.08)	47.06 (2.48)	48.40 (2.10)	49.00 (0.62)	51.39 (0.64)	51.87
Total	100.00	100.00 (4.49)	100.00 (3.05)	100.00 (2.68)	100.00 (1.53)	100.00 (0.37)	100.00 (-0.31)	100.00

Notes : (1) 0 = agriculture, hunting etc.; 1= mining and quarrying; 2 & 3 = manufacturing; 4= Electricity, gas and water supply; 5= construction; 6= wholesale and retail trade; 7= transport, storage and communication; 8= finance, insurance and real estate etc. & 9= community, social and personal services

(2) *Up to 1974, the industry groups 8 and 9 are not separately available*

(3) *Figures in parenthesis represents quinquennial average growth rate*

Source : Director General of Employment and Training (DGE&T), Ministry of Labour, Government of India

TABLE 3.2
Level and Trends of Employment Growth in Private Sector by Industry Divisions in India

Sectors	*1971*	*1976*	*1981*	*1986*	*1991*	*1996*	*2001*	*2002*
(1)	*(2)*	*(3)*	*(4)*	*(5)*	*(6)*	*(7)*	*(8)*	*(9)*
0	11.85	12.12	11.61	11.14	11.60	10.80	10.75	11.21
		(0.74)	(0.71)	(-0.95)	(1.65)	(0.67)	(0.22)	
1	5.93	1.90	1.75	1.49	1.30	1.29	0.92	0.92
		(-20.13)	(0.00)	(-3.29)	(-1.89)	(1.92)	(-6.17)	
2 & 3	58.67	60.73	61.40	60.33	58.41	59.27	57.92	64.38
		(0.99)	(1.81)	(-0.49)	(0.18)	(2.42)	(-0.16)	
4	2.07	0.58	0.54	0.54	0.52	0.47	0.58	0.53
		(-22.16)	(0.00)	(0.00)	(0.00)	(0.00)	(4.56)	
5	0.74	1.31	0.94	0.95	0.91	0.59	0.69	0.79
		(12.47)	(-4.9)	(0.00)	(0.00)	(-6.51)	(3.71)	
6	4.44	4.23	3.78	3.80	3.91	3.76	3.93	4.35
		(-0.68)	(-0.70)	(0.00)	(1.39)	(1.30)	(1.22)	

(Contd.)

TABLE 3.2 (Contd.)

(1)	(2)	(3)	(4)	(5)	(6)	(7)	(8)	(9)
7	1.48	1.02	0.81	0.68	0.65	0.70	0.92	0.92
		(-6.89)	(-3.04)	(-3.58)	(0.00)	(3.71)	(5.92)	
8	14.81	2.63	2.70	2.99	3.26	3.64	4.28	5.15
		(-29.03)	(2.13)	(1.92)	(2.59)	(4.40)	(3.60)	
9	0.00	15.47	16.14	18.07	19.43	19.48	20.00	22.96
		(1.17)	(2.85)	(1.74)	(2.30)	(2.18)	(0.83)	
Total	100.00	100.00	100.00	100.00	100.00	100.00	100.00	100.00
		(0.29)	(1.58)	(-0.14)	(0.83)	(2.12)	(0.30)	

Notes : As of Table 3.1.

Source ; As of Table 3.1.

TABLE 3.3
Changes in Employment Pattern in the Organised Sector by Industry Division between Years 2002 Over 2001

	India	
Industry	*Public*	*Private*
0	-3.6	-8.3
1	-1.6	-14.1
2 & 3	-5.6	-2.9
4	-1.3	-19.3
5	-5.1	-1.2
6	-4.0	-1.1
7	-1.1	-0.2
8	-4.0	5.8
9	-1.0	0.5
Total	-1.9	-2.5

Source : As of Table 3.1.

promote certain labour intensive activities. These sectors are agriculture and allied activities, small and medium industries, information technology, construction, tourism, financial sector etc.

The total employment growth in the organised sector during the decade 1971-81. The average annual compound rate in the public sector was 4.3 per cent, where as it was only 2.0 per cent in private sector. During the 1980s public sector recorded an annual average rate of growth about 2 per cent, the rate of growth of employment in the private organised sector was nil. During the nineties, the growth rate of employment in public sector slowed down where as it accelerated in the private sector. Private sector employment has been generated more in manufacturing sector. As on March, 2003 the total employment in the organised sector was estimated at 269.83 lakh as against 271.47 lakh by the end of March, 2002. Thus, the total employment reflect a marginal decrease. By the end of March, 2003 the public sector employed 184.49 lakh persons and the private sector employed 85.34 lakh persons. The negative growth of employment in public and private sectors is recorded.

Inter-State Disparities in Employment

These disparities can be seen in Table 3.4. During the period of 1993-94 to 1999-2000, growth of employment was highest in the state of Haryana (2.43%) followed by Gujarat (2.31%). While Kerala has the least growth of employment only 0.7 per cent. All India average during this period was 1.07 per cent. More than seven states out of sixteen states have higher

TABLE 3.4
Employment Scenario in Major States (CDS Basis)

Sl. No.	*States*	*Employment in ('000) 1999-2000*	*Employment Growth 1993-94 to 1999-2000*
1.	A.P.	30614	0.35
2.	Assam	7647	1.99
3.	Bihar	30355	1.59
4.	Gujarat	18545	2.31
5.	Haryana	5982	2.43
6.	H.P.	2371	0.37
7.	Karnataka	20333	1.43
8.	Kerala	8902	0.07
9.	M.P.	28725	1.28
10.	Maharashtra	34979	1.25
11.	Orissa	11928	1.05
12.	Punjab	8013	1.96
13.	Rajasthan	19930	0.73
14.	Tamil Nadu	23143	0.37
15.	U.P.	49387	1.02
16.	W.B.	22656	0.41
	All India	336736	1.07

Source : Planning Commission, (2002), Dr. S.P. Gupta Report, p. 145, Table, 9 also cited on Economic Survey, 2003-04.

employment growth rate like as Haryana, Gujarat, Assam, Punjab, Bihar Karnataka, M.P. and Maharashtra. This can be seen in Figure 3.1.

FIG. 3.1

Employment Growth during 1993-94 to 1999-2000 Per Annum

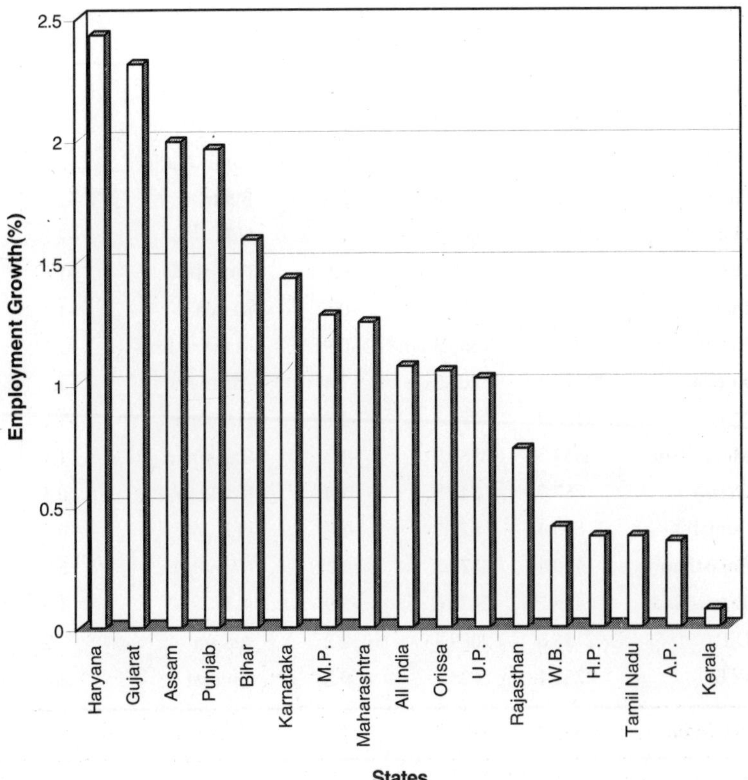

Comparative estimats of total employment in major states as on 2002-03 can see in Table 3.5. This state wise analysis reflect that only Orissa, and Gujarat recorded positive change of more than 3 per cent over previous year. Jharkhand, Assam, A.P., H.P. and Karnataka have also registered a positive change more than one per cent. Employment change over previous year decreased in West Bengal, M.P., T.N., Bihar, U.P., Punjab, Kerala and Maharashtra between (-9 to –1) per cent.

TABLE 3.5
Comparative Estimates of Total Employment in Major States as on 2002-03

States	*In Thousand*		*% change over previous year*	*States*	*% change over previous year*
	2002	*2003*	*2002-03*		
A.P.	2051.4	2077.1	1.3	W.B.	-9.3
Assam	1247.1	1272.3	2.0	M.P.	-4.8
Bihar	649.9	634.9	-2.3	Tamil Nadu	-2.9
Gujarat	1620.5	1681.6	3.8	Bihar	-2.3
Haryana	677.3	664.8	-1.8	U.P.	-2.2
H.P.	303.9	305.5	0.5	Punjab	-1.9
Jharkhand	221.7	220.3	-0.6	Kerala	-1.6
Karnataka	1850.2	1866.3	0.9	Maharashtra	-1.3
Kerala	1225.2	1205.5	-1.6	All India	-1.3
M.P.	1128.9	1074.3	-4.8	Haryana	-1.1
Maharashtra	3633.5	3587.7	-1.3	Rajasthan	-1.1
Orissa	782.7	848.5	8.4	Jharkhand	0.4
Punjab	890.4	873.2	-1.9	H.P.	0.5
Rajasthan	1190.4	1177.2	-1.1	Karnataka	0.9
Tamil Nadu	2499.2	2426.6	-2.9	A.P.	1.3
U.P.	2136.6	2089.4	-2.2	Assam	2
W.B.	2231.4	2023.6	-9.3	Gujarat	3.8
All India	27332.8	26983.2	-1.3	Orissa	8.4

Source : Same as Table 3.1.

Structure of Employment in India

The structure of employment in the organised sectors in India during the nineties is analysed below. Table 3.6 shows that public sector employment accounts for the bulk of the employment in the organised sector. However, the share of

FIG. 3.2
Comparative Estimates of Total Employment in the State during 2002-03

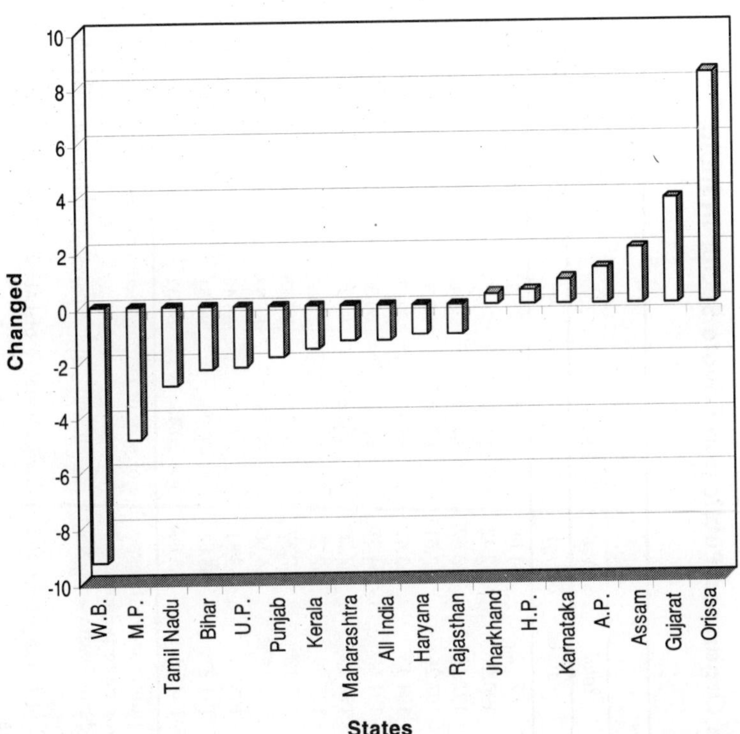

public sector in total employment in the organised sector has continuously been on decline during nineties—from 71.23 per cent in 1990 to 69.01 per cent in 2002. This is partly due to less hiring during the era of economic reforms in order to increase labour productivity. Almost all public sector units are switching over from labour intensive to capital-intensive methods of production. According to a report published in the *Economic Times*, June 1 1999, 152 PSUs have shed as many as 1,20,000 employees since 1993-94 through VRS. But statistics of 1997 and 2002 is alarming. In this period, employment in the organised sector had declined by nearly 8 lakhs, whereas this number had significantly increased in the similar period in seventies and

TABLE 3.6
Employment in Organised Public and Private Sector in India

(persons in lakh)

Year	Public			Private			All		
	Male	*Female*	*Total*	*Male*	*Female*	*Total*	*Male*	*Female*	*Total*
(1)	(2)	(3)	(4)	(5)	(6)	(7)	(8)	(9)	(10)
1990	165.22	22.50	187.72	61.88	13.94	75.82	227.09	36.44	263.53
1991	167.10	23.47	190.57	62.42	14.34	76.76	229.52	37.81	267.33
1992	167.81	24.29	192.10	63.67	14.79	78.46	231.48	39.08	270.56
1993	168.49	24.77	193.26	63.01	15.50	78.51	231.51	40.26	271.77
1994	168.80	25.65	194.45	63.41	15.89	79.30	232.21	41.54	273.75
1995	168.66	26.00	194.66	64.31	16.28	80.59	232.97	42.28	275.25
1996	167.94	26.35	194.29	67.20	17.92	85.12	235.14	44.26	279.40
1997	168.31	27.28	195.59	67.77	19.09	86.86	223.61	46.37	282.45
1998	166.56	27.62	194.18	67.37	20.11	87.48	233.93	47.73	281.66
1999	166.05	28.10	194.15	66.80	20.18	86.98	232.85	48.28	281.13
2000	164.57	28.57	193.14	65.81	20.65	86.46	230.38	49.22	279.60
2001	162.78	28.59	191.37	65.61	20.90	86.51	228.40	49.49	277.89
2002	158.87	28.86	187.73	63.84	20.48	84.32	222.60	49.35	272.05

Notes : (1) Includes all establishment in the public sector irrespective of size of employment and non-agricultural establishment in the private sector employing 10 or more persons.

(2) Excludes Sikkim, Arunachal Pradesh, Dadra and Nagar Haveli and Lakshadweep as these are not covered under the programme.

Source : *Employment Review*, Director General of Employment and Training, Ministry of Labour, Government of India.

eighties. In comparison, the overall employment in the private organised sector has only pitiably been risen. It has been growing over the last few years, and actually declined in absolute terms by the end of 2002. As on the March 2002, the total employment in the organised sector was 272.05 lakh as against 277.89 lakh at the end of March 2001. Thus, the total employment reflected a marginal decrease of 2.10 per cent.

Male-female comparison brings out certain striking features. As on 31 March 2002, a total number 49.35 lakh women employees were engaged in the organised sectors, out of which 28.86 lakh in public sector and 20.48 lakhs in the private sectors. A closer look at the table reveal that the employment patterns in the organised sector remain massively biased against women; the bias is greater in the public than in the private sector. This can be explained in terms of socio-cultural norms and prejudices, traditional values, etc. that restrict the entry of women in the labour market. However, the silver lining, it seems, is that female employment, both in the pubic and private sectors is growing 2.01 and 3.81 per cent respectively per annum, which is much faster than the male employment. Sow wages paid to women and exploitative labour relations is an issue which needs to be analysed in detail.

The importance of industrial female employment has been investigated by calculating proportional changes in 2002 over 2001 in Table 8. The figures reveal that three industries divisions namely Agriculture, Hunting, Forestry & Fishing (Div.-0), Mining and Quarrying, (Div.-1) and Manufacturing (Div. 2&3) recorded a negative growth of 9.6 per cent, 2.7 per cent and 1.4 per cent respectively. All other industry divisions showed a positive growth of women's employment though of different magnitudes. The change was as high as 4.5 per cent in Financing, Insurance, Real Estate and Business Services (Div.-8) followed by 1.9 per cent in Transport, Storage and Communication (Div.-7); 1.7 per cent in wholesale and retails trade Restaurants and Hotels (Div.-6); 1.4 per cent in Electricity, Gas & Water (Div.-4); 1.3 per cent Community, Social and Personal Services (Div.-9) and 0.4 per cent in Construction (Div.-5). However, the trends look somewhat dissimilar in Divisions 4, 5 and 6 between the public and private sectors. But a closer examination of absolute figures does not reveal any noteworthy variations in respective employment categories.

The Table 3.7 also shows that in Bihar, women employment had remained constant during 2001 and 2002. This stagnation in employment growth in Bihar owed a lot of deceleration in the overall pace of economic activity. It may be noted that during nineties, economic growth in Bihar has come almost to a halt. For instance, during 1990s, Bihar's economy has not grown at all in per-capita terms. Also, it is more alarming to find that Bihar's agricultural economy had remained stagnated in absolute terms during the same period. (i.e. it has declined at about 2 per cent per year in per-capita terms).

TABLE 3.7

Changing Women Employment Pattern in the Organised Sector by Industry Divisions between Years 2002 Over 2001

	India		
*Industry Division**	*Public*	*Private*	*Total*
0	-9.8	-9.6	-9.6
1	-0.4	-17.7	-2.7
2 & 3	-5.3	-1.0	-1.4
4	1.7	-8.5	1.4
5	0.7	-5.4	0.4
6	-0.8	3.2	1.7
7	1.8	2.9	1.9
8	3.4	8.1	4.5
9	1.2	1.4	1.3
Total	1.0	-2.0	-0.3

Note : * Industry groups as defined in Table 3.1.

Source : Calculated from *Employment Review*, Director General of Employment and Training, Ministry of Labour, Govt. of India, 2002.

However, Bihar is not the only state, which has shown inter-state variation in women's employment contains in Table 3.8. It would be observed from data that Orissa, Gujarat

TABLE 3.8
Comparative Estimates of Women Employment in Major States as on 2002-03

(In Thousand)

States	*2002*	*2003*	*% Change over previous year*	*States*	*% Change over previous year*
A.P.	437.6	461.8	5.5	Orissa	6.7
Assam	390.3	385.1	-1.3	Gujarat	6.2
Bihar	38.4	37.7	-1.8	A.P.	5.5
Gujarat	205.9	218.8	6.3	H.P.	2.9
Haryana	96.4	97.2	0.8	Karnataka	1.7
H.P.	48.5	49.9	2.9	U.P.	1.8
Jharkhand	68.6	68.7	0.1	Haryana	0.8
Karnataka	571.8	581.2	1.6	Maharashtra	0.2
Kerala	482.3	473.3	-1.9	Jharkhand	0.1
M.P.	147.3	141.6	-3.9	All India	-0.2
Maharashtra	559.4	560.8	0.3	Rajasthan	-0.9
Orissa	101.9	108.8	6.8	Punjab	-1.3
Punjab	146.2	144.3	-1.3	Assam	-1.3
Rajasthan	165.9	164.4	-0.9	Kerala	-1.9
Tamil Nadu	746.4	729.1	-2.3	Bihar	-2
U.P.	208.1	211.8	1.8	Tamil Nadu	-2.3
W.B.	258.4	227.7	-11.9	M.P.	-3.9
All India	5036.2	5024.4	-0.2	W.B.	-11.9

Source : DGET, Ministry of Labour, Government of India.

and Andhra Pradesh recorded an increase of more than 3 per cent in women's employment as on 31st March 2003 over 2002. More than one per cent increase was observed in U.P., Karnataka and Himachal Pradesh. Jharkhand, Maharashtra and U.P. female employment recorded positive growth of less than one per cent. (Figure 3.3). The highest women employment estimate in newly formed State Uttranchal (27.7%), 10.2 J & K as on March 2003 over 2002. The state of Goa registered highest decrease of 34.3 per cent of women's employment followed by 11.9 per cent in West Bengal during the same period.

FIG. 3.3
Comparative Estimates of Women Employment in the States as on 2002-03

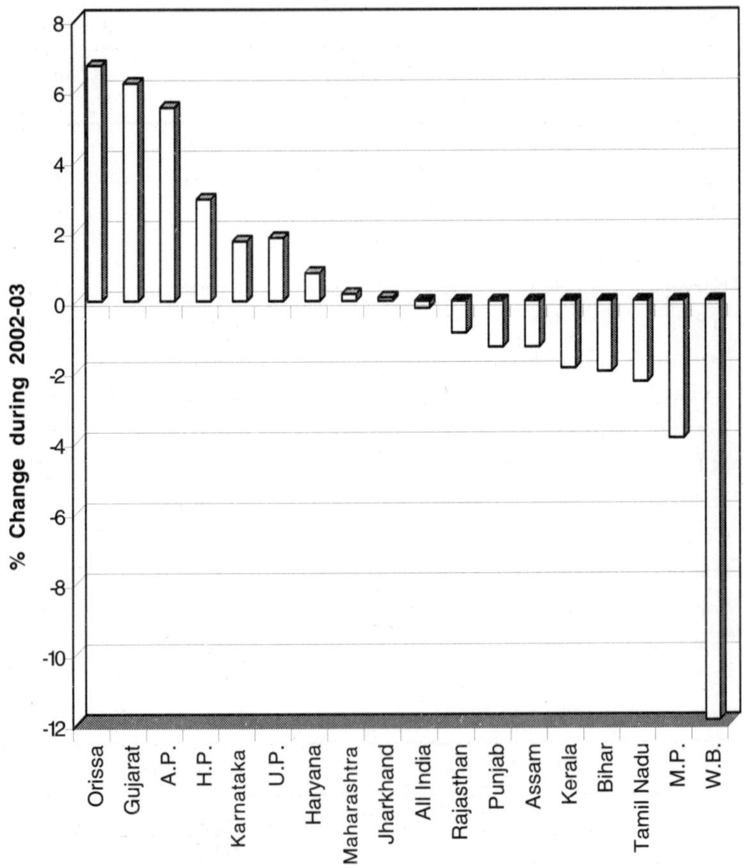

Sector-wise Women Employment

An Analysis of the structure of women employment by the broad industry groups of work is attempted in this section. The Industry divisions of NIC 1998 have been categorised as primary (01-05), secondary (10-45) and tertiary sector (50-99). These employment figures are based on 'all workers'. It may be mentioned that in NSS 50th Round NIC 1987 was used while in NSS 43rd Rounds NIC 1970 was used.

The Table 3.9 shows that during 1999-2000, in rural areas, about 85 per cent of female workers were employed in the primary sector. The tertiary sector was a more important source of employment for rural female after economic liberalisation. The secondary sector accounted for about 9 per cent of female employment in rural areas. Although the broad pattern in structure of employment remained the same during pre-post and post-liberalisation. The table shows decreasing trend in the share of employment in primary sectors. The share of female workers employed in the tertiary sector remains stagnant in the range of to 6 per cent during 1987-88 to 1999-2000.

TABLE 3.9

Female Workers by Broad Groups of Industry Per 1000 Distribution

NSS Round	*Years*	*Primary*		*Secondary*		*Tertiary*	
		PS	*All*	*PS*	*All*	*PS*	*All*
			Rural				
55th	`1999-00	841	854	93	89	66	57
50th	1993-94	847	862	91	83	63	56
43rd	1987-88	825	847	112	100	63	53
			Urban				
55th	1999-00	146	177	293	293	561	529
50th	1993-94	193	247	295	291	510	463
43rd	1987-88	218	294	324	317	458	389

Note : PS. denoted Principal Status.

Source : NSSO, 55th Round, Report No. 455.

During 1999-2000, the tertiary sector provided for maximum employment, for female workers in urban areas followed by secondary sectors. The share of employment in primary sectors reported about 15 per cent for female. Before liberalisation the share of female employment in the tertiary sectors rose steadily during the period 1987-88 to 1999-2000. This rise was much higher for female (From 39 per cent in 1887-88 to 53 per cent in 1999-2000). During this period the share of female employment in the secondary sector slightly fluctuate between 29 per cent to 32 per cent.

Rural women remain concentrated primarily in agriculture; from 1983 till date the share of agriculture in rural women's total employment is nearly 85 per cent. Since urban employment forms a very small share of women's total employment (both because majority of women live in rural areas, and also because a much smaller percentage of urban women join the workforce in India), agriculture remain the occupation of more than 3/4th of all women workers. Agriculture as an occupation for urban workers has declined sharply, for both men and women. This implies relatively faster growth of tertiary or service sector employment.

Women Employed by Status of Employment

The employed persons have been categorised in three major groups according to their status of employment. These groups are (i) self-employment (ii) Regular employment and (iii) Casual employed. These groups were formed on the basis of the activity status recorded for each person. Details have been given in the Table 3.10.

TABLE 3.10
Per 1000 Distribution of Usually Employed by Category of Female Employment

(All-India)

		Principal Status			*All*		
Years	*Rounds*	*Self-employed*	*Regular employees*	*Casual labour*	*Self-employed*	*Regular employees*	*Casual labour*
			Rural Females				
1999-2000	55th	500	39	461	573	31	396
1999-94	50th	513	34	453	585	28	387
1987-88	43rd	549	49	402	608	37	355
1983	38th	541	37	422	619	28	353
			Urban Females				
1999-00	55th	384	385	231	453	333	214
1999-94	50th	364	355	281	454	286	162
1987-88	43rd	393	342	265	471	275	254
1983	38th	373	318	309	458	258	284

Source : NSSO, 55th Round, Report No. 455 Table 10.

The Table shows that, during 1999-2000, self-employed accounted for 57 per cent of the employed females. About 40 per cent of females were employed as a casual labour. Only 3 per cent of females were regular employees. It is seen from the table that in all the survey years self-employed were maximum, regular employees the least among the employed females. The share of self-employed has steadily decreased while that of casual labour has increased. However, regular female employees constituted about 3 per cent of all employed females throughout the period.

The share of regular employees is much more in urban areas than in rural areas. During 1999-2000, it was 33 per cent among employed females. The share of self-employed was quite high, through somewhat lower than that in rural areas. About 45 per cent urban females were self-employed. The share of casual labourers was lowest in the urban females. After economic liberalisation, the share of regular employees increased among females. During 1999-2000 the share of female casual labour rose by 5 percentage point after showing a decreasing trend before economic liberalisation.

Trends of Female Employment in Agricultural Labourers

India is primarily and predominantly an agricultural economy. The primary sector accounts for nearly 40 per cent of GDP and employees nearly 69 per cent of workers. Over the years, the share of agriculture has declined and that of manufacturing and service has increased. While the increase in share of non-agriculture sector in GDP is substantial, its share in employment is less than the proportionate. This trend affects more women workforce and the economic liberalisation has miserably failed in coping with the situation which is highly unfavourable to Indian women.

The trends in the number of employment days available to agricultural labour in presented below. The changes in the relative importance of difference sources of employment like wage-paid employment (WE), self-employment (SE) and employment on salary basis (ESB) are also examined.

Table 3.12 shows the trend in the total number of employment days available to adult female labour and the

TABLE 3.11

Incidence of Sector-wise Employment

Employment	Rural				Urban			
	Male		Female		Male		Female	
	1993-94	1999-00	1993-94	1999-2000	1993-94	1999-2000	1993-94	1999-2000
	(1)	(2)	(3)	(4)	(5)	(6)	(7)	(8)
0-Primary Sector								
Self	60.4	58.1	50.1	48.20	59.1	60.6	43.5	41.2
Regular	1.8	1.9	—	1.02	4.5	3.0	—	5.9
Casual	37.8	40.0	48.7	50.26	36.7	36.4	56.5	58.8
1-5 -Secondary Sectors								
Self	36.6	36.4	52.4	66.6	28.2	29.0	41.7	50.0
Regular	18.3	18.2	9.5	9.5	47.1	42.0	19.5	23.5
Casual	45.0	45.5	38.0	23.9	24.7	28.4	38.9	26.5
6-9- Tertiary Sector								
Self	54.9	52.4	56.2	50.3	45.9	45.6	30.7	33.3
Regular	34.2	34.5	31.3	37.5	45.9	45.9	58.1	54.4
Casual	11.0	13.1	12.5	13.0	8.2	8.4	11.3	10.6

Sources: NSSO Report on Employment and Unemployment for the 50th Round 1993-94, Report No. 406.
NSSO Report on Employment and Unemployment for the 55th Round 1999-2000, Report No. 455.

TABLE 3.12
Changing Structure of Adult Female Employment of Agricultural Labourers in India

Types of Employment	*Adult Female Employment*		*(No. of employment days)*		
	1974-75	*1977-78*	*1983*	*1987-88*	*1993-94*
Wage Employment	143 (79.89)	184 (81.06)	188 (81.74)	195 (77.07)	212 (80.30)
Self-employment	35 (19.55)	41 (18.06)	39 (16.96)	52 (20.55)	48 (18.18)
Employment on Salary Basis	1 (0.56)	2 (0.88)	3 (1.30)	6 (2.38)	4 (1.52)
Total	179 (100)	227 (100)	230 (100)	253 (100)	264 (100)

Source : Rural Labour Enquiry: Report on Employment and Unemployment, 1974-75, 1977-78, 1983, 1987-88, 1993-94, Labour Bureau, Chandigarh/ Shimla.

changing importance of different source of employment like WE, SE and ESB since 1975.The total number of employment days for adult female labour increased. The table further shows that over the period the wage-paid employment and self-employment has fluctuated. The employment on salary basis for adult female remains very low. Regarding changes in the quantum of employment available to adult female labour, the total number of employment days has increased, but the availability of employment days fluctuated from one period to the other.

More women had to be engaged in agricultural sectors, not because more work was available, but because of the non-availability of work in other sectors as indicated by a decline in the number of days of work available. On the other hand, employment of women increased much faster than of men in the organised sector. Most of this increase took place in the public sector and in the tertiary sector activities. Within the tertiary sector, female employment growth was the highest in the financial services.

Policies and Programmes

Many employment theories and policies are prevatent like as The laissez-faire Policy, Demand-management Policies, Supply-side Policies, Institutional Policies etc. Among all of them Demand-management Policies, based on Keynesian Theory is more relevant in the present scenario. Demand-management Policies to reduce unemployment fall into two major categories: (i) government employment policies, in which the government stimulates employment directly by hiring people into the public sector, and (ii) Product demand policies, which stimulate employment by raising aggregate product demand (e.g. through tax reductions, increases in government spending on goods and services, or increase in the money supply.) (*Snower and Dehesa, 1997*). Keynes said that workers are unemployed because firms are not producing enough goods and services; firms are not doing so because there is too little demand; and demand is deficient because people are unemployed. *(Keynes, 1936)*

Government of India has already launched several special employment generation programmes for the country. Important are Pradhan Mantri Gramodaya Yojana (PMGY), Swarnajayanti Gram Swarozgar Yojana (SGSY), Sampoorna Grameen Rozagar Yojana (SGRY), Pradhan Mantri Gram Sadak Yojana (PMGSY) etc.

A Report of Task Force on Employment Opportunities Chaired by Montek Singh Ahluwalia explained that the aggregate employment problem in the country cannot be solved unless accelerated growth is achieved which would create additional demand for labour and also provide the increase in labour productivity needed to achieve the much needed improvement in employment quality. (GOI, 2001)

As per Special Group on Targeting Ten Million Employment Opportunities Per Year over the Tenth Plan Period, Chaired by Dr. S.P. Gupta explained that the targeted rate of Growth for SSI Sector has been kept at 12 per cent for the Tenth Plan, on the ground that economy is expected to grow at 8 per cent (GDP) in this Plan. (Gupta, 2002). The UPA government wants to go a step further and guarantee 100 days of employment to those who seek jobs in rural India. (GOI, 2004).

National Rural Employment Guarantee Act, 2004 highlighted that every household in the rural area shall have a right to at least 100 days of guaranteed employment every year for atleast one adult member. This programme has condition that every registered person shall be entitled to employment at the minimum wage, in accordance with the programme for the time being in force, as many days as the applicant requests, up to 100 days per household in a given financial year. The state government has to provide employment in accordance with the provision of the programme to every such person within 15 days of receipt of an application. If the applicant is not provided with employment within 15 days of applying, he or she will be entitled to daily unemployment allowance, unless the applicant or his/her household has already received 100 days of employment's during the current financial year. The Gram Panchayat shall prepare and maintain such registers and issue such identity cards or pass- books to the applicants.

Suggestions

Employment opportunities are going to slacken due to lack of invisible resources in this state. Bihar has considerable potential for export of agriculture/horticulture products, leather goods, silk, handloom, handicrafts, shellac, ceramics, besides hand-tools, cutting tools, forging, industrial fasteners and automobiles components etc. However, achievements on export front so far have not been commensurate with the potential of the state. One of the major reasons has been attributed to the absence of infrastructure such as Air Cargo complex in the state. The State Government has decided to promote establishment of export infrastructures such as Air Cargo Complex during VIII Plan Period.

The State would encourage Financial Institutions and Private Sector to establish and maintain industrial Growth Centres/Industrial Areas/EPIP/EPZ and such other infrastructure projects.

References

Chidambaram, P. (2003), *Financial Express*, December, 14, 2003.

Chander, Mohan, N. (2004), Labouring in Employment Generation in India, *Financial Express*, 2 September, p. 6.

GOI (2001), *Report of Task Force on Employment Opportunities*, Government of India, Planning Commission.

GOI, (2002), Planning Commission, Special Group on Targeting Ten Million Employment Opportunities Per Year over the Tenth Plan Period.

GOI (2003), *Director General of Employment and Training (DGE & T), Ministry of Labour*, Government of India.

GOI (2004), National Rural Employment Guarantee Act, 2004, Government of India.

GOI, *NSSO* Report on Employment and Unemployment for the 50th Round 1993-94, Report No. 406.

GOI, NSSO Report on Employment and Unemployment for the 55th Round 1999-2000, Report No. 455.

Keynes, J.M. (1936), The General Theory of Employment, Interest, and Money, London: Macmillan.

Rural Labour Enquiry: Report on Employment and Unemployment, 1974-75, 1977-78, 1983, 1987-88, 1993-94, *Labour Bureau*, Chandigrah/Shimla.

Snower, J. Dennis and Guillermo de la Dehera (1997), Unemployment Policy, Government Options for the Labour Market, Centre for Economic Policy Research, Cambridge, p. 20.

Uneven Growth Trends : Some Policy Concerns

KUMAR RATNESH

INTRODUCTION

The Indian Economy has undergone gradual structural changes during the post-independence period, the pace of such changes, however, being relatively rapid since the last decade. This is reflected, inter-alia, in the growth rate and in the changing soctoral composition of the real Gross Domestic Product (GDP). India's growth performance over the three decades from 1950-51 to 1980-81 saw economic growth average close to 3.5 per cent per year, the in famous 'Hindu rate of growth' is the phrase coined by la[illegible] Raj Krishna. What's worse is thàt during this long 30 year period, growth of per capita G.D.P. average was hardly 1.5 per cent a year (Table 4.1). In other words, average living standards rose painfully slowly in India during these three decades.

TABLE 4.1

Average Growth of Real GDP over 50 Years

(Per cent)

	1951-52 to 1960-61	1961-62 to 1970-71	1971-72 to 1980-81	1981-82 to 1990-91	1991-92 to 2000-01	1992-93 to 2000-01
1. Agriculture and allied	3.1	2.5	1.8	3.6	2.7	3.2
2. Industry	6.3	5.5	4.1	7.1	5.7	6.4
3. Services	4.3	4.8	4.4	6.7	7.5	7.8
4. GDP (Factor Cost)	3.9	3.7	3.2	5.6	5.6	6.1
5. Per Capita GDP	2.0	1.5	0.8	3.4	3.6	4.0

Note : Industry includes construction.
Source : Central Statistical Organisation.

There was a welcome acceleration of economic growth in the 1980s to 5.6 per cent a year, based on a clear acceleration of growth performance in all the three constituent sectors—agriculture, industry and services. Per capita growth averaged a healthy 3.4 per cent annum, bringing about a significant improvement in average living standards. There was, however, considerable volatility in the annual growth rate, and for a number of years during this period (1989-81 to 1990-91), GDP grew by less than 5 per cent. The volatility in real growth rate is most reflected in case of GDP originating in agriculture. However, the high growth phenomenon of the 'eighties' associated with a widening current account deficit, rising fiscal deficit, continuation of widespread economic control and a costly anti-export bias in trade policy, could not be sustained, as the experience of the crisis year of 1991-92 revealed, the annual GDP growth rate declined to a low of 0.8 per cent. The crisis of 1991 had cast serious doubts about the sustainability of the growth experiences of the 'eighties. Following the major shift in macro-economic policy oriented towards liberalisation, privatisation and globalisation (LPG) the economy has once again on the way towards high growth trajectory. The economy responded exceptionally well to these initiatives (i.e. LPG), with growth quickly recovering in the nine years between 1991-92 and 2000-01 averaged 6.1 per cent. It was the fastest decadal growth in India's recorded history. Furthermore, per capita growth accelerated to 4 per cent annum, taking India into the rank of 10 fastest growing countries in the world. (Table 4.1). Of late, the advance estimates released by CSO on February 9, 2004 estimated real GDP to have grown by 8.1 per cent at factor cost at constant price for 2003-04. The present high growth trend has raised certain questions for closer examination.

- What were the factors which explains this remarkable and broad based growth surge in the nineties and at the beginning years of 21st century?
- What are the recent dimensions of growth in India?
- Whether the higher growth momentum is virtuous or polarised within few states?
- How the higher growth rate be achieved and sustained under balanced regional growth doctrine?

TABLE 4.2
Growth of GDP and Major Sectors

		Annual average growth rate				
Share in real GDP 1993-94 Price (%)	*Average of 1994-95 to 1996-97*	*1981-82 to 1990-91*	*1992-93 to 2000-01*	*1992-93 to 1996-97*	*1997-98 to 2000-01*	*2000-01 to 2003-04*
Agriculture	28.9	3.6	3.2	4.7	1.2	—
Industry	27.6	7.1	6.4	7.6	4.8	—
Service	43.5	6.7	7.8	7.6	8.1	—
GDP (factor cost)	100.0	5.6	6.1	6.7	5.4	5.57

+Based on the calculation of CMIE.
Source : Central Statistical Organisation and CMIE.

There are, obviously, no easy answers to these questions. Moreover, the present paper has posed these question and tried to find out whatever indicative answers are likely to emerge.

Growth in the Nineties : A Comparative View

A Comparison of the more recent period of the 'nineties (1992-93 to 2000-01) with the 'eighties' (i.e. 1980-81 to 1990-91) reveals some notable features. The rate of growth of GDP at 6.1 per cent at factor cost during the 'nineties was distinctly, higher than 5.6 per cent recorded in the 'eighties. It is interesting to note that the acceleration of GDP growth from 5.6 per cent to 6.1 per cent is entirely attributable to the service sector where growth surged to 7.8 per cent from an already high 6.7 per cent in the 'eighties. Indeed, the growth of both agriculture and industries averages a little lower in the post crisis nine years compared to the pre-crisis decade. However, it is noteworthy that in this high growth Eighth Plan period all major sectors (agriculture, industry, services), grew noticeably faster that in the pre-crisis decade.

In developed economies, the secondary and tertiary sectors contribute a major share in GDP, with primary sector accounting for a relatively lower share. During the process of growth over the years, the Indian economy too experienced an improvement in the shares of secondary and tertiary sectors in overall GDP. The sectoral composition of real GDP at 1980-81 prices shows that the share of the agricultural sector in GDP gradually declined from 34.5 per cent in the 'eighties to 27.5 per cent in the 'nineties (1992-93 to 2000-01) (Table 4.3). In contrast, the shares of industry and services increased from 23.2 per cent to 25.9 per cent and from 42.2 per cent to 48.2 per cent, respectively during the same period. Within the service sector, the share of 'trade, hotel, restaurants, transport, storage and communication' rose from 17.4 per cent in the 'eighties to 19.3 per cent during 'nineties while share of 'financing, insurance, real estate and business services' increased from 9.4 per cent to 11.9 per cent. The share of 'construction' on the other hand, declined marginally from 4.6 percent to 4.4 per cent. Thus, there was a surge in the growth of the service sector since the early 'eighties, with the trend rate of growth being more pronounced in recent years. The recent years experience show that the growth of the service sector has imparted much of resilience to the economy, particularly in times of adverse agricultural shocks. In this context, the development experience of the Indian economy has been different from that of

TABLE 4.3

Share of Different Sectors in Gross Domestic Product at Factor Cost

(*At current prices*)

Year	*Agriculture forestry logging, & fishing*	*Manufacturing construction electricity gas & water supply mining & quarrying*	*Transport communication & trade*	*Financial services*	*Other services*
	(1)	(2)	(3)	(4)	(5)
With base : 1980-81=100					
1951-52	54.56	16.11	10.31	10.16	8.87
1961-62	44.98	21.38	12.42	11.54	9.69
1971-72	43.37	22.74	13.45	10.33	10.11
1981-82	37.19	25.79	16.72	9.17	11.13
1991-92	31.52	26.41	18.35	11.27	12.45
1999-2000 (RE)	27.52	25.98	20.31	11.71	14.13
2001-2002	24.70	26.40	20.20	12.90	15.80

Sources : (a) Planning Commission, India Planning Experience : A Statistical Profile, pp. 8-9, January 2001.
(b) Planning Commission, Tenth Five Year Plan, 2002-2007, Vol. 1.

the developed countries, as the share of services sector in the GDP surpassed that of the agricultural and industrial sectors in a relatively shorter span of time.

What are the factors which explain this remarkable and broad-based growth surge in the 'nineties particularly during 1992-97? We can suggest the following factors, in the absence of authoritative research :

- Productivity gains resulting from the deregulation of trade, industry and finance, especially in the sectors of industry and some services.
- The investment boom of 1993-96 which exerted expansionary effects on both supply and demand, especially in industry. The investment boom was probably driven by a combination of factors including the unleashing of 'animal spirit' by economic reforms, the swift loosening of the foreign exchange bottleneck, confidence in broadly consistent government policy signals and easier availability of investible funds.
- The surge in export growth at about 20 per cent per year (in Dollar terms) for three successive years beginning 1993-94 as well as for the first two months of FY 05, April-May 05, exports are up 25 per cent over April-May' 04, attributable to the substantial devaluation in real effective terms in the early nineties and a freer policy regime for industry, foreign trade and payments (Table 4.4).
- Improvements in terms of trade for agriculture resulting from a combination of higher procurement prices for important crops and reduction in trade protection for manufacturers.
- A benign world economic environment supported expansion of foreign trade, private capital flow and growth of Indian Economy. World output growth was estimated to have accelerated from 3 per cent in 2002 to 3.9 per cent in 2003 and the IMF forecasts that world GDP will grow at its highest at 4.6 per cent in 2004 alike the last time the world economy grew at a

4 per cent plus growth rate during 1996 and 1997. Strong world GDP growth raised exports and growth rate of Indian economy in 1993-96 as well as during 2002-04.

From a macro-economic perspective, however, the FY 1997-98, 2000-01, 2002-03, witnessed deceleration in GDP and exports. Moreover the FY' 1998-99 and FY' 2001-02 experienced negative growth in exports (Table 4.4). As a result, the average GDP growth rate dropped to 5.4 per cent in the four years 1997-98 to 2000-01 and 5.57 per cent during 2000-01 to 2003-04 (Table 4.2). Export growth dropped partly because of the real appreciation of the rupee and partly because of the surge in Chinese exports to the world, which took away market share from all other Asian competitors. Industrial investment stalled for several reasons. First, the investment boom of the three years (1992-95) had built-up large capacities which discouraged further expansion. Second, real interest rate had risen since 1995-96 because of sharp decline in inflation and a temporary rise in nominal interest rate driven

TABLE 4.4
Growth in Major Economic Indicators

(in per cent)

Year	*IIP*	*GDP*	*Export*
1993-94	5.8	5.9	27.4
1994-95	9.1	7.3	18.6
1995-96	13.1	7.3	20.9
1996-97	6.1	7.8	5.2
1997-98	6.7	4.8	4.6
1998-99	4.1	6.5	-5.2
1999-2000	6.6	6.1	10.7
2000-01	5.1	4.4	20.1
2001-02	2.6	5.8	-0.4
2002-03	5.8	4.0	20.2
2003-04	6.9	8.1	17.1

Note : IIP denotes Index for Industrial Production.
Source : CMIE.

by RBI in the foreign exchange market to stablise, a suddenly wobbly rupee. Third, the advent of coalition governance had heightened uncertainty and damped business confidence.

The international economic environment also weakened India's macro-economic perspective after 1997. The Asian crisis 1997-98 hurt export and private capital inflows. The problems were compounded by economic sanctions which followed the nuclear tests in May 1998. In the next two years the surge in international oil price exerted negative effects.

In addition, structural factors also influenced the decline in growth rate. Although reforms continued throughout the decade, they never regained the breadth and depth of the early nineties. Key reforms in the infrastructure, labour law, financial sector, trade, industrial policy and privatisation remained unfinished or undone. Second, despite good intimation, the bottlenecks in infrastructure became worse over the time, especially in roads, soil, power and water supply, reflecting slow progress in reforms of pricing, ownership and the regulatory framework. Third, the low quality and quantity of investments in rural infrastructure combined with distorted pricing of some key agricultural inputs and outputs to damp the growth of agriculture. Fourth, the continuing decline in governance and financial discipline in the populous states of the Gangatic plain. Lastly, the inter state variation in the growth rate is equally significant factor retrogressive effect on the economy.

Dimensions of Growth : Structural *vis-a-vis* Inter Regional

Growth depends on many variables but no one would deny the role of investment in augmenting productivity, embodying new technology and as a key component of aggregate demand. Table 4.5 shows, Gross Domestic Investment packed in the mid-nineties at around 26-27 per cent of GDP and has since retreated to around 24 per cent of GDP, which is not very different from the average recorded in the late 1980s. The prospects for an early revival are not promising, especially if we review the record on aggregate savings.

TABLE 4.5
Saving and Investment
(As per cent of GDP at Current Market Prices)

	GDCF	*GDS*	*Public savings*	*Private savings*	*House hold savings*	*Corporate savings*
Average						
1985-86	22.7	20.4	2.4	18.0	16.0	2.0
1990-91	26.3	23.1	1.1	22.0	19.3	2.7
1995-96	26.9	25.1	2.0	23.1	18.2	4.9
1999-2000	24.3	23.2	-0.9	24.0	20.3	3.7
2000-01	24.0	23.4	-1.7	25.1	20.9	4.2
2001-02	25.1	23.5	—	—	—	—
2002-03	25.8	24.2	—	—	—	—

Note : GDCF: Gross Domestic Capital Formation.
GDS : Gross Domestic Savings.
Source : Economic Survey, 2001-2002 and 2003-2004.

Gross domestic savings also peaked in the mid-nineties, at around 25 per cent of GDP and has since subsided to about 23 per cent of GDP. This is noticeably better than the late eighties record. More interestingly, private saving has held up remarkably well, even during the growth slowdown since 1997. Having climbed from 18 per cent of GDP in the late 1980s to about 23 per cent by the mid-nineties, private savings has remained strong and has even increased further in the last two years to 25 per cent of GDP by 2000-01. This strong record of private savings has been propelled by the buoyancy of household savings which has risen by almost five percentage points of GDP in the past decade. Indeed, if public savings had maintained its late 1980s level, we could well have seen aggregate savings and investments at record level of 27 and 28 per cent respectively by 2004-05.

Unfortunately over the past decade and especially since the mid-nineties, public savings has collapsed to minimum 1.7 per cent in 2000-01. Private savings, on the other hand, which remained below 2 per cent during the 'eighties', rose to 3.6 per cent during 'nineties. The investment rate of this sector, which was 4.4 per cent during the 'eighties' rose sharply to 7.4 per cent during the 'nineties'. The improved investment rate recorded in the 'nineties can be attributed to the liberalisation measures introduced in the economy and the consequent impetus afforded to the private sector in the successive budgets in the 'nineties'.

In a growing economy like India, as expected, investment has always outstripped domestic savings. However, the implied dependence on foreign savings (i.e. Saving G.D.E.F. gap) has been, on an average, within 1.8 per cent of GDP for the entire period of the study 1980-81 to 2000-01. Such dependence amounted to 2.1 per cent during 'eighties and declined to 1.4 per cent during 'nineties. However, immediately preceding the crisis year, the reliance on foreign saving rose to 3.4 per cent of GDP. Subsequent macro-economic stabilisation measures led to a fall in the saving investment gap to less than 2 per cent of GDP.

The relevant issue from a macro-economic view point, however, is not only the level of saving-investment gap but also the nature and the composition of investment. The end-use of saving into fixed capital formation and changes in stocks and inventories, thus, has important ramifications for growth process. While technical considerations and the structure of production would require certain level of inventories, excessive inventory build-up withdraws resources from circulation and locks up funds. The changes in stock (unadjusted) came down from 2.2 per cent of GDP during the 'eighties to 1.6 per cent during the 'nineties, indicating perhaps better inventory management.[2]

An important dimension of growth trends of Indian economy is the considerable variation in the performance of individual states, with some states growing faster than the average and others slower. Noteworthy thing is that the degree of dispersion in growth rates of state domestic product (SDP) across states increased significantly in the 1990s. The range of variation in the growth rate of SDP in the 1980s was from a low of 3.6 per cent per year in Kerala to a high of 6.6 per cent in Rajasthan. In the 1990s the variation was much larger, from a low of 2.7 per cent per year for Bihar to a high of 9.6 per cent for Gujarat (Table 4.6).

TABLE 4.6
Annual Rates of Growth of Gross State Domestic Product (SDP)

States	*1980-81 to 1990-91% p.a.*	*1991-92 to 1997-98% p.a.*
1. Bihar	4.66	2.69
2. Rajasthan	6.60	6.54
3. Uttar Pradesh	4.95	3.58
4. Orissa	4.29	3.25
5. Madhya Pradesh	4.56	6.17
6. Andhra Pradesh	5.65	5.03
7. Tamil Nadu	5.38	6.22
8. Kerala	3.57	5.81
9. Karnataka	5.29	5.29
10. West Bengal	4.71	6.91
11. Gujarat	5.08	9.57
12. Haryana	6.43	5.02
13. Maharashtra	6.02	8.01
14. Punjab	5.32	4.71
Cobmined SDP of 14 States	5.24	5.94
GDP (National Accounts)	5.55	6.89

Note : The growth rates have been estimated by fitting log linear trends to the State SDP data at constant 1980-81 prices obtained from the CSO and the GDP data from the national accounts.

Source : Ahluwalia, M.S. (2000).

The differences in performances across states became even more marked when we allow for the differences in the rates of growth of population and evaluate the performance in terms of growth rates of per capita SDP (Table 4.7). The variations in growth rates in the 1980s ranged from a low of 2.1 per unit for Madhya Pradesh to a high of 4.0 for Rajasthan, a factor of 1:2. In the 1990s it ranged from a low of 1.1 per cent year in Bihar and 1.2 per cent in U.P. to a high of 7.6 per cent per year in Gujarat, with Maharastra coming next at 6.1 per cent. The ratio between the lowest (Bihar) and the highest (Gujarat) is as much as 1:7.

The increased variation in growth performance across states in the 1990s reflects the fact that whereas growth accelerated for the economy as a whole, it actually decelerated sharply in Bihar, Uttar Pradesh and Orissa, all of which had relatively low rates of Growth. There was also a decleration in Haryana and Punjab, but the decleration was from relatively higher levels of growth in the 1980s, and these states were also the richest.

Six states showed acceleration in growth of SDP in the 1990s. The acceleration was particularly market in Maharashtra and Gujarat, both of which were among the richer States, but

Table 4.7
Annual Rates of Growth of Per Capita Gross State Domestic Product

States	*1980-81 to 1990-91% p.a.*	*1991-92 to 1997-98% p.a.*
1. Bihar	2.45	1.12
2. Rajasthan	3.96	3.96
3. Uttar Pradesh	2.60	1.24
4. Orissa	2.38	1.64
5. Madhya Pradesh	2.08	3.87
6. Andhra Pradesh	3.34	3.45
7. Tamil Nadu	3.87	4.95
8. Kerala	2.19	4.52
9. Karnataka	3.28	3.45
10. West Bengal	2.39	5.04
11. Gujarat	3.08	7.57
12. Haryana	3.86	2.66
13. Maharashtra	3.58	6.13
14. Punjab	3.33	2.80
Cobmined SDP of 14 states	3.03	4.02

Note : SDP and population data obtained from the CSO.
Source : Ahluwalia, M.S. (2000).

there was also acceleration in West Bengal, Kerala, Tamil Nadu and Madhya Pradesh all belonging to the middle group of states in terms of per capita SDP. It is important to note that the high growth performers in the 1990s were not concentrated in one part of the country. The six states with growth rates of SDP in the 1990s above 6.0 per cent per year are fairly well distributed regionally i.e. Gujarat (9.6 per cent) and Maharashtra (8.0 per cent) in the west, West Bengal (6.9%) in the east. Tamil Nadu (6.2%) in the south and Madhya Pradesh (6.2%) and Rajasthan (6.5%) in the north.

An interesting feature of the performance in the 1990s is that the popular characterisation of the so called BIMARU states (Bihar, Madhya Pradesh, Rajasthan and UP) as a homogenous group of poor performers, a gouping originally proposed in the context of observed commonalities in demographic behaviour, does not hold as far as economic performance is concerned. Bihar and U.P. performed much more slowly than the average, but the two members of this group-Rajasthan and Madhya Pradesh have performed reasonably better. Rajasthan actually had a good performance in the 1980s. It was the fastest growing state and though its growth rate in the 1990s was marginally lower, it remained a strong performer with above averages for the 14 states but it accelerated significantly in the 1990s.

Similarly, the perception that it is only the coastal states or the Southern States have done well in the period of liberalisation is also not valid. Orissa is a coastal state, but its growth performance is very poor while Madhya Pradesh and Rajasthan are both heartland states and have performed reasonably well. The best performers are Gujarat and Maharashtra followed by West Bengal, Rajasthan, Tamil Nadu and Madhya Pradesh. Of the Southern States only Tamil Nadu is in the top six. The Southern States as a group have done well, but they have not been the only beneficiaries of the growth acceleration harnessed in the 1990s.

The performance of Kerala deserves special attention. Kerala is justly celebrated for its achievements in human development but it has also been criticised for under performance in economic growth. However, because of the low population growth its performance in per capita SDP growth in the 1990s was actually much better than the average (Table 4.6).

While the inter state inequality as measured by the Gini coefficient has increased from about 0.16 in 1986-87 to 0.23 in 1997-98 is a substantial increase and fitting a time trend to the series shows a statistically significant positive slope.[4] The common perception that the rich states got richer and the poor states got poorer is not entirely accurate. A closer look at Table 6 and Table 4.7 shows a slightly more complex pattern of behaviour.

(i) It is not true that all the richest states got richer relative to poorer states. Punjab and Haryana were the two richest of the 14 states in 1990-91. The growth rates of per capita SDP of these two states in 1990-91 were not only lower than in the 1980s but in the both cases actually fell below the national averages. Except for Bihar, U.P. and Orissa all other states therefore narrowed the per capita income gap with the two richest states.

(ii) Maharashtra and Gujarat, which were just below Punjab and Haryana in terms of per capita income levels and therefore in the richer group, accelerated very significantly in 1990s and grew at rates much higher than the national average.

(iii) All the poor States lagged behind Rajasthan, which was also one of the pooer states, experienced much stronger growth in per capita SDP, more than double that of the other poor States. Rajasthan's performance in terms of SDP growth is actually better than the average of the 14 states (See Table 6) but it sliped below the average in per capita SDP growth because of higher rates of population growth (Table 4.7).

(iv) Performance of six middle income States (Tamil Nadu, Kerala, West Bengal, Madhya Pradesh, Andhra Pradesh and Karnataka) was clustered around the average rate. All six of these States grew faster in terms of per capita GDP than did in the 1980s, though in some cases the differences were very marginal.

IMPLICATIONS FOR POLICY PRIORITIES

The implications for policy priorities that follows from the pattern of growth observed in the recent past are: (i) First, to sustain the growth momentum and achieve and annual average growth of 7-8 per cent in the next five years; and (ii) Second, to reduce the inter-state variation in growth pattern.

Sustainable growth hinges on the availability of efficient infrastructure. Although the demand-supply gap in areas such as telecom, roads and ports have been narrowed since the first half of the 1990s, the inadequate availability of these facilities, both in terms of quantity and quality, continues to hinder economic growth. Investment in infrastructure has been grossly inadequate, despite the establishment of specialised financial institutions. In the absence of a strongly enabling environment, the private sector has not been able to compensate for the decline in public spending in infrastructure. Without a transparent regulatory mechanism, adequate private investment will not go to this sector. In addition, government must continue to play an important role even as private entry is encouraged. It should monitor for the investment flows into this sector and step into fall in the gap between intended and actual private investment. The low growth of electricity this year only highlights the need to enhance investment in energy sector.

Social infrastructure such as education and health, is as important as physical infrastructure, not only for sustaining high growth but also for enhancing human development. The root of poverty often lies in illiterary and lack of basic health. Since education and basic health development falls within the sphere of state government and there is need for much stronger emphasis on these sectors in state plans. This calls for larger allocation to these sectors and equally important, it calls for measures to ensure effective use of resources.

The full potential of agriculture as a profitable activity must be realised at the earliest not only to benefit farmers and a large section of the rural poor, but also to give a fillep to overall growth of the economy through the backward and forward linkages of agriculture with the rest of the economy. Higher yields and diversification away from cereals to high value and labour intensive agriculture and allied activities are critical for achieving sustainable annual agricultural growth of over 4 per cent. Livestock, fisheries, horticulture, organic farming, commercial crops and agro-processing are the potential areas of high growth. Rationalisation of the Minimum Support Price (MSP) regime and introduction of other risk-mitigation measures, improvements in rural infrastructure and post harvest management technologies, legislative reform to unify the Indian common market in agriculture and strengthening research and development are essential for sustaining high agriculture growth.

The decline in the capital formation in agriculture from 1.9 per cent of GDP in the early 1990s to 1.3 per cent of GDP after 2000-01 is a matter of concern[5]. The declining trend is mainly due to fall in public investment in agriculture since the mid-nineties. While there has been some reversal of this trend in recent years, public investment in agriculture needs to be augmented, especially in rural infrastructure, irrigation and agricultural research and development. Since more than 58 per cent of the population depends on agriculture, a sector producing only 22 per cent of GDP and acceleration in agricultural growth to 4-4.5 per cent is imperative. There is also a need to absorb excess agricultural labour in other sectors, notably industry. Rapid development of agro-processing industry close to the agricultural production centres can bring about this shift without moving people from rural to urban areas.

One of the most impotent challenges in Indian economy growth policy is devise strategy for otaining industrial growth over 10 per cent because annual industrial growth has been in disappointing single digits since 1995-96. Industry needs to grow rapidly not only to boost the overall growth rate in the economy but also to generate gainful employment for the entrants, who are projected to swell the ranks of labour force by .9 per cent per annum, according to an estimate. The outlook for Indian Industry is bright if–"five major constraints"—labour law rigidities, distortion in indirect tax structure, high custom tariffs, reservation for small sector and friction in creation and closure of firms are to be addressed.

Apart from infrastructure, particularly adequate and reliable power supply at reasonable cost, there is need for stepped up investment in manufacturing. A better alignment of banks lending rate with deposit rate through increased competition and better NPA resolution will strenghthen the process. Foreign investment is important in this concern not only for the funds they bring, but also for the technological knowhow, improved corporate governance practices and access to foreign markets. Suitable liberalisation of both the FDI and FII regimes, including procedural issues, needs to be considered for enhancing foreign investment flows.

Among other factors that can help in boosting industry is the removal of the remaining items from the list reserved for small scale industry. The progress in gradually dismantling the reservation policy observed over recent years should continue and the policy of protection through reservation should be replaced by promotion as the cornerstone of further policy. The move towards gradually reducing custom duty rate and aligning them with that of Asean countries should continue as it will help Indian Industry. Furthermore, a popular consensus needs to be built up on the twin issues of more flexible labour laws and less friction in the creation and closure of firms in response to normal competitive market dynamics.

On the other side, the growth pattern of 1990s witnesse differences in growth performances across States. Inter-state differences in growth may arise because some states are better managed and therefore able to create an environment which generate higher growth. The 'pay off' from superior management has also increased because of liberalisation, it is very likely that variation in the quality of economic management will lead to greater inter-state variation in management performance.

It is, therefore, necessary to reduce the inter-state in growth by increasing the rate of growth of per capita SDP in low growth states from around 1.5 per cent experienced in the 1990s to somewhat between 3.5 and 4 per cent. This requires the rate of growth of SDP to increase from a little over 3 per cent per annum observed in the 1990s, to at least 6 per cent per annum. This doubling in the growth rates of SDP is clearly necessary to deal with regional inequality since, by definition, inequality will increase if the poorer states do not grow as fast as the national average. However the acceleration in growth is also needed to tackle the problem of poverty in these states because they account for a large proportion of national poverty. There is a tendency to think that the solution to the poverty problem in these states lies in implementation anti-poverty programmes.

Doubling the rate of growth of any large economy is not an easy task the these states (Bihar, UP and Orissa), we are concerned with, have a combined population of over 300 million. The simplest growth model used to focus on investment is the critical determinant of growth. Both public and private investment are important but the efficiency of resource utilisation is at least as important as the level of investment. Efficiency in turn depends on many other factors such as the level of human resource development, the quality of infrastructure, the economic policy environment, the laws and order, the work-culture and above all the quality of governance. Last but not the least, we need to be able to explain the reasons for these differences on the basis of relevant states specific characteristics which may be economic, institutional, socio-economic or even socio-political. This would help in devising strategies that can help break the specific constraints that prevent the present poorly performing states from replicating the success of the better performers.

CONCLUSION

The process of development of the economy gained momentum during the 'nineties with the enitiation of major economic reforms in 1991. The economy has since then been successfully launched on to a higher growth trajectory and has registered an improvement in a number of macro-economic indicators in a short-span of less than a decade. The sectoral composition of GDP has undergone a change in the 'nineties. The service sector has come to occupy a place of prominence in terms of relative contribution to GDP. The higher contribution of the services sector to GDP has a number of implications for policy priorities. (i) sustaining the growth momentum and achieving an annual average growth of 7-8 per cent in the next five years, (ii) Boosting agricultural growth through higher public investment, diversification and development of agro processing, (iii) Expanding industry fast, at least 10 per cent per year to absorb the surplus labour from agriculture through softening labour rigidities, reducing distortions in indirect tax structure and promoting small-scale industries, (iv) Enforcing user charges and evolving a regulatory framework that fosters competition for attracting investment in infrastructure creation.

Further, the available evidence shows that the differences in performance across states is enormous. Some states have fared exceptionally well, several others show a strong performance while some are doing poorly. These differences may be economic, institutional, socio-economic or socio-political. Accordingly, strategies have to be devised that can help break the specific constraints that prevent the present poorly performing states from replicating the success of the better performers. In the end, a favourable socio-political management provides sufficient condition for higher and balanced growth of the economy. In a parliamentary democracy like ours, the society's design for higher and balanced growth must be reflected in the working of other major institution like the judiciary and public interest groups. Quick disposal of litigations involving key projects is essential to give credible signs to private investors. All the major wings of the government and public institutions need to provide this. The appropriate techno-economic conditions for a take off to higher balanced growth path is evident at present in India. The co-operation of the society as a whole is needed for the take off to materialise.

Notes

1. See, CSO revised estimates for 2003-04 released on February 9, 2004.
2. See Ahluwalia (2000), Kapila, U. (2001).
3. The acronym BIMARU taken from the initial letters of Bihar, Madhya Pradesh, Rajasthan and U.P. was a pun on the Hindi word *BIMAR*, meaning sick and was first used by Ashish Bose in the context of demographic analysis as these states displayed much higher fertility states than other states in the country.
4. See, Ahluwalia (2000), Kapila, U. (2001).
5. See, *Economic Survey*, (2003-04).

References

Acharya, Shankar (2002), 'Macroeconomic Management in the Nineties', *Economic and Political Weekly*, April 20.

Ahulwalia, Montek S. (2002), 'State-Level Performance under Economic Reforms in India' in Anne O. Krueger (ed.), Economic Policy Reforms and the Indian Economy, University of Chicago Press.

Bhalla, G.S. (2001), Political Economy of Indian Development in the 20th Century : India's Road to Freedom and Growth', *Indian Economic Journal*, Volume 48, No. 3.

Bhattacharya, S. and U.R. Patel (2002), 'Financial Intermediation in India : A Case of Aggravated Moral Hazard?', paper presented at the Third Annual Conference or Economic Policy Reform in India at the Centre for Research on Economic Development and Policy Reform, Stanfrom University, June 3-4.

Dollar, D.O., Goswami, *et. al.* (2002), 'Competitiveness of Indian Manufacturing : Results from a Firm-Level Survey', paper presented at a conference organised by the Confederation of Indian Industry and the World Bank, New Delhi, January.

Easterly, William (2001), 'The Elusive Quest for Growth : Economists' Adventures and Misadventures in the Tropics', MIT Press, Cambridge.

Gulati, Ashok and Seema Bathla (2001), 'Capital Formation in Indian Agriculture : Revisiting the Debate', *Economic and Political Weekly*, May 19.

Mohan Rakesh (2002), 'Small-Scale Industry Policy in India: A Critical Evaluation' in Anne O. Krueger (ed.), Economic Policy Reforms and the Indian Economy, University of Chicago Press.

Parikh, J.K. and K.S. Parikh (2002), 'Reforms in the Power Sector' in K.S. Parikh and R. Radhakrishnan (eds.), *Indian Development Report*, 2002, Oxford University Press.

An Analytical Study on Growth, Trends and Stability of Major Kharif Crops in Various Agro-Climatic Zones of Jharkhand

BAL KRISHNA JHA AND AMALENDU KUMAR

INTRODUCTION

Before division, Bihar state consisted of two dissimilar natural parts i.e. the Bihar plain and the Chhotanagpur plateau. This Chhotanagpur is now a new state named Jharkhand. The geographical area of the new state accounts for nearly 79.70 lakh hectare with nearly 2.5 crores population. Out of the total geographical area, 30.14 per cent is under forest and 29.33 per cent has been under plough. The rest land surface totaling 32.68 per cent of the area forms barren and uncultivated land, part non-agriculture use, grazing land, cultivatable waste land and other fallow lands (7.85%). Area sown more than once is 8.66

per cent of cultivable land i.e. only 2.8 per cent of the geographical area. Only 9.60 per cent of the cropped area is irrigated. This is reduced to 4.0 per cent during the rabi seasons. This has lad to mono-cropping in most of the cultivated area (90%). The cropping intensity is less than 110 per cent. Rain fed agriculture is the main feature of this area covering about 92 per cent of it.

Rice is an important and extensively grown food crop in the state. Maize remaining the next important crop and also extensively grown as food crop. About 17.50 lakh hectare of land are engaged in rice and 1.45 lakh hectare under maize cultivation. The average productivity of rice is about 8 quintals per hectare and of maize is about 8.84 quintals per hectare.

To meet the growing needs of food grains and creating additional employment opportunities in agriculture sector, several programmes like IADP, HYV, MCP, etc. were launched in the different parts of the country. The high yielding varieties of crops including hybrid maize and exotic paddy varieties were launched in the country from kharif season of 1968. The major revolution was brought about by the introduction of these programmes in Indian agricultural production. The present paper is an attempt in this direction to study the trend and magnitudes of change in cropping pattern, average yield, growth rate and variability in the two major crops i.e., rice and maize during pre green revolution period and thereafter in Jharkhand state.

Objectives

Accordingly, the broad objectives of the study are as follows :

(i) To study cropping pattern during pre and post green revolution period in different agro-climatic zones of Jharkhand state.

(ii) To measure growth rate in area, production and productivity (yield) during pre and post green revolution period (zone-wise).

(iii) To study average productivity and extent of variability in area, production and productivity in different zones of the state.

Methodology

The Jharkhand state consisting of three agro-climatic zones, i.e. zone-4, zone-5 and zone-6 were purposively selected. The study was based on secondary data collected from various sources namely, Bihar through Figures, Hand Book of Statistics and Bihar Ankro Mein, various issues of Agricultural Situation in India and Agro-climatic zone specific research, ICAR, etc. To estimate growth rate of crops under study, the periods were grouped into four. Firstly, the study period was divided into two broad period, i.e. 'pregreen revolution period' and post-green revolution period. The post-green revolution period was further divided into three periods, i.e. period-II, period-III and period-IV. As such, the periods divided and denoted for interpretation of result throughout the study are given as follows :

Period-I : Represents pre-green revolution period (From 1958-59 to 1968-69)
Period-II : Represents post-green revolution period (From 1969-70 to 1984-85)
Period-III : Represents post-green revolution period (From 1985-86 to 1999-00)
Period-IV : Represents post-green revolution period (From 1969-70 to 1999-00)

To measure the variability in respect to area, production and productivity, the periods were divided into two groups, i.e. period-I (Pre-green revolution period from 1958-59 to 1968-69) and period-II (Post-green revolution period from 1969-70 to 1984-85). The pooled period-III i.e., period-I and period-II. Thus, the period divided and denoted for interpretation of results throughout the study are given as follows :

Period-I : (Pre-green revolution period from 1958-59 to 1968-69)
Period-II : (Post-green revolution period from 1969-70 to 1999-2000)

Period-III : (Pre and post-green revolution period from 1959-69 to 1999-2000)

For estimating the growth rates of major kharif crops with respect to area, production and productivity Exponential trend equation (function) was found most suitable and was finally selected for analysis.

Limitation

Only two major kharif crops viz. paddy and maize have been selected for the present paper as about 90 per cent of the cultivated area falls under mono cropping and prominently covering these two crops.

Exponential Trend

To estimate the compound growth rates of major crops in terms of area, production and productivity following exponential function was applied.

$$Y_t = A\beta^t \qquad \ldots (i)$$

Where Y_t = value of area, production and productivity in year t (t = 1, 2, 3 .... 42)

A = refers to intercept
't' refers to years

$$\beta = 1+\frac{\gamma}{100}$$

Where 'γ' refers to the percentage compound growth of area, production and productivity per annum.

By taking natural logarithms both sides of the equation, it has been reduced to the following linear from :

$$\text{In } Y_t = \text{In } A + t \text{ in } \beta$$

When had negative value, the procedure of calculating CGR is the same but the value of growth rate will be in negative form. This negative compound growth rate indicates the decreasing growth rate over time and vice-versa.

To examine the stability with respect to area, production and yield of the crops, mean, standard deviation and co-efficient of variation were worked out for the period over 1959-69 i.e. first period before green revolution. From 1970-85 i.e., second period under green revolution and for i.e. the whole period from 1959 to 2000 third or pooled period).

$$\text{Co-efficient of variation} = \frac{\delta}{\overline{X}} \times 100$$

Where δ = standard deviation

$\overline{X}$ = mean of the sample data

Standard deviation (δ) =

Where; X - (X_1 ___ $\overline{X}$)".

N = No. of observations.

RESULTS AND DISCUSSIONS

Cropping Pattern

The cropping pattern in pre and post green revolution period of three agroclimatic zones (zone 4, zone 5, and zone 6) of Jharkhand region has been analysed and observed that rice continues to be the most important crop in all the zones of the study region contributing to more than 70 per cent to total cropped area (Table 5.1). The share of rice in total cropping area remains unchanged in all zones of the region. The range varied between 66.40 to 89.5 per cent in pre-green revolution period and between 67.89 to 91.0 per cent in post green revolution period in all zones. The next important crop is maize which during pre-green revolution period ranged between 3.13 to 9.90 per cent in all zones where as in green revolution period it ranged between 2.18 to 8.84 per cent.

Unlike rice there has been a marginal downward change in the share of maize area during green revolution period. After rice and maize, coarse millet is another important crop of all the zones. It occupied about 3 per cent to cropped area which varied from 2.20 to 4.83 per cent in pre green revolution period in all zones. After introduction of high yielding varieties

TABLE 5.1
Cropping Pattern in Pre and Post Green Revolution Periods in Different Agro Climatic Zones of Jharkhand State

(In 1000 hectare)

Sl. No.	Crops	Pre-green Revolution Period (1967-68)			Post-green Revolution Period (1999-00)		
		Zone-4	Zone-5	Zone-6	Zone-4	Zone-5	Zone-6
1.	Rice	764.40 (73.90)	565.80 (66.40)	357.0 (89.50)	770.00 (73.85)	523.90 (67.90)	354.00 (91.00)
2.	Maize	100.20 (9.20)	45.00 (5.40)	12.50 (3.13)	92.20 (8.84)	44.00 (5.70)	8.70 (2.18)
2.	Wheat	8.30 (0.86)	17.80 (2.0)	0.84 (0.20)	31.20 (3.0)	33.0 (4.27)	1.50 (0.37)
4.	Gram	16.50 (1.62)	42.50 (1.50)	3.60 (0.90)	11.10 (1.14)	16.30 (2.10)	2.40 (0.60)
5.	Barley	7.70 (0.77)	18.60 (2.18)	— —	6.90 (0.66)	11.60 (1.50)	0.10 (0.02)
6.	Other pulses	38.0 (3.90)	46.00 (5.40)	6.0 (1.50)	37.00 (3.54)	36.00 (4.66)	5.00 (1.20)
7.	Potato	9.70 (0.98)	4.80 (0.50)	0.40 (0.10)	15.80 (1.52)	9.80 (1.27)	0.80 (0.20)
8.	Sugarcane	6.00 (0.61)	2.40 (0.25)	0.50 (0.11)	2.60 (0.25)	2.20 (0.25)	0.02 (0.01)
9.	Coarse millet	39.90 (4.83)	28.0 (3.40)	9.0 (2.20)	45.0 (4.32)	63.0 (8.16)	10.00 (2.00)
10.	Ground nut	4.00 (0.42)	3.0 (1.50)	2.0 (0.06)	3.17 (0.30)	9.00 (1.16)	2.20 (0.62)
11.	Rapessed and mustard	5.0 (0.53)	0.30 (0.35)	0.80 (0.21)	3.0 (0.28)	0.80 (0.74)	0.21 (0.05)

programme, the area under this crop has reduced in all zones. There has been marked change in area of wheat and potato in green revolution period. The area under wheat crop increased from 8.30 to 31.20 thousand hectares between 1966-67 to 1999-2000 in zone-4 and from 17.80 to 33.00 and from 0.84 to 1.50 thousand hectares during same period in zone 5 and zone 6 respectively. Similarly, area of potato crop increased from 9.70 to 15.80, from 4.80 to 9.80 and from 0.40 to 0.80 thousand hectares

TABLE 5.2

Mean Value of Area, Production and Yield of Rice and Maize Crops

Zones		*Period-I Pre-green revolution period (1958-59)*		*Period-II Post-green revolution period (1969-70 to 1984-85)*		*Pooled average of period-I & period-II*		*Percentage change over period-I*	
		Rice	*Maize*	*Rice*	*Maize*	*Rice*	*Maize*	*Rice*	*Maize*
(1)		(2)	(3)	(4)	(5)	(6)	(7)	(8)	(9)
	A	790.80	107.34	778.10	96.56	747.70	99.93	-8.58	-11.16
Zone-4	P	737.40	109.00	712.50	89.58	720.30	95.67	-3.49	-21.67
	Y	921.40	1006.00	879.90	963.70	961.00	958.40	6.25	-7.20
	A	572.10	47.12	566.60	56.77	568.30	53.76	-0.96	20.47
Zone-5	P	368.90	42.71	392.90	48.96	383.50	47.01	6.50	14.63
	Y	633.60	873.26	693.70	859.40	674.70	865.70	9.43	1.58
	A	347.40	12.95	343.60	9.54	344.90	10.60	-1.03	26.33
Zone-6	P	305.80	10.84	297.90	7.83	300.40	8.77	2.53	27.50
	Y	880.00	835.80	867.40	854.20	871.30	848.50	-1.43	2.20

A = Area *P = Production* *Y = Yie!d*

in between 1966-67 to 1999-2000 in zone 4, zone 5 and zone 6 respectively. It was also observed from the analysis that area of pulse crops has considerably decreased after introduction of high yielding varieties programme in all zones. The reduction in area of maize, pulse crop and coarse millets are attributed to increased area under rice, wheat and potato and other vegetable crops during green revolution period. Overall, it is observed from the analysis of cropping pattern that after introduction of HYV programmes (green revolution), the cropping pattern shifted in favour of wheat, potato and other vegetable crops in Jharkhand region.

Zone 4

The Mean value of area, production and productivity of rice and maize for different periods, i.e., pre-green revolution and post-green revolution period indicates that the average annual area under rice was 747-70 thousand hectares which varied from 728.10 to 790.6 thousand hectares during period-I & II. The area covered by rice was more during period-I that than of period-II. Whereas in case of maize crop during the same period area has declined in post green revolution period in all zones except zones-5. The area under this crop decreased from 107.34 to 96.56 thousand hectares in zones-4.

The table further shows that the total production of rice was also higher in period-I as compared to period-II. The higher total production of rice in period-I was positively associated with higher area. But productivity analysis also indicates that the average productivity per hectare of this crop was higher (6.25%) in period-II as compared to period-I.

The total production of maize in zone-4 decreased from 109.00 to 89.58 thousand tones and also declined in yield per hectare as observed. The average yield declined from 1006 kg. to 934 kg. during the reference period.

Zone 5

Table indicates that during period-I annual average area under rice was marginally higher than that of period-II. Inspite of higher area during period-I, the total production of rice was lesser the level of total production of period-II. This was mainly because of higher productivity per hectare during period-II. The average productivity per hectare was 633.60 and 693.40 kg. respectively in Period-I and Period-II.

Whereas in case of maize the total production increased from 42.71 to 48.96 thousand tones due to increase in area between 1958-59 to 1999-2000 920.47 per cent). Like area and production, yield per hectare of maize in this zone also found to be declining from 873 to 859 kg./ha.

Zone 6

There was almost constant but marginal decline in respect of area, production and productivity of rice during period-II. The area declined from 347.4 to 343.80 thousand hectares, production from 305 to 298 thousand tones and productivity from 880 to 868 kg. ha.

The area under maize in this zone was also found declining. The crops are decreased from 12.95 to 9.54 thousand hectares. Also the production decreased from 10.84 to 7.53 thousand tones. But the average productivity is found increased due to large decline in area.

At overall level these results indicate that the average productivity per hectare of rice during green revolution (period-II) has increased in all zones except zone-6. Whereas in maize, results indicate that there has been considerable decline in area and production of maize while marginal reduction in productivity per hectare in post-green revolution period was observed in Jharkhand region.

Zone 4

The estimated annual compound growth rate of rice and maize in respect of area, production and productivity are presented in Table 5.3. The figures in the table reveals that during period-I the area, production and productivity registered decreasing compound growth rate i.e. 1.18, 5.63 and 3.89 per cent per annum in the case of rice, while during period-II of green revolution, the growth rate of area, production and yield was moderately increased being 0.081, 0.87 and 0.79 per cent at compound rate. Inspite of negative growth rate of area during period-III, production and productivity showed positive growth rate being 3.17 and 3.79 per cent per annum during the same period. The magnitude of growth rate of production during this period was marked by more than that for all the period considered for the study. This was mainly due to higher growth rate of productivity which neutralised the effect of area of the total tonnage of rice. The overall pooled period experienced negative growth rate of area and production being 0.61 and 0.019 per cent per annum. But during the same period, the rate of increase in productivity significantly neutralised the effect of area on total production of rice showing a dismal decrease (0.019%) per annum.

The annual compound growth rate of maize in Jharkhand state shows that area of maize in pre-green revolution period was larger in this zone with growth rate of 1.05 per cent per annum. After advent of green revolution the area of maize was

TABLE 5.3

Annual Compound Growth Rate of Area, Production and Yield of Rice and Maize in Different Zones of Jharkhand Region

	Period-I Pre-green revolution period		*Period-II Post-green revolution period*		*Period-III Post-green revolution period*		*Pooled of Period - I& period-II*	
Zones	*Rice*	*Maize*	*Rice*	*Maize*	*Rice*	*Maize*	*Rice*	*Maize*
A	1.81	1.05	0.081	0.27	-0.59	-6.22	-0.62	-2.51
P	-5.63	9.27	0.87	1.35	3.17	-4.78	-0.02	-1.00
Y	-3.89	8.13	0.79	1.10	3.79	1.53	0.60	1.55
A	1.10	1.87	0.21	-0.82	-0.86	-2.34	-0.46	-1.96
P	1.10	10.34	7.80	-6.52	0.47	2.18	1.29	-2.62
Y	1.10	8.30	7.57	-6.52	1.28	4.64	1.77	-0.67
A	-0.03	-0.27	0.63	-11.19	-0.35	-6.08	-0.47	-3.99
P	-0.75	8.06	2.79	-2.83	3.95	-3.69	0.69	-4.60
Y	-3.72	8.36	2.14	-1.28	4.32	-0.25	1.17	-1.90

A = Area P = Production Y = Yield

considerably decreased (2.51%) in this zone. The data also indicates that in period-II the rate of decline was more pronounced than the period-I. But the yield rate was observed increasing trend at 1.55 per cent per annum which could be attributed to improved seeds and better farm techniques/ management.

Zone 5

The result reveals that unlike zone 4, the agricultural performance of zone 5 in respect to area, production and productivity of rice was positive during period-I. the area, production and productivity grew at annual compound rate of 1.10 per cent each. The table further indicates that compound growth rates of area, production and productivity of rice during period-II were positive being 0.21, 7.80 and 7.57 per cent. The same trend was maintained in all cases except area during period-III. For the pooled period, the area experienced negative growth rate (0.046%) while positive growth rate was obtained in case of production and productivity.

The result for maize in this zone indicates declining trend during post green revolution period over that in pre-green revolution period. The same results like zone 4 was observed in case of period-II in area which indicates negative trends in more pronounced manner. The negative trend also observed in case of production and yield rates which were -2.62 and -0.67 per cent per annum.

Zone 6

In case of rice in period I was recorded negative rates in area, production and productivity at 0.027, 3.75 and 3.72 per cent respectively per annum. But in period-II trend was positive. The pooled period experienced positive growth rate in production and productivity while negative in case of area.

Whereas in case of maize in pre and post green revolution period area shows negative trend, in period-II the rate of decline was observed more in comparison to other periods including pooled period. In period-I the production and yield were observed increasing trend while in period-II, period-III and pooled period it was observed negative trend, i.e., 11.19, 6.08 and 3.99 per cent respectively and in production 1.28, 0.25 and 1.09 per cent in productivity.

It is indicated from the analysis of agricultural performance during pre- and post-green revolution period that the area of rice crop declined during pooled period while productivity increased in all zones of Jharkhand state during the same period. In case of maize, the overall results of growth rates indicate that after advent of green revolution programme production of maize declined accompanied by decline in area and yield of maize in the all agro-climatic zones of the region.

The two statistical methods used are standard deviation and co-efficient of variation to give magnitude of variation in absolute term as well as percentage term. It is evident from Table 4 that the magnitude of variability in terms of absolute as well as percentage for area, production and productivity in rice in zone 4 found to be higher during period-I as compared to period-II. Among area, production and productivity the minimum variability was recorded in area and maximum in case of production in both the period. The average variability was recorded at 8.31, 17.80 and 15.48 per cent in case of area, production and productivity of rice respectively. Whereas in zone 5, variability in case of area, production and productivity was found to be more during period-I as compared to period-II. Among them variability in area as minimum (22.29%). On an average the magnitude of variability was recorded to be 6.68, 22.29 and 21.51 per cent respectively in case of area, production and productivity. Whereas in zone 6 in same cases variability percentage were 4.50, 19.12 and 19.6 in area, production and productivity respectively.

Table also presents the variability in area and productivity of maize. The data clearly indicates that the minimum variability was observed in case of area in period-I in all zones. While the reverse situation was observed in case of production and productivity (yield) in all zones except zone 6. The high variability in case of yield was accompanied by high variability in production also in period-I. The green revolution period, which is denoted by period-II, was accompanied by minimum variability term, i.e., absolute and percentage in all zones except zone 6 of the region. 'The instability in productivity or yield risk

Table 5.4
Variability in Area, Production and Yield of Rice and Maize Crops

Zones	Period	Area				Production				Yeild			
		Standard deviation		CV		Standard deviation		CV		Standard deviation		CV	
		Rice	Maize	Rice	Maize	Rice	Maize	Rice	Maize	Rice	Maize	Rice	Maize
(1)	(2)	(3)	(4)	(5)	(6)	(7)	(8)	(9)	(10)	(11)	(12)	(13)	(14)
	Period-I	64.15	6.52	8.11	6.07	176.17	40.29	23.89	36.94	179.80	339.9	19.52	33.13
	Period-II	51.50	19.14	7.08	19.82	104.78	26.27	14.70	29.77	133.10	248.5	13.60	26.53
	Period-III	62.15	16.92	8.31	16.93	128.70	32.21	17.80	33.66	148.80	276.3	15.48	28.83
	Period-I	48.62	5.92	8.52	12.00	82.03	23.09	22.60	54.07	139.90	356.0	22.07	40.76
	Period-II	33.20	7.70	5.86	13.56	87.26	15.25	22.10	31.15	143.78	218.6	21.11	25.43
	Period-III	37.95	8.43	6.68	15.68	85.50	17.97	22.29	38.12	145.14	263.09	21.51	30.45
	Period-I	12.00	0.63	3.45	5.50	70.74	3.63	23.13	33.54	205.60	284.5	23.37	34.03
	Period-II	17.00	0.43	4.90	25.50	52.03	2.86	17.46	36.55	151.59	331.9	17.47	38.86
	Period-III	15.54	2.59	4.50	24.46	57.45	3.37	19.12	33.43	166.98	313.4	19.16	36.93

in production of maize was estimated to be about 29.30 and 37 per cent in zone 4, 5 and 6 which ranged from 25 per cent. This analysis indicates that there is still high risk in production of maize in the region when three and half decades of green revolution has passed. Although, instability in yield of maize crop has been reduced during green revolution period at the country level.

CONCLUSIONS

- There has been positive shift in cropping pattern in favour of wheat and potato crop after introduction of green revolution programmes.
- The average yield of paddy per hectare has increased during green revolution period in all zones of the region.
- The average yield per hectare of maize in green revolution period did not show superiority over pre green revolution period in all zones.
- The growth rate in case of rice productivity is found to be positive during green revolution period, while the negative growth rate was observed before green revolution period in all zones of the region.
- In case of maize, the growth rate of area, production and yield were found to be negative in green revolution period in all zones.
- The reverse situation was observed during pre green revolution in all zones.
- In general, the magnitude of variability of area, production and productivity in case of rice is observed to be small in green revolution period as compared to pre revolution period in all zones of the region.
- However, production and productivity have been comparatively noticed more stable during green revolution period than that of pre green revolution period.
- In case of maize the variability in yield per hectare is recorded to be minimum during green revolution as compared to pre green revolution period.

NOTES

1. Various Issues of Bihar Through Figures, Directorate of Statistics and Evaluation, Government of Bihar (1960-96).
2. Hand Book of Statistics, Bihar (From 1960-2001).
3. *Bihar Ankro Mein, Bihar Ek Jhalak,* Directorate of Statistics and Evaluation, Government of Bihar (1960-96).
4. Various issues of Agricultural Situation in India, Directorate of Economics and Statistics, Ministry of Agriculture, Government of India (1958-2001).

WTO and Indian Agriculture

SITA RAM SINGH

PREAMBLE

Established on the 1st January 1995, the World Trade Organisation (WTO), a successor of GATT (General Agreement on Tariff and Trade), 1947 is the embodiment of the result of Uruguay Round (UR) held during 1986-93. WTO is one of the multilateral institutions like I.M.F., World Bank, UNO etc. In the backdrop of global wave of liberalisation, privatisation, marketization, and globalisation (LPG) WTO has been playing a very crucial role and making concerted efforts in inducting radical shifts in the development paradigm at national and international levels. The Uruguay Round (UR) was uniquely distinct from the earlier rounds in so far as it covered new areas such as: trade related intellectual property rights, agriculture, trade textiles etc. But the most fundamental features of UR and WTO are the fact that an institutional mechanism for enforcement of the commitments has been established in 1995 in the form of WTO whose long arm of jurisdiction stretches beyond the conventional border-level policies of tariff and non-tariff barriers to trade up a member of truly domestic policies thereby impacting on the pace pattern of development in the developed and developing countries. Removal of quality restrictions (QRs), reduction of tariffs, removal of subsidies, changing in patent regimes, shift in investment regimes, new rules of dumping and anti-dumping measures, provision of safeguards measures etc. have all imp laced radical shifts in the development paradigms of developing countries. WTO encompasses rules of 30,000 pages consisting of 60 agreements and separate commitments (called schedules). Whole the broad objectives of WTO, in bringing about a rule based liberalised world trading system are laudable, the practical experience of the emerging policy actions is in sharp context to the perceived expectations. The theory of comparative advantage based on factor endowments and factor intensities, as no longer valid. Competitive strengths are determined by new factors such as access to information, knowledge intensity and aggressive policies in marketing and R&D intensity.

Knowledge and WTO

Knowledge is power and information is a valuable resource. In a market system, price change with varying frequency and price dispersion is a manifestation and a measure of asymmetric information in the market. Asymmetric information in a market distorts the market price. The information asymmetry also plays significant role in the development process.

The information age has heralded a new way of doing business. Few could have guessed how the individual components of information technology (IT)–hardware, software, networks, etc. could come together to create a whole New World of virtual reality. Information Technology has the power to change the most well entrenched business paradigms. It has the power to link and connect people and enable the exchange of products, services and capital in an entirely different manner than in the past.

Information Technology

Today IT has become largest industry in the world with

companies such as Microsoft leading the way to the future. Increased accessibility to IT has melted barriers of time, space and place and has created new areas of opportunity. According to P. Galgan, "It is anticipated that products, interconnected workers, and intellectual capital will influence each other in many ways in the future." Similar View was stated by Prof. Galbraith, "Today's technology can tie people and databases together, the company's entire knowledge base and computer power can be delivered to any person or team on the firing line."

Information Technology is also a powerful catalyst and tool for managing change. The strategic use of Infotech is a business decision and not a technology choice. Indian managers need to take a fresh look at the current state of information management in their respective organisation and take the help of Information Strategy Planning to manage their most important resource-information more effectively.

Enabling technologies will allow human resource departments to manage important organisational issues such as cost cutting, employee-communications, recruitment, training, retention and reengineering in a better way.

Under present age of globalisation and WTO organisations have a mix employees, i.e. some educated in the industrial age and others nurtured in the information age. Both the older and the younger generations need to synergise their activities and speak each other's language. The continuing education programmes in IT is necessary due to the everchanging nature of technologies.

The appropriate application of the tools of IT have just begun to permeate different functions in Indian industry. It has only had a trickle-down effect to the human resource function and other support functions.

Today human resource management faces challenges and opportunities of paradigm shift, a change that can revolutionise human resource policy and practice.

Information Technology can enable the human resource function to have a more integrated reach and influence over the organisation and thus play the role of strategic partner.

IT has become a valuable decision making tool. The technology can further help in increasing connectivity between divisions in an organisation. In other words, IT serves as an important tool to improve efficiency and productivity. It is necessary that human resource professionals in Indian Companies fully exploit the opportunities which are provided. This makes it necessary to communicate the benefits of IT for departments/divisions and functions.

Intellectual Property: Concept and Relevance

The corporate world in the new economic environment of WTO regime is experiencing a paradigm shift in management especially of intellectual property. Strategic intellectual property management is recognised as an important tool to achieve competitive advantage.

The era of WTO of fierce competition and overcharging global markets has resulted a shift in organisational design from command, control and compartmentalization to:

(a) service orientation with a sharper focus on customers;
(b) a network of specialists—a far cry from bureaucratic ways of functioning and integrated hierarchies;
(c) employing fewer people with greater emphasis on team work;
(d) a redefined work culture that focuses on constant learning and continuous improvement; and
(e) performance-linked pay rather than seniority-based pay.

Concept of Intellectual Property

Under WTO Regime, it is clear that the importance of intellectual property (IP) has long been widely appreciated in most of the world economies though, the approach towards the protection of the intellectual property varies from economy to economy. The protection of IP in developed economies, has been obviously recognized as the solid basis of promoting inventions so as to ensure dynamism in their economies through new commercial and industrial enterprise which produce the own cascading effects on economic growth and employment therein.

According to GATT (1994, p. 365). "The term 'Intellectual Property' is defined to refer to all categories of intellectual property that are subject to Sections 1 to 7 of part-II of the Agreement". Article-3 defines 'persons' who shall be accorded the national treatment. They are 'nationals' both natural and juridical (legal) persons, that would meet the criteria or eligibility for protection for under the earlier convention.

Intellectual property refers to the creation of the human mind and of human intellect. In other words, IP is the product of the mind. The rights granted of creations of innovative work are known as IPR. The unauthorised use of IP is an infringement of the right of the owner to protect these rights. IPR consists of: (a) Patent; (b) Copyright; (c) Trademark; (d) Industrial design (e) Geographical indications; (f) Trade secret; (g) Layout designs of integrated circuits; Patent provide rights to inventions. An invention may be defined as a noval idea which permits in practice in the solution of a specific problem.

Strengthen the Institutional Basis of IPR Regime

According to V. R. Panchamukhi, "As per the commitment under the trade related intellectual property's (TRIP) agreements, India is all set to move towards a comprehensive intellectual property right regime, with product patent system and a region's copy-right-enforcement framework. The issues of widening the scope of patentable matter, protection and promotion of bio-diversity, protecting the farmer's right as against the plant breeders rights, etc. would continue to figure prominently at the national and international fora.

We need to develop greater clarity in regard to the identification of our long-term interests without creating large damages for the short-term ones. In this context, one important initiative that needs to be launched without further delay is that of strengthening our institutional facility for patent registration, copyright protection and legal process of dispute settlement. It is learnt that China has established a facility under roof for dealing with all the aspects of IPR regime. In contrast to this, our patent registration system is cumbersome. There is no R&D (Research and Development) activity with linkages with industrial applications and patenting facilitation.

Our music and entertainment industry can earn huge amount of foreign exchange if our copyright regime is tightened.

We have not mapped our bio-diversity resources property. Inventory on the profile of community knowledge sector is non-existent. We need to invert more in bio-technology research to make it a leading sector of global strength. We have already opted for the option of Exclusive Marketing Rights (EMR Route), in the transition period of moving towards Product Patent system in the case of pharmaceutical and agro-chemical. We have, however, not tightened our internal systems for ensuring fair place to domestic producers and traders in these products. Our investment on R&D activity as a proportion of GDP is one of the lowest in the world.

Since Technology would be the prime engine of growth and competitiveness in the coming years a sound national technology promotion policy both at the governmental and corporate levels is called far.

Soon after the WTO came into existence the accord on TRIPS has raised a whole range of apprehensions in the country.

TRIPS Agreement covered eight types of intellectual property under various sections of the agreement viz: licenses.

(a) Patent (Section-V)
(b) Trademark (Section-II)
(c) Copy right (Section-I)
(d) Industrial design (Section-IV)
(e) Integrated Circuits
(f) Geographical Indication (Section-III)
(g) Protection of Undisclosed (Section-VII)
(h) Information and
(i) Control of anti-competition practice contractual licenses.

A. *Patent*

Patent provides rights to invention under Article 27 of the WTO. It is a novel idea which, in practice, permits the solution of a specific problem. Invention to be registered as a patent must be-a) new; (b) involved in an inventive step; and (c) capable of industrial application.

TRIPS Agreement stipulates that the countries shall grant patents for inventions in all fields of technology for both. (i) Products and (ii) Process including those used in manufacturing the products.

Patents are to be granted without discrimination as to place of invention and whether products are imported or locally produced.

The product/process which countries are permitted to exclude from patentability consists of: (a) Diagnostic, Therapeutic and Surgical methods for the treatment of humans and animals; (b) Plants and animals other than micro-organisms; (c) Essentially biological process for the production of plants; (d) Animals other than non-biological and microbiological process.

Patent gives patent owners exclusive property rights allowing them to prevent others from using the inventions covered. Manufacturers willing to use patented inventions must obtain licences or authorizations from the patent owners, who normally will require them to pay royalties.

The term of patent failing within the category of drug, medicine and food is 5 years, from the date of grant or 7 years from the date of filing and 14 years for any other invention from the date of grant.

B. Copyrights : Articles 9 to 15 Provide Copyright

Copyright can be acquired in terms of works of authorship that include literary work including Computer software under Indian Law, Musical works and accompanying lyrics, dramatic works and dialogues, partomines and choreographic work, architecture, works of applied art, maps plans, sketches, motion pictures and other audio-visual work and sound recording. This copy right is basically a proprietary right and comes into existence as soon as the work in created.

India Copyright Act of 1957 was ended in 1984 and subsequently in 1995. Under this Act, registration of work is not compulsory. There is no requirement of completion of any formality of registration.

Copyright provides proprietor exclusive right to make copyright provides proprietor exclusive right to make particular use of the work. Original literary dramatic, musical or artistic work enjoy copyright protection for the lifetime of the author plus 60 years if they are published within the lifetime of the author.

C. Trademark

A Trademark is a visual system in the form of a word, a symbol of a label applied to an article of manufacture scale with a view to indicating to the consumer the origin of manufacture. Articles 16 to 21 of WTO deal with trademark in J.P.

As such, Trademark helps to distinguish such goods from similar goods manufactured by others in the same trade. As Trade Mark creates a link between manufacturer and the customer its registration is significant. It is an excellent instrument of publicity and a symbol of goodwill apart from being a property which can have an enormous economic potential.

The duration of Trade Mark is for a period of 7 years from the date of filing of the application. This period can be renewed from time to time for a period of 7 years from the date of expiry of original registration of subsequent renewal.

Therefore, a registered Trade Mark can be kept in force perpetually by paying the prescribe renewal fees. It is followed because continuous use of the mark over a long period of time helps in making the mark popular amongst the customers generating both publicity and goodwill.

D. Industrial Design

Industrial design as provided in Articles 16 to 21 is also one of the most important part of IPR. A design is an idea of conception relating to the features of shape, configuration pattern or ornamental features applied to an article by any industrial process or means, whether manual, mechanical or chemical, separate or combined; which is in the finished article appeal to and are judged solely by vision. It is clear that design means features of shape etc. applied to an article itself. These features are conceived in the creator's intellect. The ideas conceived are given material form as a pictorial illustration, or as a specimen, prototype or as a model. These features can then be protected as design.

Designs in India are covered by the Design Act of 1911 which confers exclusive right to apply to any article in any class in which the design is registered.

The design has some basic features:

(h) Design must be new or original;
(i) It must have been previously published in India prior to the date of registration.

But the registration of design is possible only when it is reduced to visible form so as to identifiable.

E. Undisclosed Information

Trade secrets or know how are referred as undisclosed information which has commercial value because it is secret. It has also been subject to reasonable step to keep at secret. TRIPS Agreement stipulates that person lawfully in control of such information must have the possibility or preventing it from being disclosed to, acquired by or used by others without his or her consent in a manner contrary to honest commercial practices.

Furthermore, the agreement has provisions on undisclosed test data and other data whose submission is required by governments as a condition of approving the marketing of pharmaceutical or of agricultural chemical products. Member Government must protect such data against unfair commercial use.

Natural and legal persons shall have the possibility of preventing information lawfully within their control from being disclosed to acquired by or used by others without their consent in a manner contrary to honest commercial practices.

Paradigm Shift of Intellectual Property in Borders

Human resource assets now, need to imbibe general

business capacities in addition to their specialisation. These changes call for a shift in approach from reactive intellectual property management to proactive and innovative one.

Intellectual property managers should be able to go beyond nearly responding to business strategies and be able to anticipate and to prepare for the future needs. As organisations move away form traditional, hierarchical systems of management, the following capabilities become increasingly important teamwork shared goals, individual and group learning and planning for team action.

Under present WTO regime the colour and complexion of organisation has changed due to change in technology and expansion of world market. With globalisation and technological transformations feeding each other, business paradigms have undergone a major shift. Intellectual property and information technology have resulted in flatter structures and less hierarchical control in global organisation.

Policy Charges in IP

As a result of domestic and international competition, intellectual property management in borders is being given a key role. Under WTO regimes, following changes in the management of intellectual property and their policies and programmes are expected to be highlighted.

(i) With manpower costs going up and the need to bring product prices down to meet completion, manpower productivity has become a central issue in organisation and human resource professional will have to play a critical role to fulfill this need.

(ii) There is increasing emphasis on training and retaining to tap latent talent.

(iii) Global companies have started playing attention to career—growth and career planning for employees.

(iv) These companies are showing increasing willingness to retain talent and deploy manpower when necessary.

In a era of constant environmental change, total quality management is the need of the hour. While greater emphasis on product quality is required to survive in any business in India's competitive environment, customer service has to be given equal importance. For this, new management tools of intellectual property need to be developed.

Benchmarking

Benchmarking is one of such structured management tools. It involves the simple act of comparison and learning for organizational improvement. It contains four categories : (a) Product benchmarking; (b) Functional benchmarking; (c) Organisational benchmarking; and (d) Strategic benchmarking.

The nature of benchmarking can be stated in following form : (i) planning phase; (ii) analysis phase; (iii) integration phase; (iv) action phase; (v) maturity phase.

The management of intellectual property offers a wide latitude for the benchmarking process as it is amenable to internal, competitive, functional and generic benchmarking.

An organisation should benchmark to develop a holistic model for its intellectual property function which is turned to its corporate objective edge. This model should include an appraisal of intellectual property function in terms of its both direct as well as indirect contribution.

IP Strategy

A well defined intellectual property strategy can transform a business into a profitable venture in borders under WTO Regime i.e.: (i) participation of management; (ii) open style of management; (iii) delegation-work-taking powers to managers; (iv) composition of top management team; (v) training of managers; (vi) incentives for top management; (vii) succession planning and (viii) performance appraisal.

It is strange that in WTO regime, as obvious from Doha and Cancum Conferences, despite having a seat and democratic right of vote, actual decision-making occurs by consensus, heavily influenced by the largest and richest countries.

Global Democratic Deficits

The democratic deficit in global organisations is unavoidable, as people do not directly elect their representatives to the WTO, IMF, World Bank or UN Security Council, etc.

It is also argued that the imbalances of global political and economic powers also make unrepresentative decision-making inevitable at the intergovernmental level. Notably the influence of the United States over these institutions especially on WTO has little to do with formal voting power and much to do with global standing of United States.

It is perfect reality that powerful countries, crucial to the success of any international institution, tend to gravitate towards institutions that give them the most influence. And they take their power with them whether it is to the WTO's green room meeting or the meeting of IMF executive board.

However, there is still considerable room for making such global institutions particularly WTO more democratic, fruitful and transparent.

Global Goals

As such, if the global goal is peace, economic growth or environmental sustainability, international efforts to promote changes do not work if national actors feel excluded. Increasingly leading global powers may recognize that a wide speed sense of exclusion and powerlessness in developing countries can threaten economic growth and security in industrial countries as well as developing economies. IP may be helpful in global perspective while deciding global goals.

Sustainable Development

Sustainable development is about enhancing human well-being through time. What constitutes a good life is highly subjective and the relative importance accorded to different aspects of well-being varies from individuals, societies and generations. IP may help in promoting sustainable growth.

The capacity of any society to meet the requirements of individual well-being depends on the level and quality of range of assets and to how society deploys them.

Knowledge Assets

Human assets and knowledge assets are the basis of intellectual property. Human assets consist of the inmate skills, talents, competencies and abilities of the individual as well as the effects of education and health knowledge asset contains codified knowledge which is easily transferable across space and time.

Summing UP

The significance of Intellectual property has long been appreciated in most of the economics of the world. The approach, towards the protection of the property, however, varies from country to country.

The protection of intellectual property has been recognized as the basis for promoting inventions in the developed countries so as to ensure dynamism in their economics through new commercial and industrial enterprise which produce their own cascading effects on economic growth and employment therein.

No doubt, knowledge is the sole basis origin of intellectual property. It has the rest opportunities and scope of market value. Through well-managed intellectual property a sound, solid and fruitful combination and co-ordination can be established between the Saraswati and the Laxmi as stated by the Then Union Finance Minister of India in Union Budget, 2001-02. The Economy like India can get a massive benefit through well managed intellectual property in terms of foreign exchange and sustainable development in the present era of globalisation and WTO. It is pertinent to refer the issues of IPR stated in WTO provisions as explained by S. Narayan, Ex-Indian Ambassador to Geneva and an Expert of WTO in following ways :

- In the case of Intellectual Property Rights, the original limited mandate gct expanded during the mid-term review.

- Many developing countries were made to fall in line by the US through threat of action under Section 301—India was the last one to fall in line.
- Out of different types of intellectual property rights India's concern was basically with regard to patents, that too regard to product patents for pharmaceuticals.
- India's interest in different kinds of intellectual property were different—opposed to patents but comfortable with copyright.
- Ten years transition period for Product Patents.
- Current Situation in India—Many Pharmaceutical companies are trying to patent their products.
- Hardly any pharmaceutical product has been given exclusive marketing rights during the transition period.
- There is a general recognition that balance between private profits and public interests is a very delicate one in the area of intellectual property rights.
- Recent Doha Ministerial Declaration on TRIPS and Public Health.

However, on the basis of the resolutions adopted at Doha and Cancun Conferences and the behaviour of the developed nations the provisions of IPR require reassessment and proper amendment for maintaining balances between developed and developing countries.

References

Panchmukhi, V.R. (2001), "World Trade Organisation and India Challenges as Prospectives", In G.K. Chadha (ed.) WTO and Indian Economy; Deep and Deep Publications (P) Ltd., New Delhi.

Alagh, Y.K. (2001), "Globalisation Debates", 84th Annual Conference of Indian Economic Association.

Eric, W. Veltor (1967), "Manpower Planning for Higher Talent Personnel", Bureau of Industrial Relations, Graduate School of Business Administration, p. 15.

Cohen, D. (2002), "Fear of Globalization: The Human Capital Nexus", Annual World Bank Conference on Development Economics, Washington D.C., World Bank pp. 69-93.

Stiglitz, E. (1998), "Knowledge and Development, Economic Science, Economic Policy and Economic Advice", In B. Pleskvic IF. Stiglitz (eds.) Annual World Bank Conference, Washington D.C.

Radrik, D. (2001), Development Strategy for the 21st Century' *op. cit.* Washington D.C.
Kumar Rajesh (2001), TRIPS and Indian Agriculture, 84th Annual Conference Volume of I.E.A., Vellore, pp. 50-65.
Methapand, S. (1998), "India and WTO—The Management Accountant 33 (July pp. 491-96.
Narayan, S. (2003), "India and the WTO", Paper Presented in a National Conference on 15th November, 2003 at A.N. College, Patna.
Gelegan, P. (1996). "Trading and Development", Vol. 50 No. 11.
Galbraith, J.R. (1995), Designing Organisations, San Francisco.
WTO and TRIPS, *Virgirnia Journal of Intellectual Law*, Vol. 37, p. 453.
TRIPS Agreements and Developed Countries—UNCT AD.
Singh, Jaya (2003), "WTO in Indian Perspective".
World Development Report, 2003, U.N. Publication, Oxford.
World Development Report, 1996, U.N. Publication, Oxford.
Human Development Report, 2002, U.N. Publication, Oxford.
Tenth Five Year Plan 2002-07, Planning Commissions, New Delhi.
Economic Survey 2002-03, Ministry of Finance, Govt. of India.

Agricultural Growth and Indian Economy

Krishna Nand Yadav

Agriculture is the backbone of the Indian economy desspite the industrilisation. Indian agriculture accounts for about one-fourth of gross domestic products and is source of livelihood of more than two-third of the Indian population. It provides employment to around sixty to sixty-five percent of total workforce in the country.

Growth Performance in Agriculture

The growth of total production under principal crops based on index, prepared by the Directorate of Economics and Statistics (DES), Ministry of Agriculture, Government of India has decelerated during 90s. The growth in agriculture output was 2.26 per cent per annum during the nineties as against 3.17 per cent during the eighties. But if one take into account the aggregate crop output at 1993-94 prices, a different picture emerges; the growth rate works out to be slightly higher at 3.08 per cent during nineties as compared to 2.94 per cent during the eighties.

There has been appreciable increase in agricultural exports after economic reforms were initiated. Aggregate agricultural exports increased from $ 3.2 billion in 1991-92 to $ 6.86 billion in 1996-97, but thereafter declined to $ 5.5 billion in 1999-2000. Thus, during the nineties agriculture exports increased at 8.96 per cent per annum as compared to only 2.43 per cent during the eighties. Appreciable increase in exports has come about mainly due to the devaluation of the Indian rupee and opening of economy due to significant reduction in the import duties. The decline in the agricultural exports in the latter half of the nineties is probably due to sharp reduction in the international prices of agricultural commodities. The growth performance may be justified in the light of Table 1.

The appreciable increase in agriculture performance contains mainly two factors, i.e. (a) Investment and (b) Recent Policy Development. The economic reforms of 1991-did not contain an explicit agricultural component, it created favourable conditions to agriculture through the trade policy reforms of the rupees. The former has helped in reducing the protection to manufacturing, eliminating thereby anti-agricultural bias and improving the terms of trade to agriculture. These economic reforms seem to have helped the agricultural sector probably because of increasing business transactions between the agriculture sector and rest of the economy over the years.

Recent policy development is determined mainly by trade policy, exchange rate, monetary policy and relative weighted average support price.

Overall annual growth rate of agriculture declined to 3.6 per cent during the 1990s from 3.9 per cent during the preceding decades, and that of its allied sectors declined to 3.7 per cent from 4.2 per cent during the corresponding periods. Despite favourable terms of trade for agriculture and a normal south-west monsoon, the growth of food production remained sluggish during the 1990s and the process of diversification of agricultural production from coarse cereals to oilseed crops in the rainfed areas also slowed down. These trends may be

TABLE 7.1

Growth Performance of Indian Agriculture from 1978-79 to 1999-2000

Item	*Annual Growth Rate (%)*		
	1978-79 to 1989-90	*1990-91 to 1999-2000*	*1978-79 to 1999-2000*
1. Aggregate crop output at 1993-94 rates.	2.94	3.08	3.02
2. Principal crop production based index triennium ending 1981-82.	3.17	2.26	3.10
3. Index of Yield of principal crops based on triennium ending 1981-82.	2.54	1.19	2.14
4. Per hectare crop output at 1993-94 prices, based on net area sown	3.03	3.08	2.94
5. Total agricultural exports in million $	2.43	8.96	5.56
6. Income velocity of money	(-) 2.66	(-) 1.67	(-) 2.03
7. Nominal exchange rate (Rs. per dollar)	6.70	8.97	9.02
8. Real exchange rate (Rs. per dollar)	(-) 1.90	0.37	0.30
9. Gross terms of trade at 1993-94 prices	(-) 0.59	1.23	0.59
10. Import duties as per cent of total imports (i.e. tariff level)	6.37	8.96	(-) 1.76
11. Relative average weighted procurement support prices at 1981-82 price	0.17	0.58	0.95
12. Relative manufacturing prices (regd.) at 1993-94 prices	0.81	(-) 1.57	(-) 1.05
13. Per capita of aggregate crop output at 1993-94 prices, based on total population	0.81	1.15	0.96
14. Public gross fixed capital formation at 1993-94 prices	(-) 3.49	0.43	(-) 2.99
15. Private gross fixed capital formation at 1993-94 prices	1.75	2.99	3.77
16. Real agricultural wages	3.99	2.35	2.90
17. Wages weighted per hectare crop output at 1993-94 prices based on net area	7.02	5.46	5.84

Source : *Economic and Political Weekly*, October 25, 2003.

attributed to: (a) a decline in public investment in agriculture since the early 1980s (the annual growth rate being 1.9 per cent during the 1990s as compared to 4.0 per cent during the 1980s) which slowed the expansion of irrigation; (b) low public investment in R & D (0.5 per cent of agricultural GDP as against the norm of 1 per cent as recommended by the ICAR) thus affecting technological progress; (c) decline in the annual growth rate of fertilizer use from 7.8 per cent during the 1980s to 4.3 per cent during the 1990s; (d) deceleration in the annual growth rate of area under HYV from 4.9 per cent during the 1980s to 2.8 per cent during the 1990s; (e) fall in soil fertility due to intensive cultivation and wheat-rice rotation year after year in the north-western region; and (f) the over-exploitation of groundwater due to an unregulated expansion of tubewells. More than a decade of high growth in food production has led to a slackening of investments in agricultural research, irrigation and rural infrastructure that would provide productivity growth in the crop sector.

The study of annual growth rate of agriculture as well as GDP can be made with the help of Table 7.2.

TABLE 7.2
Annual Growth Rate

(Percentage)

Years	*Agriculture %*	*GDP %*
1999-00	0.6	6.1
2000-01	0.1	4.4
2001-02	6.1	5.8
2002-03	-4.0	4.0
2003-04	8.6	8.1

Source : *The Economic Times*, Kolkata, July 2004.

The country may have graduated to second stage of development and agricultures, influences in the economy has gradually weakened—its share in GDP. has declined steadily over the years–but it still plays a dominant role in shaping the GDP trend.

Last years records 8.1 per cent GDP growth, infact, was largely due to sharp 8.6 per cent farm growth. Our back experiences show that growth in farm output is followed by a growth in GDP.

Present Trend of Agricultural Production and its Determinants

As we have seen in the ahead that agriculture plays an important role in the growth of GDP of Indian economy. The present central government has also relied upon agricultural sector to achieve 7-8 per cent growth of GDP. Hence, it is essential to study the present pattern of agricultural production and its determinants with the help of tables below.

Table 7.3 clearly shows a fluctuating trend in the production of foodgrains between 1996-97 to 2003-04. The table indicates that production of foodgrains during 2001-02 and 2003-04 remained better in comparison to 1996-97 and 1997-98. The production of foodgrains during 2003-04 has been estimated at 210.05 million tonnes according to the fourth

TABLE 7.3
Agricultural Production

(*Million Tonnes*)

	1996-97	*1997-98*	*1998-99*	*1999-2000*	*2000-01*	*2001-02*	*2002-03*	*2003-04*
Foodgrains	199.4	192.3	203.6	209.8	196.8	212.0	174.2	210.8
Rice	81.3	82.5	86.1	89.7	85.0	93.1	72.7	86.3
Wheat	69.4	66.3	71.3	76.4	69.7	71.8	65.1	72.7
Cereals	185.2	179.3	188.7	196.4	185.7	198.8	163.1	195.9
Pulses	14.5	13.0	14.9	13.4	11.1	13.2	11.1	14.9
Khariff Foodgrains	103.9	101.6	102.9	105.5	102.1	111.6	87.8	110.5
Rabi foodgrains	95.5	90.7	100.7	104.3	94.7	100.5	86.4	100.3
Oilseeds	25.0	21.3	24.7	20.7	18.4	20.8	15.1	25.0
Sugarcane	277.6	279.5	288.7	299.3	296.0	300.1	281.6	244.8

Source : Same as Table 7.2.

advanced estimates released by the Agricultural Ministry but the third advanced estimate for the year released in July 2004 put the grain production for 2003-04 at 210.78 million tonnes.

The Table clearly explains that irrigated area for different crops occupies a very small portion in the country in comparison to gross land available for production of different crops. Hence, it is necessary to expend the portion of irrigated area under the country for maximum production of crops. It is necessary to mention here that the percentage irrigated area for rice production was 38.4 million hectare in 1970-71 which increased to 54.0 million hectare in 1999-2000. This clearly reflects that area of irrigated land could not increase in compared to the growing demand of foodgrains. That is why, the present Finance Minister of India has pledged to increase the spread of irrigation too.

Despite reforms and sharp rises in industrial and service sector investment, agricultural still provides livelihood to the large part of our population. That is why, the Finance Minister has signaled out agricultural to meet the objective of growth. The economy has lift-forged agricultural to service sector—the share of service sector in gross domestic product has increase sharply at the expense of agricultural—but the people have been left behind and the agricultural sector was also left to itself for development.

Finance institutions did not find agricultural sector locality enough to put their money in and capital formation, which was already very low at 1.6 per cent of GDP in 1995-96 as result, has declined further to 1.3 per cent of GDP 2002-03. Therefore, it is necessary to increase the share of GDP for capital formation in agricultural to meet the demand of increasing population and achieved the goal of 8 per cent GDP of the economy. The decline in the capital formation in agricultural from 1.9 per cent of GDP in the early 1990s to 1.3 per cent of GDP after 2001 is a matter of concern. The declining trend is mainly due to a fall in public investment in agricultural since the mid nineties while there has been some reversal of this trend in recent years, public investment in agricultural meet to be augmented, especially in rural infrastructure, irrigation and agricultural research and development.

During the course of budget speech in 2004-05, the Finance Minister accepted the need for maximum flow of credit to

TABLE 7.4
Irrigated Area under Different Crops

(Million Tonnes)

Crop	*1970-71*	*1980-81*	*1990-91*	*1995-96*	*1996-97*	*1997-98*	*1998-99*	*1999-00*
(1)	*(2)*	*(3)*	*(4)*	*(5)*	*(6)*	*(7)*	*(8)*	*(9)*
Rice	14.3	16.4	19.4	21.5	22.2	22.1	24.2	24.4
% in are under the crop	38.4	40.8	45.5	49.9	51.10	50.7	53.9	54.0
Jowar	0.6	0.8	0.8	0.8	0.8	0.8	0.7	0.8
% in are under the crop	3.6	4.7	5.6	6.8	7.0	7.3	7.1	7.7
Bajara	0.5	0.6	0.5	0.6	0.5	0.6	0.6	0.7
% in are under the crop	4.0	5.5	5.1	6.2	4.9	6.1	6.3	8.3
Maize	0.9	1.2	1.2	1.4	1.3	1.3	1.4	1.5
% in are under the crop	15.9	20.1	19.7	22.6	20.3	20.3	22.2	22.9
Wheat	9.9	15.6	19.5	21.6	22.4	22.9	23.8	24.1
% in are under the crop	54.3	70.0	81.1	85.8	86.2	85.8	86.5	87.2
Barley	1.3	0.9	0.5	0.5	0.5	0.5	0.5	0.5
% in are under the crop	52.0	50.6	54.5	60.3	62.5	55.6	62.5	60.7
Total cereals	28.1	35.8	42.3	46.5	47.9	48.5	51.5	52.4
% in are under the crop	27.6	34.1	41.0	46.6	47.0	47.7	50.3	51.0

(Contd.)

TABLE 7.4 (Contd.)

(1)	(2)	(3)	(4)	(5)	(6)	(7)	(8)	(9)
Total pulses	2.0	2.0	2.6	3.0	3.0	2.7	3.5	3.8
% in are under the crop	8.8	9.0	10.5	12.9	12.9	11.3	14.3	16.1
Total foodgrains	30.1	37.8	44.9	49.5	50.8	51.2	55.1	56.0
% in are under the crop	24.1	29.7	35.1	40.1	40.6	40.8	43.5	44.8
Oilseeds	1.1	2.3	5.8	7.3	7.4	6.8	6.8	6.8
% in are under the crop	7.4	14.5	22.9	26.0	26.2	24.4	23.9	25.0
Cotton	1.4	2.1	2.5	3.2	3.3	3.3	3.3	3.1
% in are under the crop	17.3	27.3	32.9	35.0	35.9	37.1	34.7	35.2
Sugarcane	1.9	2.4	3.4	3.9	3.9	3.8	4.0	4.1
% in are under the crop	72.4	81.3	86.9	87.4	88.6	90.5	90.9	92.0

Source : Same as Table 7.2.

TABLE 7.5
Capital Formation in Agriculture

(*Rs. Crores*)

Sector	*1995-96*	*1996-97*	*1997-98*	*1998-99*	*1999-2000*	*2000-01*	*2001-02*	*2002-03*
Public sector	4849	4668	3979	3870	4221	3927	4127	4538
Private sector	10841	11508	11963	11025	13083	12979	13201	14119
Total	15690	16176	15942	14895	17304	16906	17328	18657
Share of Pub. Sec. (%)	30.9	28.9	25.0	26.0	24.4	23.2	23.8	24.3
Share of Pvt. (%)	69.1	71.1	75.0	74.0	75.6	75.6	76.2	75.7
Inv. in agriculture as% of GDP	1.6	1.5	1.4	1.3	1.4	1.3	1.3	1.3

Source : Same as Table 7.2.

agricultural to achieve the desired goal of GDP. The Finance Minister stated "it is my intention to doubled the flow of agriculture credit in three years". Lack of funds, of course, is not the sole impediment of agriculture prosperity. In 2003-04, the flow of agriculture credit from landing institutions is estimated act 8,0000. The number of Kishan Credit Card (KCC) increased from 1.1 lakh at end of March 1999 to 413.79 lakh at the March 2004. To strengthen credit delivery to rural areas a pilot project of linking Self Help Group (SHGs) of the rural poor with the banking system was launched in 1992. A unique future of programme is absence of subsides. By March 2004, 10.8 lakh SHGs where linked with banks and 30,000 branches of 504 banks that participated in the programme amounted to rupees 3905 crore by March 31st 2004.

The agriculture occupies an important place in the determination of GDP of Indian economy as well as SDP of different state. Indian agriculture contribute a share of 25 per cent to the GDP of the country while Punjab, Bihar, U.P., Assam and Haryana contributed is share of 39.30, 38.50, 35.10, 32.80 and 31.10 respectively to its state domestic products during. 2001-02. In West Bengal, Orissa and Rajasthan the agriculture has contributed 26.20 per cent, 30.50 per cent and 29.50 per cent respectively. Hence, agriculture plays an important role in determining the growth of GDP.

TABLE 7.6

Flow of Institutional Credit to Agriculture

(Rs. Crore)

Institutions	*1996-97*	*1997-98*	*1998-99*	*1999-2000*	*2000-01*	*2001-02*	*2002-03*	*2003-04*
(1)	(2)	(3)	(4)	(5)	(6)	(7)	(8)	(9)
Co-op. Banks	11944	14085	15957	18363	20801	23604	24296	30080
Regional Rural Banks	1684	2040	2460	3172	4219	4854	5467	6080
Commercial Banks	12738	15831	18443	24733	27807	33587	41047	43840
Total	26111	31956	36860	46268	52827	62045	70810	80000
Per cent Share in total Co-op. Banks	45.2	44.1	43.3	39.7	39.4	38.0	34.3	37.6
Regional Rural Banks	6.4	6.4	6.7	6.9	8.0	7.8	7.7	7.6
Regional Banks	48.4	49.5	50.0	53.5	52.6	54.1	58.0	54.8
Total	100.0	100.0	100.0	100.0	100.0	100.0	100.0	100.0

Source : Same as Table 7.2.

TABLE 7.7

Share of Agriculture in State Domestic Product

(Per cent)

States	*1994-95*	*1995-96*	*1996-97*	*1997-98*	*1998-99*	*1999-2000*	*2000-01*	*2001-02*
Andhra Pradesh	31.0	31.10	31.00	26.20	29.20	27.30	28.80	27.60
Assam	38.70	38.30	37.10	38.00	36.50	35.20	33.60	32.80
Bihar	51.00	46.40	50.00	41.70	45.60	40.70	18.70	38.50
Chhattisgarh	32.10	29.60	29.10	22.40	23.40	22.40	39.80	23.80
Goa	13.50	12.50	11.30	10.90	9.00	8.90	9.80	8.00
Gujarat	26.60	22.10	25.90	23.30	23.00	15.70	13.60	17.30
Haryana	42.20	39.30	38.90	35.40	34.70	33.70	32.60	31.10
Himachal Pradesh	29.60	28.30	26.90	25.40	23.90	21.20	22.00	0.00
Jammu & Kashmir	3560	34.60	35.20	32.10	32.20	33.00	32.10	0.00
Jharkhand	24.00	22.40	24.10	18.90	18.30	21.70	0.00	0.00
Karnataka	33.50	32.20	31.00	26.80	28.20	30.00	29.90	26.20
Kerala	30.70	29.10	28.80	26.50	25.40	24.30	23.70	23.20
Madhya Pradesh	37.90	36.70	36.40	35.40	33.90	32.50	26.70	28.90
Maharashtra	18.70	17.50	19.30	15.10	16.10	16.10	15.60	15.10
Manipur	33.90	32.60	30.30	30.90	31.20	27.30	28.30	27.50
Meghalaya	25.00	26.10	26.90	25.50	24.10	25.50	24.60	23.60
Nagaland	25.30	21.90	23.10	24.60	27.10	30.50	0.00	0.00
Orissa	37.40	36.10	33.50	35.60	34.20	30.10	28.10	30.50
Punjab	45.70	43.90	43.80	40.60	39.80	40.50	40.30	39.30
Rajasthan	36.20	33.60	36.40	34.00	32.80	27.90	25.80	29.50
Tamil Nadu	23.80	20.10	19.00	19.10	19.90	17.80	17.30	16.40
Tripura	33.10	33.00	32.10	29.50	28.90	28.10	23.30	21.70
Uttar Pradesh	38.00	37.20	36.70	34.70	35.10	36.00	35.20	35.10
West Bengal	32.70	31.20	30.90	30.90	28.20	27.20	26.00	26.20

Source : Sam as Table 7.2.

What is significant is that the present government emphasis to raise farm output will help the government to achieve its bigger objective too, mainly a 7-8 per cent annual GDP growth. Despite a fall in its share in GDP, agriculture still remains a decisive driver of GDP growth. Infact, the country achieved its record 1.8 per cent of GDP growth last year largely due to a 8.6 per cent growth in farm output.

And this was not an isolated happening. Way back in 1988-89 when GDP grew an all time of 10.5 per cent (at 1993-94 prices) farm output too grew by an all time high of 15.4 per cent. In the post reform period too this second highest GDP growth of 7.8 per cent in 1996-97 too was accompanied by sharp 8.8 per cent rise in agricultural output. At the other end, a fall in farm output 2002-03 and 1997-98 witnessed a sharp deceleration in GDP growth too.

In a year when the government was complaining of excess food stock and exporting them at a subsidy, the total availability of food actually when down sharply in 2002-03. Not only was there less wheat and rice to eat, the amount of pulses *(dal)* available for every one daily is now the smallest in 53 years.

Barring the drought in 2001, the last time such abysmally low levels of availability where seen, was just before the World War II in the hungry thirties in colonial time and again briefly for two years during the food crises of the mid sixties. As the population increased by 18 million in 2003 while foodgrain production dropped by 32 million tonnes obviously India's agriculture has failed to keep pace with demand. Even the availability of cooking oils was significantly lower as it fell from almost 9 Kg. Per capita to 7.2 kg. in 2003.

The net availability of Cereals dropped to 160 million tonnes in 2003, down from 175 million tonnes in 2002. The net

TABLE 7.8

Per capita Net Availability of Foodgrains

Year	*Population*	*Cereals*	*Pulses*	*Total*
1999	996.4	429.2	36.5	465.7
2000	1014.8	422.7	31.8	454.4
2001	1033.2	386.2	30.0	416.2
2002	1050.6	457.3	35.0	492.2
2003	1060.2	409.9	28.2	438.2

Source : The Economic Times, Kolkata, 8 July 2004.

availability of pulses fell from 13.4 million tonnes to just 11 million tonnes in 2003. As a result the daily per capita availability of Cereals dropped a serious 10 per cent from 457 gm. to 409 gm. in 2003. The availability of pulses fell from 35 grams to 28 grams. Hence, the per capita net availability of foodgrain has fallen by over 11 per cent in 2000 at 438 grams per day this decline is the highest since 1991. Decline of similar magnitude was observed in 1998 but the per capita availability then was at a higher level of 447 grams per day. The per capita availability of cereals and pulses had reached a low of 416 grams per day in the year 2001—the lowest since 1980.

Decline in per capita availability of foodgrains is certainly not indicative of a progressive economy.

India's Agricultural Export Scenario

Exports of some agriculture commodity showed better performance while other showed declining trend during WTO regime. It was expected that under WTO, the entry of agriculture products from India in the world market would be without much restrictions owing to market productivity, reduction to AMS and export subsidies. Undoubtly, their significant improvement in the structure India's balance of payment after the adoption of new EXIM Policy in 1991. The annual average growth of India's total exports increase upto 10 per cent during the period 1992-93 to 1999-2000 but export of agricultural products reduced gradually. There are many reasons due to which the share of agricultural export reduced. The main reasons are devaluation of Indian currency, disguise subsidies provided to agriculture by developed countries and withdrawal agricultural subsidies in India. We can understand the scenario of agricultural exports under Table 7.9. As shown in Table 7.9 the volume agriculture exports in rupees term has been increasing, but in terms of dollar it has shown a declining trend in recent years. After having the share of 20.4 per cent in total export during 1996-97, it decline to 18.8 per cent 1997-98, 18.1 per cent in 1998-99 and 14.6 per cent in 1999-2000.

As a percentage of total merchandise exports, the share of agricultural export declined rom 13.5 per cent in 2001-02 to 12.8 per cent in 2002-03.

TABLE 7.9

India's Export of Agricultural Product

Year	*India Total Export*	*Total Agriculture Export*	*Percentage Share of Agriculture Exports to Total Export*
1996-97	33470	6828	20.4
1997-98	35006	6594	18.8
1998-99	33218	6014	18.1
1999-2000	37599	5457	14.6

Source : GOI, Economic Survey 2000-01, Table 8.30, p. 168.

The share of farm exports in India's total exports is now 15.2 per cent in 2003-04, down from 16.7 per cent in 2002-03. However, farm imports continued to rise from $2.3 billion in 2001-02 to 2.8 billion in 2002-03.

Impact of Infrastructure on Agriculture Productivity

It can be seen from Table 7.10 that Punjab, which has the highest index of infrastructure, also has the highest yield of foodgrains. Tamil Nadu and Haryana which have second and third highest index of infrastructure, have also higher yields of foodgrains. Rajasthan and Madhya Pradesh that have a very low index of infrastructure have also very low level of foodgrain production. Gujarat and Maharashtra that have a relatively better infrastructure development index have lower productivity is partly attributed to millet based cropping pattern with low production potential and partly to poor irrigation infrastructure development. It is also worth nothing that in almost all the states the productivity is increasing over the period. But in many of the states a reverse trends is observed in case of infrastructure development even though agriculture production is showing as increasing trend over time as observed in case of Bihar, West Bengal, etc.

TABLE 7.10
State-wise Index of Infrastructure Development and Foodgrain Productivity

(*Per cent*)

State	*Infrastructure Development Index*			*Foodgrain Productivity (Kg/ha)*		
	1980-81	*1990-91*	*1995-96*	*1980-81*	*1990-91*	*1995-96*
(1)	*(2)*	*(3)*	*(4)*	*(5)*	*(6)*	*(7)*
Andhra Pradesh	33.54	50.34	54.94	11.40	1590	1690
Assam	21.58	47.21	44.64	1070	1210	1310
Bihar	33.96	47.34	45.84	990	1300	1440
Gujarat	35.95	54.20	57.82	1000	1050	1090
Haryana	49.11	65.88	71.96	1520	2350	2540
Karnataka	33.74	46.93	49.97	890	910	1260
Kerala	44.51	60.30	71.04	1540	1870	1940
Madhya Pradesh	17.29	33.08	38.76	700	1000	1030
Maharashtra	33.17	56.33	61.37	690	850	870
Orissa	20.32	38.82	38.99	870	1000	1200
Punjab	62.59	74.40	78.43	2460	3399	3470
Rajasthan	26.72	38.47	40.20	530	860	800
Tamil Nadu	52.47	76.32	77.83	1340	1910	1920
Uttar Pradesh	32.78	52.97	57.11	1220	1740	1890
West Bengal	41.30	52.23	52.06	1360	1740	1960
India	34.97	55.50	58.64	1020	1380	1490

Source : The Bihar Journal of Agricultural Marketing, Vol. IX, No. 2, April-June 2001.

Vision of Indian Agriculture 2025

With rapid changing global, economic environment it is now necessary to shift the focus from self-sufficiency to export orientation. In order to accomplish the vision and achieve the targets set for Indian agriculture by the year 2025, a carefully designed strategy of increasing total factor productivity growth in agriculture and simultaneously raising the growth of factor supplies to agriculture should be followed.

- High rate of technological progress in agriculture;
- High rates of public and private investment in agriculture;
- Significant growth in total cropped area, which can be achieved by increasing the area under irrigation; and
- Increasing the effective applications of high yielding variety of seeds in dry-land farming.

The policy initiative required for this purpose should focus on the utilisation of the created irrigation capacity by putting in place a comprehensive irrigation management system. Further, there is an urgent need to involve the corporate sector formally in the cultivation of high value, capital intensive and modern technology based crops with potential for exports. Corporatisation of farming will not only facilitate technological upgradation, but would also ensure rapid growth of private investment in Indian agriculture. Corporatisation of the farm sector would also result in a significant quality upgradation and growth of value added products and, in the process, it would significantly enhance the export orientation of Indian agricultural sector.

Conclusion

If Indian agriculture has to emerge globally competitive, it does not need sops of free power or even cheaper credit. What it desperately requires is investment in rural infrastructure, agriculture R&D, and effective institutions that can promote efficiency by reducing transaction cost in market risks.

There are some important issues which needs to be addressed. First productivity must improve. India's productions of crops like rice, sugarcane, maize, cotton, banana, pulses and many others is much lower than that of Egypt, Peru, Kuwait and Israel. Large investments in irrigation are obviously needed. There is over use of urea, as it is subsidies, and phosphorous and potassium are under utilised. Even worse, our soils are very deficient in micro-nutrients like zinc. Application of zinc sulphate and other micro-nutrients is still rare. Our soils are not even mapped for these micro-nutrient deficiencies. Research in new high-yielding, disease-resistance varieties is flagging. Our extension machinery is inept and generally ignored by farmers. All these need to be set right to enhance productivity.

Second, a proper and healthy credit system is the necessary pre-requisite for sustainable agriculture. Whenever credit institutions do an outstanding job farmer's distress is minimal.

Third, proper marketing facilities are the key to agricultural propriety. Horticulture farmers in many states, fish farmers in West Bengal and the North-east and other producer are fleeced by the mafia controlling local market.

Fourth, value edition needs to be promoted. This is particularly vital for perishable commodities. Infrastructure building, R & D, technology, transfer, promotion of processing industry through social incentives, new mechanisms to ensure input supply, proper storage and transport facilities and easy credit for agro-industry are all necessary to transform Indian agriculture. Short-term sops and populism are not substitutes to sensible policies and well-considered actions.

Lastly, India being a founder member of the WTO is bound to under-take further economic reforms in agriculture. These would include removal of barriers to internal trade in agriculture commodities, abolition of zonal restrictions and compulsory procurement, opening future market and protecting patent right.

By considering the above discussed facts India can over come the challenges faced by Indian agriculture and succeed in getting the maximum production of foodgrains.

CHAPTER

8

Economic Growth and Agricultural Development in 20th Century : Some Reflections

ASHWINI KANT JHA AND BHAVNA JHA

India recorded a significant acceleration in the growth rates of GDP and per capita income after independence. Taking the entire period 1950-51 to 1999–2000, whereas the gross domestic product of India recorded a growth rate of nearly 4.16 per cent per annum at 1980-1981 prices, the per capita income grew at a rate of 1.77 per cent. India launched its First Five Year Plan in 1951, but this was only a collection of British schemes. It was in the mid-fifties that a systematic attempt was made for the planning of the country, with the strategy of Nehru-Mahalanobisian industrial development. A heavy investment in infrastructure and in heavy industry, machine building in power, irrigation, scientific research establishments, roads, transports and communications etc. were made under public sector with a view to establish socialistic pattern of society.

TABLE 8.1
Growth Rates of GDP 1950-1951 to 1998-1999 at 1980-1981 Price

Years	*GDP*	*Agriculture*	*Secondary*	*Tertiary*	*Per Capita Income*
1950-51 to 1998-99	4.16	2.61	5.61	5.15	1.77
1950-51 to 1990-91	3.77	2.49	5.49	4.76	1.41
1967-68 to 1990-91	4.20	2.80	5.20	5.20	1.64
1950-51 to 1964-65	4.00	2.65	7.73	4.61	1.69
1967-68 to 1979-80	3.45	2.10	4.43	4.49	1. 1 1
1980-81 to 1990-91	5.46	3.94	6.86	6.58	3.01
1990-91 to 1998-99	6.23	1.95	7.45	8.24	4.30

Source : Economic Survey, Various Issues.

During the period 1950-51 to 1964-65, gross product from industry rose at a rate of 7.7 per annum, which is one of the highest rate growth recorded. During the above period the GDP of India recorded a growth rate of 4 per cent per annum and per capita income grew at a rate of 1.68 per cent per annum. The growth rates of income from the primary, the secondary and the tertiary sectors were 2.65 per cent, 7.73 per cent and 4.01 per cent per annum respectively. Whereas, agricultural output recorded a growth rate of 3.2 per cent, industrial output rose at the rate of 7.5 per cent per annum. But the population growth rate, agricultural output, food availability emerged as major constraints. Thus, India has to impose large quantity of food grains under PL480. The crisis of 1965-67 was triggered by two successive droughts in 1965-66 and 1966-67.

The Indian economy witnessed a turn around and recorded a very high growth during this period. The income growth rate increased from 3.45 per cent in seventies to 5.46 per cent in eighties. Per capita income increased at 3.01 per cent per annum compared with a partly figure of 1.2 per cent during the previous 30 years. Agricultural GDP grew at 3.94 per cent per annum; income from the secondary and tertiary sector grew at 6.58 per cent per annum respectively while agricultural output grew at a rate of 3.47 per cent per annum. The industrial growth rate, rose to 8 per cent per annum, the highest in the Indian history not only that the export growth rate touched 10 per cent per annum in real terms.

The crisis of 1990 was mainly due to the unsustainable level of expenditure in the economy. The high level of expenditure can be controlled only by the internal or external savings. The government was incurring large capital expenditure unmatched with its revenue collection. During 1980-81 to 1990-91, while revenue receipts grew at a rate of 16.6 per cent per annum, revenue expenditure recorded at a growth rate of 17.1 per cent. The deficit on revenue account kept on increasing from 1.5 per cent of GDP during 1980-81 to 3.5 per cent of GDP by 1990-91. There were several reasons like fiscal irresponsibility, rising interest payment on internal and external debt, inefficient functioning of the public enterprises both at central and states levels and amounting expenditure on subsidies which affected the situation more adversely. By 1990-91, internal liabilities had increased to 53.3 per cent of GDP compound with 35.6 per cent of GDP in 1980-81, the gross interest payments accounted for as much as 2.37 per cent of total expenditure (4% of GDP) compared with 11.6 per cent (1.9% of GDP) in 1980-81. Large-scale expenditure on defences, huge amount borrowings from the RBI led to increase in money supply and inflationary pressure, deficit created balance of payment problems which have all aggravated the situation. In addition to internal borrowings, import of machinery and raw materials like oil, machines and tools necessitated foreign borrowings, which led to huge interest payment on foreign debt and made the situation worse.

Although, export rose in real terms by 10 per cent per annum during 1985-90 but these increase were insufficient to finance mounting expenditure on import of machinery and raw materials. In this period higher investment expenditure made the gap between domestic savings and investment wide that resulted into accumulation of large current account deficits, which were financed by the foreign borrowings (Economic Survey 1999-2000). The above situation led to the large enlargement in India's external debt from $ 23.5 bn in 1980-81 to $ 63.40 bn by 1989-90 further increased to $ 97.68 bn by 1999. The total external debt as percentage of GDP had increased from

TABLE 8.2
Macro-economic Indicators of the Indian Economy

Indicators	*1990 - 91*	*1991 - 92*	*1992 - 93*	*1993 - 94*	*1994 - 95*	*1995 - 96*	*1996 - 97*	*1997 - 98*	*1998 - 99*	*1999-2000*
(1)	*(2)*	*(3)*	*(4)*	*(5)*	*(6)*	*(7)*	*(8)*	*(9)*	*(10)*	(11)
GDP annual % growth	5.4	0.8	5.1	5.0	7.0	7.3	7.5	5.0	6.8	5.9
Agriculture	4.1	-2.5	5.3	3.0	5.0	-0.9	9.6	-1.9	7.2	0.8
Secondary	–	–	–	–	9.2	11.8	6.0	5.9	4.0	6.9
Manufacturing	5.0	-1.8	2.3	3.6	10.7	14.9	7.9	4.0	3.6	7.0
Services	4.3	4.5	4.4	5.4	7.0	10.3	7.1	9.0	8.3	8.2
Inflation % per annum	10.3	13.7	10.8	10.8	10.2	4.4	6.9	5.3	4.8	2.9
Broad money annual % incr.	15.1	19.3	15.7	18.4	22.3	13.2	16.2	18.0	18.4	16.6
Gross Dom. Inv. % of GDP	27.1	23.6	22.0	21.6	26.1	27.2	24.6	26.2	23.4	—
Gross Dom Sav. (% of GDP)	23.7	23.1	20.0	21.4	25.0	25.5	23.3	24.7	22.3	—
Real GFCF (% of GDP)	21.3	20.3	20.6	20.8	21.6	23.8	23.6	23.6	25.1	—
Public	8.6	8.7	7.7	7.9	8.8	7.8	7.0	6.5	6.7	—
Private	12.7	11.6	12.1	12.6	14.9	18.8	15.1	17.5	16.7	—

(Contd.)

TABLE 8.2 (Contd.)

(1)	(2)	(3)	(4)	(5)	(6)	(7)	(8)	(9)	(10)	(11)
Export annual growth %	9.0	1.1	3.3	20.2	18.4	20.3	5.6	4.5	-3.9	12.9
Import annual growth %	14.4	-24.5	15.4	10.0	34.3	21.6	12.1	4.6	-7.1	9.0
Trade deficit (US $ billion)	-9.44	-2.8	-4.37	-4.06	-9.05	-1 1.35	- 14:8	-15.5	-13.25	—
Curr. account deficit (%)	3.2	0.4	1.8	0.1	1.0	1.7	1.2	1.4	1.0	1.5
Foreign exch. reserve ($ Bn)	2.3	5.7	6.7	15.3	20.81	17.04	22.37	25.98	29.52	31.94
Fiscal deficit % GDP	8.3	5.7	7.4	6.1	5.7	5.1	4.9	5.9	6.4	5.4
Revenue deficit % of GDP	3.5	2.6	2.6	3.8	3.1	2.5	2.4	3.1	3.7	2.8
Fiscal deficit (% of GDP)	10.0	–	–	–	6.9	6.4	6.2	7.1	8.5	7.6
Central and State										

Source : Government of India, CSO (1999), National Accounts Statistics, Govt. of India, Economy Survey, Various Issues, Govt. of India.

13.7 per cent in 1980-1981 to 27.3 per cent by 1990-91, this really aggravated the debt burden on the economy by 1990-1991, actually total 28 per cent of export were required to service the payment of interest and repayment of capital. Gradually high interest rates attracted the NRI and foreign private bank to finance the Indian economy, which became more onerous (Bhagwati and Srinivasan, 1998).

The gulf war in the second half of 1990 which led to a sharp rise in oil prices and an increase in payments made for oil imports, the drying down of remittances from workers in the gulf and disruption of trade and drastic reduction in export to middle east were some of the causes which led Indian economy to the edge of a precipice. Above situation aggravated by the political situation because of a weak government at centre led to downgrading of India's credit rating. In spite of borrowings from the IMF, the foreign exchange reserve declined from Rs. 5480 crores in August 1990 to only Rs. 1666 crores on January 16, 1991. In fear of defaulting first time to pay foreign liabilities in time, the government of India had to send Gold physically to finance its necessary foreign exchange transactions. It was the background 'under which New Economic Policy was introduced. The multilateral agencies like the International Monetary Fund and World Bank had, for a long time, been advocating a radical change in India's economic policy and a programme of structural adjustment.

India initiated economic reforms in June 1991 with two components. The devaluation of rupee, drastic fiscal compression and credit squeeze and continuation of severe import controls were the short term measures adopted by the congress government. Under the medium term Structural Adjustment Programme (SAP) a package of trade reforms, exchange rate reforms, reforms in industrial policy, capital market reforms, reforms in financial policy, tax reforms, public sector reforms including a move towards disinvestments and privatisation of public sector enterprises and gradual dismantling of the process of the planning in favour of the market were introduced. The second phase of reforms currently being envisaged are designed to carry forward the process of economic liberalisation and globalisation and is aimed to put market and market institutions as the prime movers in the development process replacing the state and public agencies in as many spheres as possible.

At the time of undertaking reforms in 1991, the Indian economy was going through one of the severest economic crisis in its history. The stabilisation polices initiated in 1991 were highly contradictory and controversial and were designed to reduce inflation from the current level of 17 per cent per annum, improve precarious balance of payment situation, reduce fiscal deficit and help to pick-up sagging industrial growth. The rate of inflation came down from 13.6 per cent in 1991-92 to 10.1 percent next year. After staying at this high level till 1993-94, inflation came down to about 4.4 per cent per annum during 1995-1996 but stayed within a range of 4.8 to 6.9 per cent since then. The fiscal deficit of the centre decreased from 8.7 per cent of GDP in 1990-91 to 5.7 per cent of GDP in 1991-92. Since 1993-94, the fiscal deficit has honoured around 6 per cent of GDP, really a much too large. The axe of fiscal compression has largely fallen on investment in physical infrastructure and social sectors like power, irrigation and other infrastructures and on health and education and human capital formation. High revenue expenditure was high due to large payment to interest debt. The internal debt accounts for 47 per cent of GDP in 1998-99 in comparison to 52.9 per cent in 1990-91. The interest. payments accounted for about 47 per cent of non-plan revenue and 48 per cent of plan expenditure during 1998-99. The policy makers have been unable to resist the pressure of the vested interests be it government administration, Parliamentarians, rich farmers or other elite groups. Due to vote bank or populist reasons, successive governments could not curtail major subsidies or unnecessary expenditure. The acceptance of Fifth Pay Commission Report is one of the blunderous steps, though inevitable, taken by the government, which has affected the public exchequer adversely. The reduction of fiscal deficit through reducing investment physical and in human capital including higher education is bound to adversely affect the long-term economic growth (Bhagwati and Srinivas).

The new policy has succeeded in restoring the confidence of foreign investors. The root cause of crisis of 1990-91 was India's inability to finance the large current account deficit in the country which was managed and a large exchange reserves of above $ 30 bn was built which is now nearly $ 120 bn. Export did show large buoyancy immediately after devaluation and increased by 20 per cent in 1995-96 but the growth has stagnated to only about 5 per cent per annum. The slow down in industrial export is due to non-competitiveness of Indian manufacturers and lack of modernisation.

During the post reform period an important development is that both the gross domestic product and per capita income recorded a significant acceleration during 1990-91 to 1998-99 as compared with the earlier period 1950-51 to 1990-91 (Table 8.1). During 1990-91 to 1998-99, while the GDP recorded a growth rate of 6.23 per cent per annum, per capita income rose at 4.30 per cent per annum. These are significantly higher than the growth rate of GDP and per capita income of 3.77 per cent per annum respectively recorded during the pre-reform period 1950-51 to 1990-91. But the growth rates during the nineties are not significantly higher than the one achieved

TABLE 8.3
Export of Major Agricultural Commodities from India

(Value in million $)

Year	*Agriculture*	*Coffee*	*Tea*	*Oil Cakes*	*Cotton*	*Rice*	*Fish*
1960-61	596	15	260	29	25	0	10
1970-71	644	33	196	73	19	7	40
1980-81	2601	271	538	158	209	283	274
1990-91	3521	141	596	339	471	257	535
1991-92	3338	135	491	374	124	306	585
1992-93	3265	130	337	534	63	337	602
1993-94	4151	174	410	741	209	410	814
1994-95	4367	335	384	573	45	384	1126
1995-96	6320	449	1366	702	61	1366	1011
1996-97	6828	402	894	985	444	894	1129
1997-98	6840	456	505	924	221	907	1207
1998-99	6219	405	547	454	53	1474	1038
Growth Rate (per annum)	11.12	20.28	-0.848	8.79	-6.95	25.03	11.07

Source : Economic Survey of India, Various Issues.

during the eighties, when gross domestic product and per capita income rose at a rate of 5.6 per cent and 3.01 per cent per annum respectively. But there are distinct differences with regard to the sectoral patterns of growth between the eighties and nineties. During both the periods, highest growth was recorded by the secondary and tertiary sectors. Actually during the nineties, the tertiary sector, with a growth rate of 8.6 per cent per annum, has emerged as the leading sector of the economy followed closely by a growth rate of the 7.5 per cent by the secondary sector.

During the eighties also, the secondary and tertiary sector grew at a rate of 6.58 per cent and 6.86 per cent per annum respectively. But what is different is that there has taken place a notable deceleration in the growth rate of gross products from agriculture during the nineties, which decelerated for 3.9 per cent per annum during 1980-81 to 1990-91 to only 1.95 per cent per annum during 1990-91 to 1989-90. Since agriculture accounts for nearly 26 per cent of GDP and 60 per cent of the total labour force is engaged in it, the slow down in its growth has serious implications, which need further analysis. The liberalisation of the Indian economy gave increasing hopes to the agriculture sector in the early nineties. Policy-makers arranged that the opening-up of the economy, devaluation of money and increase in output would give benefit to export oriented agricultural products. The signing of GATT accord during December 1994 would be instrumental in promoting multiliberalism and in increasing international trade in agriculture. The reduction or complete withdrawal of domestic and export subsidies by the developed countries would result in raising prices and bringing immense increase in agricultural export of developing countries. Being labour oriented agricultural export would help in increasing employment and help in reducing poverty. It was further assumed that increased prices combined with efficiency of production would lead to increase in private investment leading to increase in aggregate agricultural output. A decade after the beginning of economic liberalisation, instead of expiring an unprecedented boom in growth, the agricultural sector in India is facing some serious crisis. The growth rate of agriculture both in terms of gross product and in terms of output has visibly decelerated during the nineties. This has resulted in immense hardship to farmers motivating some of them for committing suicide. The Food Corporation of India does not procure crops in time during the past years has also caused serious concern. The diversification of cereal crops towards oil seeds crops in some of the poor rain fed states of India has slowed down considerably during the recent past. Despite a fair growth in GDP, the process of shifting away of labour force from agriculture to non-agriculture has not gathered any momentum after 1987-1988. Non-agriculture employment in rural areas has virtually collapsed and dependence on agricultural activities has increased. With the introduction of new economic policy the land tenure, land reforms, land-ceiling methods seems to be backtracking. Agricultural exports also rose sharply initially after devaluation of Indian currency but stagnated after 1995-1996. This was due to the large subsidies and the developed countries to their agriculture sector gave high protection. Both the trade deficit and the current account deficit have remained quite high, with trade deficit running at about $ 13 bn an year and the current account deficit at about $ 4 bn to $ 6 bn a year. The current account deficit is being financed by aid, borrowings and through inflows as FDI and FII current account deficit has come down from 3.2 per cent of GDP in 1990-1991 to between 1.4 to 1.7 per cent of GDP during the second half of the 90's. Increased borrowings have resulted in accumulation of large debt, which had accumulated to $ 87.68 bn by 1999. External debt constituted about 24 per cent of GDP during the latter half of 1990's and debt service at 2.5 to 2.7 per cent of GDP. The above figures and facts give a bird's eye view of performance of Indian economy during the 1990's. The growth rate of gross product from agriculture including allied sectors declined sharply from 3.2 per cent per annum during 1980-1981 to 1990-1991 and only 1.93 per cent during 1990-1991 to 1998-1999. Again, taking the output of crop sector alone, as compared with a growth rate of 3.5 per cent per annum during the eighties, the growth rate of agricultural output decelerated to only 2.37 per cent per annum during the nineties. This is the lowest growth rate achieved during any period.

A more serious development during the 90's was that the yield growth for all crops taken together decelerated from 2.65

per cent per annum during the eighties to 1.38 per cent per annum during the nineties. Growth rate of rice decelerated from 3.21 to 1.27 and in wheat from 3.15 to 2.32 per cent per annum. After green revolution regional pattern of growth was visible but during 1970-1973 to 1980-1983 in almost all the states of India growth rate in agricultural produce increased. During the nineties almost all the states except J & K, Bihar, Gujrat and Kerala have experienced deceleration in their growth rate.

The deceleration in agricultural growth is one facet of the emerging crisis in agriculture. The lack of work force diversification in India and increasing burden of work force in low productivity agriculture is yet another dimension of the crisis. One of the very disturbing features of the growth pattern in the post liberalisation period is very low employment generating potential growth in the secondary and the tertiary sectors. The emergence of rural non-farm sectors as important provider of employment in rural areas during 1987-1988 but it could not be sustained. The woman workforce in primary sector (88.5%) has increased which is not a good sign.

Deceleration in agricultural growth has strong case of public sector investment, which has been neglected during last two decades. The availability of adequate institutional credit is another means that would foster investment by the small and marginal farmers. Simple procedures, cutting down the red tape and village panchayat's involvement would help the investment in farms. There needs removal of barriers to internal trade in agricultural commodities, abolition of zonal restrictions, compulsory procurement, opening of future markets, patenting rights and abolition of subsidy by the developed countries for international marketing. Competitiveness and increased productivity needs in investment in agricultural research, biotechnology, rural infrastructure and creation of rural institutions, which can provide benefits to the cultivators, small and marginal farmers. Land ceiling, tenancy Act and consolidation of land holdings and other reforms are the need of time because 70 per cent of the farmers are of small and marginal category. Though Kulaks support consolidation of land holding. There is a need to constitute and strengthen the institutions like cooperatives,

Regional Rural Banks and some NGOs, which can face the challenges of export possibilities and involve small and marginal farmers in the process.

Efforts should be made to develop new technologies for the farming sector enabling them to diversify their production of export oriented high value commercial goods to face the challenges. They should be supplemented by trading and warehouses, market, intelligence services and network of information of market demand and prices at national and at international level. There is also need to create infrastructure in processing, grading and marketing of produce. Deceleration in agriculture needs technological innovation so that productivity and growth can be accelerated to feed millions of people through scarce resources like land. Lack of diversification and pressure on agriculture of vast workforce has led to the productivity population nexus. But the policy of liberalisation has bias inclination of rich farmers towards agriculture and farming sector, which may endanger the socio-economic structure of rural economy.

References

Ahluwalia, Isher J. (1989), Industrial Growth Rate in India, Stagnation since the Mid-Sixties, Oxford, Delhi.

Ahluwalia, M.S. (1978), Rural Poverty and Agricultural Performance in India, *Journal of Development Studies*, Vol. 14, No. 3, (April), pp. 298-323.

Bhagwati, Jagdish (1998), The Design of Indian Development, (eds.) India's Economic Reforms and Development Essays for Man Mohan Singh, edited by Isher, J., Ahluwalia and IMD, Little Oxford University Press, New Delhi.

Bhagwati, J. and S. Chakravarti (1969), Contribution to Indian Economic Analysis, *American Economic Review*, Supplement, 5.

Chakravarty, Sukhamoy (1978), Development Planning—The Indian Experiences, Clarendon Press, Oxford.

Chandra, B. (1970), Colonialism and Modernisation, Presidential Address to the Section-III, Indian History Congress, 32nd Session, 1970.

CSO (1990), Govt. of India, New Delhi.

Economic Survey (various issues), Govt. of India Publication, New Delhi.

Gadgil, D.R. (1972), The Industrial Evolution of India in Recent Times, Oxford University Press, Bombay, 10. Little, IMD & Vijoy, Joshi (1996), India's Economic Reforms 1991-2001, Oxford University Press, Bombay.

National Accounts Statistics, Govt. of India, New Delhi.

Raj, K.N. (1996), Some Reflections on Economic Growth in India over the Period 1952-1953 to 1982-1983, *Economic and Political Weekly*, 19, 13th Oct., 1984.

Rao, V.K.R.V. (1983), India's National Income, 1950-1980, An Analysis of Economic Growth and Change, Delhi.

Rao, V.K.R.V. (1962), Changes in Indian National Income : A Static Economy Under Progress reprinted in paper on Natinoal Income and Allied Topics, Vol. II, V.K.R.V. Rao, A.K. Ghosh, M.V. Divatia and Uma Dutta (Eds.), Bombay, pp. 6-11.

Thorner, D. (1955), Long Term Trends in Output of India, in Ed. Simon Kuznets, W.E. Moore and J.J. Spengler, Economic Growth of Brazil, India and Japan North Corolina, 1955, pp. 103-128.

Indian Agriculture : Growth, Yield and Output

K.B. PADMADEO AND SRI NIWAS PANDEY

INTRODUCTION

The agriculture sector is the backbone not only of our economy but also our society. Agriculture had made significant progress after independence, the annual food grains production increased about 4-fold by adopting import substitution policy rather the export promotion. However, this pattern of growth mounted-up certain crisis and this is aggravated after fully liberalisation of Indian economy including Agriculture Sector, as per recommendation of Uruguay Round of GATT-WTO (1994). India maintains Quantitative Restriction (QR) on the import of agriculture though there is a strong recommendation to dismantle the QRs. Ultimately India has eliminated QRs from 714 items on 200 and remaining 715 items were made free from 1st April, 2001. This may arise specific agricultural crisis. Firstly, the QRs elimination will pressurise the balance of trade as because higher level of import the market of our foodgrain production of the affected sector get squeezed. Thirdly, the adverse effect of Globalisation and Liberalisation may cause a possible decline in production, income; employment is well as the overall agricultural growth.

The liberalisation of the Indian economy during the early nineties gave increasing hopes to the agricultural sector. The policy-makers who initiated the process argued that the opening-up of the economy combined with large real devaluation of the currency and increase in output prices would go a long way in remedying the age-old discrimination against tradable agriculture. It would bestow immense benefits to this sector through increased exports. Further, the signing of GATT accord during December 1994 would be instrumental in promoting multilateralism and in increasing international trade in agriculture and other commodities and services. The reduction or complete withdrawal of domestic and export subsidies by the developed countries would result in raising prices and bringing immense increase in agricultural exports of developing countries. Being labour intensive, agricultural exports would help in increasing employment and help in reducing poverty, it was further assumed that increased prices combined with efficiency of production would lead to increase in private investment leading to increase in aggregate agricultural output. By the beginning of the 'nineties', the Economic Survey was in an upbeat mood and predicting a substantial gain to India running into billions of dollars from increased agricultural exports. A decade after the beginning of economic liberalisation, instead of experiencing an unprecedented boom in growth, the agricultural sector in India is facing some serious crisis. Firstly, the growth rate of agriculture both in terms of gross product and in terms of output has visibly decelerated during the nineties. For some crops and in some regions, the deceleration has been quite steep. This has resulted in immense hardships to farmers driving some them to commit suicide. The refusal of FCI to procure paddy on time during the kharif harvesting season of 2000 has further added to the woes of the Indian farmers. Secondly, the diversification of the cropping pattern from coarse cereals towards oilseed crops in some of the poor rained states of India, has slowed down considerably during the recent years. Thirdly, the initial spurt in agriculture exports after liberalisation and devaluation has now almost come to a halt. Fourthly, despite a fairly high growth in GDP, the process of shifting away of labour force from agriculture to non-agriculture has not gathered any momentum after 1987-88. Non-agricultural employment has collapsed in rural areas and dependence on agriculture has actually increased. Finally, with the new policy paradigm, there seems to be backtracking on institutional issues like land reforms, ceilings on holdings and on security of land tenure. The absence of a cohesive and strong peasant movement has enabled many a state government to bring about retrogressive legislation. The policy-makers have completely failed to grasp the complexities of the agricultural sector and have designed a mix of policies, which have landed this sector into serious difficulties.

Deceleration in Growth Rates of Agriculture

As discussed above the growth rate of gross product from agriculture including allied sectors declined sharply from 3.2 per cent per annum during 1980-81 to 1990-91 to only 1.93 per cent during 1990-91 to 1998-99. Again, taking the output of crop sector alone, as compared with a growth rate of 3.5 per cent per annum during the eighties, the growth rate of agricultural output decelerated to only 2.37 per cent per annum during the nineties. This was the lowest growth achieved during any period.

Secondly, a more serious development during the 90's was that the yield growth for all crops taken together decelerated from 2.65 per cent; per annum during the eighties to 1.38 per cent per annum during the nineties. There was a sharp decline in the yield growth rates of wheat, rice and cotton. Growth rate of yield in rice decelerated from 3.21 to 1.27 and in wheat from 3.15 to 2.32 per cent per annum In the case of cotton yield growth rate has gone down from 4.15 per cent per annum during the eighties to only 0.59 per cent during the nineties (Table 9.1, See also Figures 9.1 and 9.2).

Third, the regional pattern of growth shows that the green revolution which was mainly confined to the northwestern and the southern region, during 1970-73 to 1980-83. Spread to almost all the states of India during the period 1980-83 to 1990-93.

TABLE 9.1

All India Compound Growth Rates of Area under Cultivation and Yield of Major Crops

Crop	1949-50 to 1964-65			1967-68 to 1980-81			1980-81 to 1990-91			1990-91 to 1998-99		
	Area	Prod.	Yield	Area	Prod.	Yield	Area	Prod.	Yield	Area	Prod.	Yield
(1)	(2)	(3)	(4)	(5)	(6)	(7)	(8)	(9)	(10)	(11)	(12)	(13)
Rice	1.21	3.5	2.25	0.77	2.22	1.46	0.53	3.76	3.21	0.53	1.81	1.27
Wheat	2.69	3.96	1.27	2.94	5.65	2.62	0.51	3.68	3.15	1.70	3.30	1.58
Coarse Ce	0.90	2.25	1.23	–	–	–	–	–	–	-2.12	0.18	2.09
T. Cereals	1.25	3.21	1.77	0.37	2.61	1.7	-0.21	3.02	3.25	0.05	2.00	1.51
T. Pulses	1.72	1.41	-0.18	0.44	-0.4	-0.67	0.23	1.87	1.63	-0.14	0.81	0.55
Foodgrains	1.35	2.82	1.36	0.38	2.15	1.33	-	3.04	2.82	0.05	1.86	1.39
Sugarcane	3.28	4.26	0.95	1.78	2.6	0.8	1.87	3.27	1.37	1.37	2.87	1.23
Oilseeds	2.67	3.2	0.3	0.26	0.98	0.68	2.85	5.99	3.06	1.51	2.83	1.60
Cotton	2.47	4.55	2.04	0.07	2.61	2.54	-0.96	3.15	4.15	3.25	3.06	0.18
Non-Foodgrains	2.44	3.74	0.89	0.94	2.26	1.19	1.46	4.16	2.42	1.51	3.11	1.34
All Crops	1.58	3.15	1.21	0.51	2.19	1.28	0.26	3.46	2.65	0.37	2.38	1.37

Source : GOI, 1999, Agricultural Statistics at a Glance, Ministry of Agriculture.

Fig. 9.1
Growth Rate is Crops Production During 80s and 90s

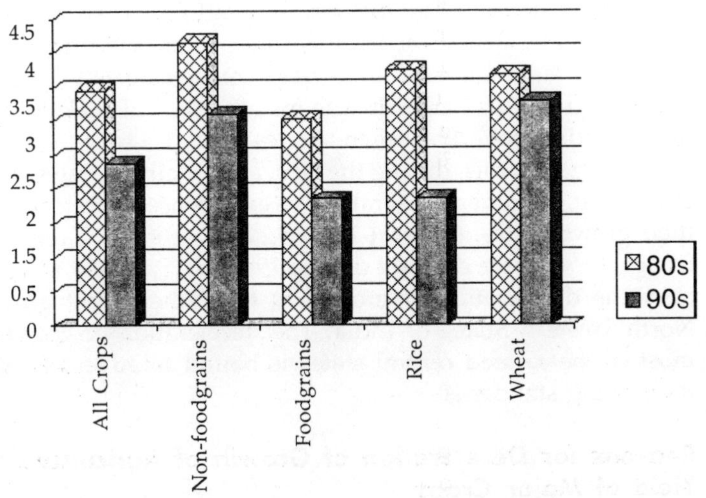

Fig. 9.2
Growth Rate of Production During 1980s and 90s

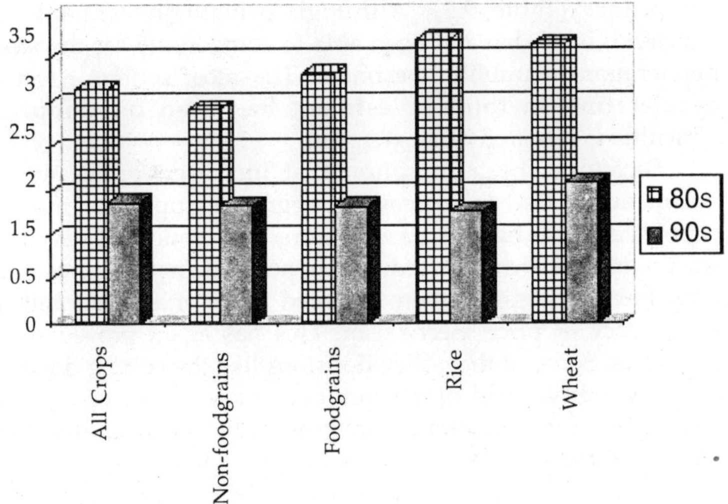

Specially creditable was the performance of eastern states in general and West Bengal, in particular, where the growth rate increased to an unprecedented level of 5.4 per cent per annum. The rainfed states of Madhya Pradesh and Rajasthan and many southern states also recorded high rates of growth primarily as a result of large shifts of areas from coarse cereals to oilseeds. Higher agricultural growth was instrumental in making a big dent on rural poverty in many states.

As against this, during the 90's, almost all the states except J&K, Bihar, Gujarat and Kerala have experienced deceleration in their growth rates. (Gujarat is a special case since it recovered from a very severe drought during 1980-83). Specially steep has been the deceleration of growth in the hitherto fast growing North Western States of India. The deceleration of growth in most of the rainfed central states is bound to adversely affect their living standards.

Reasons for Deceleration of Growth of Agriculture and Yield of Major Crops

There are many reasons for the recent deceleration in the growth of agricultural output and yield of major crops in India. The most important among these was the sharp deceleration in total investment and more so in public sector investment in agriculture (Table 9.2). Although private investment has increased, but it has not been able to compensate for the steep deceleration in public investment. The most serious effect of deceleration in total investment has been on crippling agricultural research and extension.

Secondly, the assumption that increased prices would automatically lead to increase in aggregate supply because of supply response has not proved correct. Although all empirical studies had already rejected this hypothesis, nevertheless after economic liberalisation there emerged a new misplaced faith in the efficacy of price mechanism. This has again proved to be erroneous. Some of the policy decisions like the cutting down of duty on edible oils of 15 per cent have also been partly responsible for deceleration in growth in the poor dry land regions of India.

TABLE 9.2

Public and Private Sector Investment in Agriculture (At 1980-81 Prices)

Year	*Public sector*	*Private sector*	*Total GCF in agriculture*	*Total GFCF in agriculture*	*% Share of agriculture sector*	*% Share in Public sector GCF*	*% Share of agr. GCF in total GCF*
(1)	*(2)*	*(3)*	*(4)*	*(5)*	*(6)*	*(7)*	*(8)*
1980-81	1892	2972	4864	4765	38.9	16.1	18.9
1981-82	1878	2863	4741	4587	39.6	12.4	13.9
1982-83	1857	3008	4865	4676	38.2	11.2	14.6
1983-84	1843	2563	4406	4259	41.8	11.9	14.1
1984-85	1822	3066	4888	4597	37.3	10.4	14.8
1985-86	1631	3010	4641	4374	35.1	9.0	12.1
1986-87	1550	2810	4360	4147	35.6	7.9	11.3
1987-88	1580	3202	4782	4577	33.0	8.8	11.8
1988-89	1485	3252	4737	4651	31.3	7.7	10.5
1989-90	1298	3484	4782	4614	27.1	6.3	10.8
1990-91	1315	3741	5056	4925	26.0	6.4	10.2
1991-92	1135	4017	5152	5147	22.0	5.7	11.2

(Contd.)

TABLE 9.2 (Contd.)

(1)	(2)	(3)	(4)	(5)	(6)	(7)	(8)
1992-93	1179	4694	5873	5770	20.1	5.7	11.3
1993-94	1269	4295	5564	5542	22.8	5.9	10.8
1994-95	1426	5397	6823	6686	20.9	5.7	9.6
1995-96	1394	6193	7587	7406	18.4	6.1	9.9
Growth Rate (% per annum)							
1970-71 to 1979-80	9.07	4.92	6.13				
1980-81 to 1990-91	-3.85	1.77	-0.20				
1990-91 to 1996-97	-3.09	4.86	2.46				

Suggestions : Some Reflective Suggestions are given below

1. Keeping in view the deceleration of growth rate in agriculture during the 90's, there exists a strong case for increasing investment in rural infrastructure. It is essential to accord very high priority to public sector investment in agriculture, which has been neglected during the last two decades. Since there exists a strong complimentarily between public and private sector investment in agriculture, increasing public sector investment is also likely to foster private sector investment. The availability of adequate institutional credit is another means that would foster investment specially by the small and marginal farmers. Streamlining the procedures, cutting down the red tape and involvement of Village Panchayats would help local participation.
2. India being a founder member of the WTO is bound to undertake further economic reforms in agriculture. These would include removal of barriers to internal trade in agricultural commodities, abolition of zonal restrictions, and compulsory procurement, opening future markets, and protecting patent rights etc. But India should also do hard bargaining on the issue of market access and removal of subsidies by the developed countries. But the real gains from trade can only accrue if the country improves its competitiveness by increased productivity. This requires large investment in rural infrastructure, in agricultural research and in biotechnology, and creation of institutional arrangements for reaching the benefits of research to all the cultivators including the small farmers.
3. There is a need to proceed further with consolidation of holdings and other land reforms. One of the lessons that can be learnt from East Asian and Chinese, experience is that through land reforms become instrumental in fostering more rapid and equitable growth in agriculture. Keeping in mind the interests of existing

occupancy tenants, steps should be taken to gradually free the lease market. On the other hand, despite the pressure by industrial interests, kulak lobby and some liberalisers for their abolition, under no circumstances should be legislation on ceilings on land holdings be diluted This is because a country where small and marginal farmers constitute 70 per cent of the land holders, it would be disastrous to endanger their only source of livelihood.

4. Since the reforms in agricultural sector are likely to open up export possibilities, there is a need to design a pro-active policy to foster exports and to involve the small and marginal farmers in increasing productivity and in deriving benefits from increased agricultural exports. There is a need to create innovative institutions including integrated co-operatives like the mother dairy, and other service co-operatives. Special efforts should also be made to develop new technologies for the farming sector and reach these to the small farmers for enabling them to diversify their production towards high value commercial and export commodities. The efforts on the production front should be supplemented by creation of institutions like trading houses, market intelligence services and creation of net work of information on national and international prices, reforms in agricultural sector are likely to open up export possibilities. There is also a need to create necessary infrastructure in processing, marketing and grading of produce. Investment in information infrastructure through market committees would percolate the information to the local levels.

CONCLUDING OBSERVATIONS

The crises in Indian agriculture are manifest in various ways. First the growth in agriculture has decelerated. More serious is the fact that because of absence of any technological breakthrough, there is stagnation in yield levels of various crops. This can have very serious implications for a land scarce country where land area is limited and there is a need to accelerate growth rates in agriculture for feeding increasing population. Furthermore, the aspiration to increase exports in a big way would also need growth in agriculture to accelerate for generating adequate surpluses. The crisis in agriculture is manifest in lack of diversification and increasing burden of workforce on agriculture. This has led to a state of low productivity employment for a large section of agricultural population and the persistence of large-scale rural poverty in most of the states in India. The hope that export boom as a consequence of economic reforms would lead to increasing incomes and employment has also been belied to large extent. It has to be underlined that a market driven liberalisation process in agriculture is bound to be strongly biased towards rich farmers and prosperous regions. The peasant movement would have to intervene effectively and play a crucial role in assuring that the interests of small farmers and of disadvantaged regions are also protected and they enabled to partake the benefits of trade liberalisation.

CHAPTER

10

Agricultural Economy of Bihar : Potential, Compulsion and Options

Anjani Kumari Jha and Niranjan Kumar Jha

INTRODUCTION

It would not be wrong to say that true Indian culture is agriculture. It is the backbone of Indian economy. Though, since independence share of agriculture to GDP has declined, but it is the largest contributor with 26.5 per cent as per the year 2001-02. In Bihar, agriculture's contribution to GDP is 43.8 per cent. The rural population in India is 72.2 per cent whereas it is 89.5 per cent is Bihar. The workforce participation in agriculture as per 1999-00 NSS survey is 60.4 whereas this figure stands at 73.1 per cent in Bihar. These figures and facts are testimony to the fact that to what extent agriculture is the mainstay of the economy of Bihar. It is the largest sector which has the potential as well as compulsions to absorb the maximum workforce. Agricultural potential is explicit as the state has vast fertile land, abundant water resources and hard working workforce. The element of compulsion is evident from the dismal industrial growth and consequent backwardness in the service sector. It makes the state one of the BIMARU States, the epithet coined for Bihar, Madhya Pradesh, Rajasthan and Uttar Pradesh.

Gloomy Picture

The Per Capita income of the state at 1993-94 prices stands at meagre Rs. 3574 against the all-India figure of Rs. 8941. The per capita agricultural income in Bihar is Just Rs. 1508 against the corresponding all-India figure of Rs. 2552. The value of agricultural output per hectare at 1993-94 Prices in Bihar is Rs. 5939 against Rs. 11839 in India. These figures present the gloomy picture of the state which occupies the lowest rank on the basis of Hùman Development Index. This Pathehtic situation was further worsened by the partition of the state. The mineral-rich and industrialised region was carved out as Jharkhand. It resulted into the increase in the population dependence on agriculture in absence of industries and the consequent service sector. It has created the 'Push' factor for the inglorious migration of skilled and unskilled workforce to richer states like Punjab, Haryana, Delhi, Maharashtra etc. where they have to bear the brunt of hard lives and derogatory behaviours meted out by people of host states. Strange! Bihar, the fifth largest state with an area of 8.99 million hectare and gifted with fertile land, and abundance of water, is counted as one of the BIMARU states. Is it not a big paradox which boggles the minds of thinkers, planners, social activists and all concerned? Really there is no riddle which can not be unriddled. There are constraints, no-doubt, but those are not beyond solution.

Productivity

The land productivity per hectare in Bihar can be divided into three categories. In some distinct, it is less than Rs. 5000, in a few it is between Rs. 5,000 and Rs. 7,000. A few districts witness per hectare land productivity between Rs. 7,000 and 10,000. This fact is revealed by datas provided by the

Directorate of Statistics and Evaluation, Government of India at 1993-94 prices. The land productivity depends on various inputs and their utilisation. Now, let us have a glance on this front.

Fertilizer Consumption

The NPK fertilizer consumption in Bihar varies in three different zones. The fertilizer consumption in Zone-I is 104 kg. per hectare. It is 78 kg. in Zone-II and only 69 kg. per hectare in Zone-III. There was steep rise in the NPK Consumption in 1980s. It shot up from 22 kg. in 1982 to 63 kg. in 1991. By 1998 the figure reached to 82 kg. per hectare. Vermicomposting and biofertilizers have not gained popularity among farmers due to ignorance and lack of awareness and incentives for the adoption of this poor-friendly and eco-friendly technology.

Agricultural Implements

Technological and institutional reforms are the prelude to the Green Revolution. On both these fronts, Bihar is on the backbench. Land reforms measures have not succeeded. Land disputes, fragmentation of land and inability to execute the policy of consolidation have rendered the cultivable land unsuitable for modern farming. The numbers of tractors per thousand hectares was 20 in 1980. The figure increased to 30 in 1990 and further to 45 in 1999. Similarly the number of pumpsets increased at snails pace from 27 in 1980 to 39 in 1990 and 47 in 1999. This is more disturbing when we consider the reality that ironically the diesel tube well is the biggest source of irrigation in the water abundant state of Bihar.

Infrastructure and Public Investment

On the infrastructure and public investment fronts too, the picture is not worth rejoicing. Market accessibility of agro-products is less due to bad condition of roads especially in the Kosi affected region of north Bihar. Lack of cold storage facilities deter the fruits and vegetables growers from earnings more prices for their products. In the 5th five year plan, public investment per hectare of Net Sown Area (NSA) at 1980-81 prices was Rs. 196 whereas the all-India average was Rs. 311. Bihar occupied 18th rank. By the eighth plan the figure declined to just 79 against the all-India average of 197. Thus, the state was relegated to the 23rd rank. The growth rate was witnessed at -4.78 against the all-India average growth rate of –3.16.

Research and Development

R&D is the pre-requisite for the modernisation of agriculture. It reflects the ability and aptitude to introduce scientific farming in order to increase the agricultural productivity. On this front, Bihar stands almost nowhere. Public Research Investment of agricultural GDP remained at 0.14 against the all-India figure of 0.52 Needless to say, universities shade tears on their own pathetic condition. They are faced with the paucity of funds to improve seed varieties or any new techniques to modernise the traditional farming.

Market Arrival of Food-Grains

The soil and climatic conditions of Bihar is ideal for rice production. But the quantum of rice production in the state can be gauged by the fact that market arrival of rice was just 71 per cent in 1999-2000 whereas, the same figure for states like Andhra Pradesh and Punjab are 83 and 71 per cent respectively. The market arrival of wheat was just 17 per cent which is just half the all-India figure of 37 per cent. Needless to mention Punjab stands first at 51 per cent followed by Haryana at 45 per cent and MP at 41 per cent.

Water Management

Bihar is blessed with many perennial rivers like the Ganga, the Gandak, the Kosi, the Ghaghra, the Sone and many other small rivers but the management of surface water has remained a riddle even after 50 years of planned development. As a result, diesel tube wells constitute the major source of irrigation with 45.22 per cent followed by Canal irrigation with just 28.18 per cent. Canal Irrigation occupies the second rank sarcastically in the state endowed with many perennial rivers. If the water of these rivers could have been channelised, the running cost of diesel pumpsets could have been saved and the furry of flood could have been checked to a large extent. This sad state of affairs exist despite several major and medium irrigation projects launched in the state. It, certainity, points finger at the competence, sincerity and honesty on the part of project implementing authorities from the top to the bottom.

Flood and Droughts

Districts like Araria, Begusarai, Bhagalpur, East Champaran, Darbhanga, Gopalganj, Katihar, Khagaria, Kishanganj, Lakhisarai, Madhepura, Munger, Muzaffarpur, Purnea, Saharsa, Samastipur, Saran, Sitamarhi, Vaisali and West Champaran are badly affected by flood whereas 11 districts have to bear the brunt of severe draughts. These include Aurangabad, Bhojpur, Buxar, Gaya, Jamui, Lakhisarai, Munger, Nalanda Nawadah, Rohtas and Shekhpura. The ambitions Kosi Project was started in Collaboration with the Government of Nepal in 1950s to protect the state from its sorrow but the poor management of Kosi Canals and embankments have thrown the people to the mercy of Lord Indra, the legendary God of rain and water. Similar is the fate of other projects launched in the state. The silting of Kosi river bed has raised its level to the extent that its banks are not able to check the overflow of water innundating large areas every year. The hopeless people have been taught only the rhetoric of relief, relief and relief. The task of water management as a permanent solution is almost deleted from the priority list of planners, legislators, administrators and political activists who are at the helm of affairs. Due to water logging in *Diara, Tal* and *Chaur* lands are kept fallow during Kharif season due to no timely outlet of water as a result of poor water management.

Policy Options

The salvation of Bihar lies in its agricultural growth. It has the potential and compulsion for the growth of agriculture. The Agriculture Research and Extension services must be given impetus to enable the state in finding its rightful place in the modernising Indian agriculture and globalising scenario. Fund allocation to Research institutes should be doubled and tightly monitored. Needful support should be accorded to extension services and manpower training to make the R&D more fruitful. Although the Diary Cooperative Societies (COMFED) gives some ray of hope but most of the institutions concerned with agriculture and rural development are almost paralysed. Legal provisions governing the institutions are outdated and irrational in context to the changing needs of the time. Land disputes redressal agencies should shed off their lathergic and delaying modus operendi. Government policies should be people friendly and goal oriented rather than populist gymicks. The lack of coordination can be noticed at everysteps of integration and programme. Government machineries should be greased to make them sensitive to peoples needs and aspirations. NGOs with proven record and missionary zeal should be associated in research, awareness and project implementation. In sum and substances, the development of state should be kept above partisan attitude. There should be sincere efforts by everyone with the mantra of "lighting a candle rather than cursing the dark".

CHAPTER

11

Role of Fertilizer in Indian Agriculture : An Analysis

BIRENDRA KUMAR AND MEERA RANJAN LAL

As far as economic reforms are concerned, the country is at crossroads. No strategy of economic reforms and regeneration can succeed without sustained and broad-based agricultural development. Such development is critical to raise standard of living of the masses, alleviating abject poverty, providing food to the millions, generating a buoyant market for expansion of other two important segments of Indian economy i.e. industry and services.

There are distinct signs that the green revolution launched in the late sixties, which was instrumental in transforming a crisis-prone food economy into one of reasonable self sufficiency, is now running out of steam.

We have already celebrated Golden Jubilee of our Independence and have entered in the 21st century, still about 200 million children, women and men will go to the bed undernourished to night. In India 167 million are exposed to risk of iodine deficiency of which 54 million have goitre. Micronutrient malnutrition is most devastating for pre-school children and pregnant women but it is debilitating the national economy as well.

About 40 years after the term Green Revolution, which was coined by Dr. William Gadd of USA, we are in a position to draw a balance sheet and chalk out a strategy for future. Apart from erasing the begging 'bowl' image of India thanks to the use of fertilizer in the soils.

It has been estimated that in order to achieve a growth of more than 8 per cent in GDP, the agriculture production should increase at annual rate of 5.5 per cent and industrial production by more than 10 per cent. The growth of GDP in tenth. Five Year Plan has been targetted 8 per cent which requires more than 5 per cent increase in agriculture and 12 percent in industry.

After signing the GATT on December 16, 1993 the world has become a vastly different place with a rapidly changing economic order. At this juncture agriculture sector is destined to make a substantial contribution to the national economy.

The significance of agriculture also arises from the fact that it has been the source of supply of raw materials to our leading industries. The proportion of agricultural goods, which are being exported, is about 14 to 19 percent of our total exports of the country. India ensured a record export of foodgrains during 2001-2002, which gave foreign exchange of worth 742.08 million US dollar.

Ever since Malthus wrote his celebrated, Essay on Population, attention was Focused on the problem of population versus food supply. There is no doubt that per capita cultivated area is gradually on the decline in India. During 1921 to 2001 the cultivated areas per capita dropped from 1.11 acre to 0.49 acre indicating a fall of more than 50 per cent. The total geographical area of the country is about 328.7 million hectares but statistical information regarding land classification is available for only about 305 million hectares. The total cropped area is about 190.2 million hectares.

While the government is claiming that India has enough foodgrains to feed the masses, the total availability of food

TABLE 11.1

Year	*Population*	*Cereals*	*Pulses*	*Total*
1991	846.3	437.3	40.7	478 gms.
1999	996.4	429.2	36.5	465.7 gms.
2000	1014.8	422.7	31.8	454.4 gms.
2001	1033.2	386.2	30.0	416.2 gms.
2002	1050.6	457.3	35.0	492.2 gms.
2003	1068.2	409.9	28.2	438.2 gms.

actually went down sharply during recent years. The following chart made us to ponder over the actual condition regarding per capita net availability of food in grams.

As per the Indian Council of Medical Research norm 650 gram per person per day is essential for his survival. For feeding of more than 109 crore population 240 MT foodgrains will be require... Meanwhile rising trend of population and deceasing trend of arable land in the country boosting of agricultural outputs pose a problem.

In any scheme for boosting agriculture output, use of fertilizers has an important role. India's soil though varied and rich is deficient in Nitrogen Phosphorus. As population is rising at faster rate and a[illegible]le land is declining, for augmenting foodgrain production larger dozes of chemical fertilizer is required. Indian soils are being continuously depleted of plant nutrients nearly to the tune of 9-10 million tones per annum. Hence soils may have to be supplied with more and more nutrients to make-up for the depleted soil fertility level and for additional harvest required in future. It has been estimated that by the end of the Tenth Plan for the required agricultural production more than 20 million tones of fertilizer will be essential.

Dr. M.S. Swaminathan in his article published in Economic Times 20th July 1994 wrote:

"The secret increase in genetic advancement of yield potential of several economic plants have stemmed from success in improving the capacity to utilize more nutrients and convert them into economic product."

Similarly Dr. Norman Borlang, a Nobel laureate, has stated, "If HYV's are the catalyst, fertilizer is the fuel for green revolution."

Dr. Saburo Okita, former Managing Director, International Development Centre of Japan, has pointed out that secret of success in Agriculture is making full use of water and fertilizers. According to Food and Agriculture Organization "50 per cent of the recent increase in foodgrain production could be attributed to fertilizer use alone."

It is open fact that like men and animals, plants also need food for their growth and development. But with a difference. Animal including man can only subsist on food in organic form. Plants, on the other hand, have power of building-up organic tissues directly from in-organic materials. The leaves of the plants are the most miraculous chemical laboratories in the world. From a limited number of chemical elements, drawn from the soil and air, plants build up a vast array of grains, fruits, fibres, flowers, timbers, gums, sugar, drugs etc. These chemical elements are known as plant nutrient.

Sixteen nutrient elements are recognised, at present, being essential to all plants for their normal growth and development. These elements are Carbon, Hydrogen and Oxygen, which are derived from the air and Soil, Water and Nitrogen, Phosphorus, Potassium, Calcium, Magnesium, Sulphur, Iron, Zinc etc. are supplied by the soil in varying quantities either from the reserves in the soil or through application of manures and fertilizers.

Nitrogen, Phosphorus and Potassium are used in large quantities by plants. That is why they are known as primary nutrients, while Calcium, Magnesium and Sulphate are secondary nutrient required in relatively less. Rests are known as micronutrients. Nitrogen is an important constituent of chlorophyll, protoplasm, protein and other acids, which increases growth and development of all living tissues and improves the quality of leafy vegetables and fodders. Another chemical fertilizers are Phosphatic which contains the nutrient element Phosphorus. It is essential for the development of plant roots as well as it stimulates flowering.

Potassic fertilizer is the third major plant nutrient. It is obtained by mining and purification of natural deposits containing potassium salts. Muriate of potash is an activator of enzymes involved in protein carbohydrate metabolism. It brings about a greater utilisation flight during cool and cloudy weather and thereby enhances plant ability to resist cold and other adverse conditions. Apart from these three chemical fertilizers, complex fertilizers are also important. In India variety of complex fertilizers are being produced which are known as Ammonium Phosphates, NPK etc. Mixed fertilizers are also significant in plants growth.

These are the chemical fertilizers, which are inorganic materials of a concentrated nature. It forms a wide group of materials. Secondary nutrients are concerned they have distinct role to play in augmenting the production. With the adoption of multiple cropping system and use of high yielding varieties of crops, requirement of these elements has been increased.

Micro-nutrients did not receive much attention due to various reasons. The deficiency of nitrogen in Indian soils is more wide spread compared to Phosphates and Potash fertilizers. The use of these inputs in proper proportion is salubrious impact on production. According to recent survey made by some Agronomists published in *Economic Times*, the use of one unit of Nitrogen leads to additional production of 12 units of foodgrains, one unit of phosphate to 8 additional unit of crop and simultaneous application of one unit of potassic fertilizer gives five additional units of crop.

According to agriculture scientists, different types of fertilizers (NPK) should be used in a balanced proportion to maintain the productivity of the soil. For India, the standard ratio for the use of various fertilizers has been assumed to be 4:2:1.

Table 11.2 indicates the NPK ratio in different years:

No doubt, the use of fertilizers has increased leaps and bounds especially after the advent of green revolution in the country. The fertilizer off take doubled in every successive plan till the fifth plan. There after it took nine years for the consumption to further double from 5.5 MT in 1980-81 to 12.5 MT in 1990-91 it has gone up to 15.3 MT in 2002-03. The NPK ratio in India is eight times the application of nitrogen and 2.5 times application of phosphate to potash, whereas the world average is 3.7:1.6:1

TABLE 11.2
NPK Ratio in Various Years

Year	*N*	*P*	*K*
1960-61	7.2	1.8	1
1970-71	6.5	2.0	1
1980-81	5.9	1.9	1
1990-91	6.0	2.4	1
1997-98	7.9	2.8	1
1999-00	6.9	2.9	1
2000-01	6.4	2.7	1
2001-02	6.2	2.5	1
2002-03	8.0	2.5	1

of NPK. The consumption of NPK by major countries of the world in 2002-03 is indicated in the following Table 11.3.

TABLE 11.3
Fertilizer Consumption Ratio

(Metric tonnes)

Countries	*N*	*P*	*K*	*N*	*P*	*K*
Canada	1507400	622100	306700	4.9	2	1
USA	11110300	4087900	4915100	2.2	1.8	1
UK	1394000	384000	486000	2.9	0.8	1
China	23598500	8823700	3105000	7.6	2.8	1
Japan	528000	631400	482200	1.1	1.3	1
France	2392000	1032000	1491000	1.6	0.7	1
Germany	176900	40000	649000	2.7	0.6	1
Australia	650000	870000	215000	3	4	1
World	78736400	31018400	21110400	3.7	1.6	1
India	—	—	—	8.5	2.5	1

The ratio is more balance in countries like Canada, USA, Japan etc. The balance use of NPK fertilizers has a good impact on production of agricultural commodity. It is evident from the Table 11.3.

It is evident from the Table 11.4 that the balance dose of NPK ratio is quite significant for the agricultural production. The ideal ratio of NPK should be 4:2:1 for more production. If the NPK ratio is not maintained at the optimum, it will affect the yield. Dr. B.C. Biswas of Fertilizer Association of India indicated that if the imbalances of nutrients were not corrected it would have a deleterious affect on the production of crops. It is estimated that nearly 50 per cent of increase in foodgrain production is due to increase in fertilizer use.

Though the consumption has gone up, inter regional disparities still persists. The off take in majority of states in the Western and Eastern parts of the country is still much less than the national average of 76.8 kg per hectare. The five states (Punjab, Haryana, A.P., U.P. and Tamil Nadu) account for 51.5 per cent of the total fertilizer consumption in the country. Whatever the Government Policy regarding chemical fertilizers,

TABLE 11.4

Fertilizer Consumption Per Capita Per Hectare and Yield of Commodities

Countries	*Consumption of Fertilizers (Kg.) N*	*Yield Per Hactare (Kg.)*			
		Paddy	*Wheat*	*Maize*	*Potato*
Canada	53.5		2419	6759	26162
USA	107.1	6860	2442	7975	39093
Australia	35.9	6788	2136	5197	29818
France	252.6	5273	7134	8357	36385
UK	379.2	–	8113	–	40785
Japan	375	6192	3548		32048
China	370.7	6062	3759	5173	13146
India	81.8	2811	2493	1408	16478
Pakistan	113.1	2451	2018	1469	13466
Srilanka	105.9	2801	–	1069	10993
Russia	12.8	2762	1397	1375	11801

the increase in food production over last 35 years or more has been based on more quantitative use of available land. The scope of additional land is inevitable; but due to the decreasing land-man–ratio has forced the agriculturist to involve in intensive cultivation. For the intensive cultivation more balanced use of fertilizers is needed.

It is evident from the Table 11.5 that use of fertilizers and foodgrains production is positively correlated.

While the fertilizer consumption in India in 1951-52 was 65.6 thousand tones and the production was 52 MT. After third five year plan or the starting of green revolution the consumption of fertilizer began to increase and the food production also showed a rising trend. With the dawn of 21st century the food production was crossed 200 MT mark because of enhanced use of fertilizers. It is quite evident from the region-wise consumption of fertilizers. The northern region's contribution of foodgrains production has shown a rising trend due to increase in fertilizer consumption.

Table 11.5
Fertilizers and Foodgrains Production

(Metric tonnes)

Year	*Consumption (000 Tonnes)*	*Agricultural Production (Mt)*
1951-52	65.6	52
1961-62	338.3	66.3
1971-72	2656.8	100
1981-82	6067.2	140
1991-92	12728	168.37
1995-96	13876.2	191.2
1998-99	1483 8.3	194.1
1999-2000	14308.1	200.1
2000-2001	16721.3	200.2
2001-2002	17845.5	203.1
2002-2003	18733.9	174.2 (due to draught in several part of the country)
2003-2004	19343.2	210.8

Even the state-wise consumption of fertilizers and production of foodgrains shows the positive correlation between fertilizers use and agricultural production.

Hence the foodgrain production is closely connected with the use of fertilizers in holding. There is a very high magnitude of positive correlation between them (i.e.= +0.98). This type of positive relation can also be gauge by the consumption pattern of fertilizers and the food production in major countries of the world. While five developed countries, i.e. Canada, USA, Australia, UK and Japan used almost balanced ratio of NPK its production of foodgrains are also high.

The use of fertilizers, not only increases the foodgrain but it can engage more labour resources, can solve the problem of acute unemployment of the country like India. In 1980-81 about 70.6 thousand persons had directly engaged in the fertilizer industries, which has gone-up to 84.2 in 1996-97. However due to closure of several fertilizer units of the North-Eastern region thousands of labour forces have become jobless. Keeping in view of population increment and requirement of food, use of fertilizer is invitable. A number of fertilizer experiments carried by the India Council for Agricultural Research have shown that the Contribution of Phosphorus and Potassic fertilizer in the extra yield from fertilizer application is substantially high.

The President of India A.P.J. Kalam exhorted the agronomists and scientists to make all out efforts to bring another green revolution in the country for feeding the, growing

TABLE 11.6

Consumption of Fertilizers and Region-wise Food Production in 2002-03

Region	*Consumption of Fertilizers (%)*	*Production of Foodgrains (%)*
Northern	34.90	45
Southern	28.60	28.20
Western	22.90	16.80
Eastern	13.60	10.00
Total	100	100

population. It has been widely acknowledged that the additional of one rupee on fertilizers it should give at least of Rs. 2.75 from the additional crop production. It will be better to motivate the farmers to fertilizers in balanced quantity.

Apart from chemical fertilizers natural manures are important inputs for the growth of agriculture. India since ages has been the users of environmental manures. Only after independence, the country has gone in for the massive production and use of chemical fertilizers. In India, still the rural households, while going for toilet prefer to go to their own fields since it enriched the soil.

There is no doubt that the raison d'etre for fertilizer industry in India is its crucial role in increasing agricultural production. The increase in food production for feeding the enhancing population is the need of the hour. The increase in food production over last 35 years has been on more intensive use of available land. As the scope for additional area, which can be brought under cultivation, is limited. The continued need for increased supply of fertilizers is inevitable for self reliance in agricultural output in one hand and earns a sizeable foreign exchange by exporting it.

It is observed that for making more profit in agriculture sector seeds, water and fertilizer are more significant. More than 60 per cent of crop yields are influenced by fertilizers product pattern as well as time and methods of application. It is said that fertilizer is one of the important factors for green revolution.

TABLE 11.7
Consumption of Fertilizers and State-wise Food Production in 2002-03

States	*Consp. of Fert. (KG Per Hactare)*	*Production of Food-grain (MT)*
Punjab	158.4	37.8
U.P.	108.4	25.3
M.P.	39.2	10.21.04
A.P.	139.4	27.4
West Bengal	103.2	24.6
Bihar	80.6	19.2

AS soil alkalinity is one of the factors, which adversely affect crop production and restrict the economic utilisation of the available land and water resources particularly in the acrid and semi-acrid regions of the country. Out of an estimated area of 8.5 million hectare of degraded salt affected soils of the country, over 40 per cent is affected with soil alkalinity.

Fertilizer, machinery and irrigation are significant positives regression coefficients, indicating a large scope for increasing the wheat output with higher level of fertilizers. A vast area of India soil is rain-fed, which is said to be impoverished. There is no other way to achieve sound soil fertility then by the judicious fertilizers' use. In India there are different soil conditions such as vertisols, alfisols etc. While vertisol soils have low organic matter content and are deficient in Nitrogen, Phosphorus and Zinc. All crops grown during the rainy season need N fertilization. Higher application of N is warranted in wet years. Deeper placement of N is required in case of post rainy season. Phosphorus is second soil contain only 2 to 10 pm of available P fertilization strategies for vertisols in respect of major limiting nutrients have been suggested.

So far Alfisols and related soils are concerned they are shallow. They have limited moisture and nutrients storage capacity. They have low organic matter. Most of these soils are deficient in available P organic manures enhance the efficacy of applied chemical fertilizers.

Fertilizer use in rained areas is surer way to make the efficient use of limited available water and thereby improving productivity of these areas. As the population bomb is tickling away and the Economic Survey, 2003-2004 has warned against the dubious distinction of becoming the world's most populous country by 2050.

The Indian Prime Minister in his address to the Nation on August 15, 2004 promised a New Deal for agriculture and rural India. For the second green revolution apart from other ingredients balance use of fertilizers is the need of the hour. Side by side diversification from cereals to high-value and labour intensive crops, agro processing, livestock, fisheries, horticulture, etc. are also needed for second green revolution in the country.

As the eleven million new livelihoods will have to be created every year in India and these have to come largely from the farm and rural sectors. Importing food and other agriculture commodities will hence have the same impact as an importing unemployment. Thus for achieving second green revolution in the country the role of balanced dozes of fertilizers are inevitable.

CHAPTER

12

Role of Fertilizers on Indian Agriculture

N.K. THAKUR

INTRODUCTION

Indian the second most populus country of the world having its population more than *one billion*, resides in 6.5 lac villages and contributes 23 per cent to GDP at present which were used to be more than 50 per cent (1951-56). It has a total of 329 million hect. of land out of which only 143 million Hect. are cultivable. Average irrigation is only 32 per cent and rest is dependent on rain GOD. India, sharing 1/4th of world's total land but her burden of 16.44 per cent of world's populations.

Agriculture

Agriculture is the foundation of our economy which occupies a place of price in the country's progress. Agriculture is the mainstay of the economy of any developing country of the world and the performances of other sectors are largely dependant on the progress of the Agriculture sectors. Agriculture is the "backbone" of Indian economy in terms of gross national produce and proportion of population which depends upon it for their livelihood.

To meet the nutritional security of India, it is only Agriculture sector which has brought this country from "SIP to mount" to self sufficiency in foodgrain production.

Agriculture plays a pivotal role as antiforce against *Migration* of rural population to urban area and have its impact on the balance of payment of the country's progress. Agricultural Production has increased several folds in last four decades since "Green Revolution" period. Prior to that there was scarce level of food and fiber.

Indian Agriculture has been revolutioned in food production from 50 million tonnes (1950-52) to 211 million tonnes (2001-02).

Role of Fertilizers

Dr. Norman E. Borlogue has rightly said "If high yielding wheat and rice varities were catalysts than that ignited the "Green Revolution" is the "Chemical Fertilizers" was the fuel that powered its "forceful thrust".

Fertilizer being key input in increasing production of food-grain and other agricultural crops has an inextricable linkage with Agriculture. This is also amply borne out by the broadly similar trends in the consumption of fertilizers on the one hand and production of foodgrain on the other.

Fertilizer being key input in increasing production of good grains contributes more than 50 per cent increase alone apart from HYV seeds and irrigation.

India's self reliance in food production can primarily be credited to Green Revolution, which has led to increase in cropping intensity, nutrient consumption per hectare, chemical fertilizes have played a vital role in success of Green Revolution.

India is blessed by nature through diverse agroclimatic conditions and having vast resources Green Revolution was a boon to Indian Agriculture.

TABLE 12.1
Nutrient Consumption and Growth Rate per annum in India

Year	Consumption (000' mts)			Total	Compound Growth rate %
	N	P_2O_5	K_2O		
1951-52	58.7	6.9	—	65.6	—
1961-62	249.8	60.5	28	338.3	17.8
1971-72	1798	558.2	300.6	2656.6	22.9
1981-82	4068.7	1322.3	676.2	6067.2	8.6
1991-92	8046.3	3321.2	1360.6	12728	7.7
1992-93	8426.8	2843.8	883.9	12154.5	4.5
1993-94	8788.3	2669.3	908.7	12366.3	1.7
1994-95	9507.1	2931.7	1124.8	13563.6	9.7
1995-96	9822.8	2897.5	1155.8	13876.2	2.3
1996-97	10301.8	2976.8	1029.6	14308.2	3.1
1997-98	10905	3917.2	1372.6	16194.8	13.2
1998-99	11353.8	4122.2	1331.5	16797.5	3.7
1999-2000	11592.5	4797.9	1678.4	18068.9	7.9

Source : FAI Fertilizer Statistic, 2002-03, Table 6.

TABLE 12.2

Consumption of fertilizers (NPK, in kg/hec)	*Total foodgrain production (million tonnes)*		*Population (Millions)*
Year	*NPK consumption*	*Foodgrain production*	*Population*
1951-52	0.55	51.99	363
1960-61	1.9	82.02	432
1970-71	13.6	108.42	551
1980-81	32.0	112.3	684
1990-91	67.6	176.3	846
2001-02	90.1	211.32	1027

Source : *FAI Fertilizer News*, Sept. 2003.

Fertilizer use in India started in 1920 and was a limited use. The everfirst fertilizer factory of SSP started in 1906 at Ranipet (Tamil Nadu). During late 40's synthetic Ammonia plant developed at Sindari (Jharkhand).

During 60's saw a rapid growth in indigenous fertilizer production of Nitrogenous and Phosphatic complex fertilizers.

Chemical Fertilizers were not much in use before independence and even after independence. It is the Green Revolution of 60's, the use of chemical fertilizers sparked and boosted the foodgrain production. Wheat and Rice are the major crops grown in India after Green the production of these two major crops have increased.

TABLE 12.3

Year	*Fertilizers consumption*		*Crops (Yield in kg/hect)*
	per kg/hect.	*Rice*	*Wheat*
1950-51	0.55	668	663
1964-65	1.93	1078	913
1975-76	16.90	1235	1410
1985-86	47.50	1552	2048
1990-91	67.50	1740	2281
1995-96	74.00	1797	2483
1997-98	75.50	1900	2485
1998-99	84.90	1921	2590
1999-2000	95.23	1985	2621
2000-01	88.03	1901	2708
2001-02	91.49	2086	2770

Source : FAI Fertilizer Statistic, 2002-03.

But this fertilizer consumption kg./hect. and yield kg./ hect. are for below than most of developed countries which is mentioned below:

Fertilizer Industries in India played a supportive role in sustaining the green revolution all the years making the country "Self Sufficient" in food and fiber from "Scarce level".

TABLE 12.4

(Yield in kg/hect)

Country	Fertilizer consumption kg/hect.	Crops	
		Rice	Wheat
Netherland	450.00	—	8741
Korea Rep	407.00	6930	3279
Egypt	385.80	8769	6357
Belgium	343.00	—	7672
Japan	301.00	6659	3864
China	254.20	6361	3832
India	90.00	2086	2770

Source : Same as Table 12.3.

It is heartening to note that India is the third largest producers and consumers of fertilizers in the world after China and USA. India has increased its production and consumption of chemical fertilizers (Nitrogenous and Phosphatic).

Production capacity of Nitrogenous and Phosphatic Fertilizers.

Fertilizer Consumption Trend in India

Fertilizer use was negligible the pre-independence era. It was in the early 1950 that fertilizer use got an impetus with the introduction of planned economy beginning from 1951-52 and its has increased to about 280 times to touch a level of 18.1 million tonnes of N.P.K. in 1999-2000.

In the beginning of First Five Year Plan, fertilizer consumption in the country was merely 65000 mts. The fertilizer consumption increased at an annual compound growth rate of 17.8 and 22.9 per cent from 1951-52 to 1961-62 to 1971-72 respectively. After a reasonably good base year annual growth in fertilizer consumption was 8.6 per cent in 80's and 4.7 per cent in 90's. Due to decontrol of phosphatic and potassic fertilizers in 1992 the growth in the consumption was adversely affected contributing to the slow growth rate during 90's.

TABLE 12.5

(000′ MTs)

	N		P_2O_5	
Year	*Capacity*	*Production*	*Capacity*	*Production*
1951-52	90	29	78	10
1961-62	283	154	182	65
1971-72	1487	949	534	290
1981-82	4719	3143	1408	950
1991-92	8282	7302	2806	2562
1992-93	8510	7431	2806	2321
1993-94	8844	7231	2817	1874
1994-95	8998	7944.3	2873	2562
1995-96	9134	8768	2982	2593
1996-97	9468.2	8593.1	3027	2578
1997-98	10473	10083	3347	3205
1999-2000	11077.8	10873.2	3761	3448
2000-01	11032	10942.8	4987	3734
2001-02	12166	10689.5	5112	3835
2002-03	12285	10507.6	5536	3907

Source : FAI Statistic, 2002-03.

The consumption of fertilizers is one of the most important determinants of agricultural growth. The increase in fertilizer consumption has contributed significantly to a sustainable production of food grains in the country. The over all consumption of fertilizer from 0.55 kg./hect. tonnes (1950/51) to about 90.12 kg./hect. (2001-02).

The fertilizer industries in India has grown tremendously in last 30 years. The Government is keen to see that fertilizer reaches the farmers in the remote and hilly areas.

To ensure the availability the Government has introduced the Essential Commodity Act, 1955 and for the protection of industries Retention Pricing Scheme in 1977 to provide subsidy to manufacturers a difference between unit-wise cost of production fixed on normative basis and MRP of fertilizers which was 12 per cent post tax return on net worth.

Table 12.6
Nutrient Consumption and Growth Rate per annum in India

Year	Consumption (000' mts)			Total	Compound growth rate %
	N	P_2O_5	K_2O		
1951-52	58.7	6.9	—	65.6	—
1961-62	249.8	60.5	28	338.3	17.8
1971-72	1798	558.2	300.6	2656.6	22.9
1981-82	4068.7	1322.3	676.2	6067.2	8.6
1991-92	8046.3	3321.2	1360.6	12728	7.7
1992-93	8426.8	2843.8	883.9	12154.5	4.5
1993-94	8788.3	2669.3	908.7	12366.3	1.7
1994-95	9507.1	2931.7	1124.8	13563.6	9.7
1995-96	9822.8	2897.5	1155.8	13876.2	2.3
1996-97	10301.8	2976.8	1029.6	14308.2	3.1
1997-98	10905	3917.2	1372.6	16194.8	13.2
1998-99	11353.8	4122.2	1331.5	16797.5	3.7
1999-00	11592.5	4797.9	1678.4	18068.9	7.9

Source : FAI Statistic, 2002-03.

Government also introduced equated freight to make available fertilizers at block level.

At present there are about 2.83 lac sales points scattered through out country and fertilizer is being sold through institutional agencies including co-operative, as well as private trade. A limited quantities are also being sold through company's own retails depos.

Though fertilizers have played a vital role in rapid growth of Indian Agriculture after Green Revolution and crisis of nutritional thret has to come to sufficiency level providing food and fiber to all. Food scarcity for a huge country like India with high density of population is of vital importance which growing @ 2.3 per cent and it has crossed the level of one billion.

This unprecedented increase in population will lead to increase in demand of food and fiber mainly in 21st century when per capita land has reduced to 0.12 hect.

To feed this mass at present 17.5 million tonnes of N.P.K. are used to produce 211 million tonnes. By the end of 2011-12 it is expected to have a rapid increase in population and to agricultural production and would continues to be in future also to provide nutritional security to the second most populus country of the world.

CHAPTER

13

Trend in Total Factor Productivity of Crop Sector in Bihar during Green Revolution Period

R.K.P. Singh, A.K. Choudhary and Vinod Kumar

INTRODUCTION

Bihar has made impressive progress on the agricultural front during the last two and half decades. Public strategies, investment in research and farmers efforts have helped achieving almost self-sufficiency in food production. Irrigated eco-system is the mainstay of Bihar's agricultural economy, sharing more than 50 per cent of net sown area and contributing more than 65 per cent to the total foodgrain production.

Irrigated ecosystem is dominated by the rice-wheat cropping system. Over the past three decades, the continuous rotation of rice and wheat, the staple food grains, has increased dramatically and contributed substantially to the food security of one of the most populous state of the country. But the impact of Green Revolution technologies has not been uniform across the district, mainly due to bio-physical and socio-economic factors. Grains in productivity were higher in the Rohtas, Aurangabad, Nalanda, Begusarai and West Champaran districts in contrast to the districts of Sitamarhi, Supaul, Sheohar, Nawada and Jamui where the benefits are not evident.

However, the indiscriminate exploitation of natural resources in these intensively cultivated districts has raised concern about the long-term sustainability of the agricultural production system and environment. In the recent past several indicators highlight that natural resources of the region, especially land, water and bio-diversity are under severe pressure to meet the growing food demand due to increasing population and income (Singh, 2004). At the same time the productivity of this system has now started showing stagnation in many districts. There is also concern of declining soil health and other related environmental problems.

The irrigated agriculture, in general and the rice-wheat system, in particular are confronted with several economic and ecological problems, threatening the very sustainability of agricultural production. Several studies have highlighted that the Total Factor Productivity (TFP) growth of important crop like; rice and wheat in the Indo-Gangetic region is decelerating and the future production growth is input based in many regions of the country (Kumar *et al*. 1998, Kumar and Rosegrant, 1994, Kumar and Mruthyunjaya, 1992). Besides, the widespread cultivation of paddy and agricultural intensification resulting from spread of irrigation are observed to have an adverse impact on the natural resources and ecology (Pingali *et al*. 1997).

At the farmers' level, sustainability concerns are being expressed in several ways. Many farmers believe that the input levels have to be continuously increased in order to maintain the yield. In the 1970s, most farmers used only nitrogenous and phosphatic fertilizers to achieve high yields. Due to the occurrence of increasing deficiencies of several secondary and micro-nutrients most farmers now apply phosphorus, potassium, sulphur, zinc, boron, iron, and manganese to mitigate the nutrient constraints. Results from many long-term experiments on the rice-wheat cropping system show declining yield trends when input levels were kept constant. This situation poses a threat to the sustainability of the crop sector. It is felt that if urgent measures to address the problem of sustainability and natural resource degradation are not undertaken, it would jeopardize the future growth of agriculture in the irrigated areas of Bihar, which is the backbone of food security in State. Under this backdrop, the present study was taken up to provide information on TFP trends for the crop sector at the district level. The study was taken up to provide information on TFP trends for the crop sector at the district level and identify the sources of TFP growth.

The present study has analysed the performance of irrigated agriculture by measuring TFP indices at district level. The district level analysis will capture the location-specific differentials at the micro level. No study has been undertaken in the recent years to analyse the trend in TFP at the disaggregated district level. Rosegrant and Evenson (1995) have used the district level data to study TFP at all-India level but they have not analysed TFP for the crop sector of different districts of Bihar. Secondly, their study covered Post-Green Revolution period up to 1987 whereas the serious concerns of sustainability have emerged during the late 1980s and early 1990s. This study is an attempt to analyse changes in TFP at the district level in the irrigated agriculture in Bihar the most recent period.

Objectives

1. To measure the district-wise total factor productivity (TFP) indices of the crop sector in an irrigated agro-ecosystem.
2. To examine the changes in TFP of the crop sector and to identify the factors affecting the same.

Methods and Data

The increased use of inputs, to a certain extent, allows the agricultural sector to move along the production surface. The use of modern inputs may also induce and upward shift in the production function to the extent that a technological change is embodied in them. TFP measures the amount of increase in the total output, which is accounted for by increases in the total inputs. It serves as an excellent indicator of the performance of any production system and sustainability of the growth process. It overcomes the limitations of partial input productivity measures as well as partial output productivity especially when the production of one activity affects the production of other activities. This TFP concept, which implies an index of output per unit of total factor inputs, measures the shifts in output properly, holding all other inputs constant. TFP measures the amount of increase in the total output that is not accounted for by increases in the total inputs. TFP is influenced by changes in technology, institutional reform, infrastructure development, human resource development and other factors. The crop-related technology changes are often embodied in the seed adoption by the farmer that can be divided into two components: the "quality" and the "quantity". The former represents productivity improvement and cost reduction, while the latter is the extent of area on which the farmer adopts the technology. The "quality" reflects the research output that is determined by investment in research and is an exogenous variable in explaining TFP. The "quantity" of technology is linked to its adoption and is affected by the extension, literacy, infrastructural development, as well as the on-farm and off-farm characteristics. The accounting approach is popular because it is simple to calculate and requires no econometric estimation and, therefore, the data requirement is minimal. The use of TFP indices gained prominence since Diewert (1976, 1978) proved that Theil-Tornquist discrete approximation to the Divisia index is consistent in aggregation and superlative to a linear homogeneous trans logarithmic production function. Thus, the Divisia-Tornqvist index is used in the present study for computing the total output, total input and TFP for the crop sector by district and agro-eco region. The total output, total input, and TFP indices are computed as :

Total output index (TOI)

$$TOI_t/TOI_{t-1} = \Pi_j (Q_{jt}/Q_{jt-1})^{(R_{jt} + R_{jt-1})1/2}$$

Total Input Index (TII)

$$TII_t/TII_{t-1} = \Pi_i (X_{it}/X_{it-1})^{(S_{it} + S_{it-1})1/2}$$

Where,

R_{jt} is the share of output j in total revenue,
Q_{jt} is output j (j =1) for main product and j = 2 for by - product),
S_{it} is the share of input i in total input cost,
X_{it} is quantity of input i and P_{it} is price of input i, all in period t.

For the productivity measurement over a long period of time, chaining indexes for successive time periods is preferable. With Chain-linking, an index is calculated for two successive period t and t-1, over the whole period t_0 to T, (sample from time t = 0 to t = T) and the separate indexes are then multiplied together :

TOI (t) = TOI(1).TOI(2) .... TOI (t-1).

TII(t) = TII (1), TII (2) ....TII (t-1)

Total factor productivity index (TFP)

$TFP_t = (TOI_t/TII_t)$

Chain-liking index takes into account the changes in relative values/costs throughout the period of the study. This procedure has the advantage that no single period plays a dominant role in determining share, weights and biases which are likely to be reduced. The above equations provide the indices of total output, total input, and TFP indices for the specified period 't'.

The following crops are included in the output index. These crops account for more than 90 per cent of the gross cropped area (GCA) :

Paddy, Wheat, Maize, Barley, Murua, Small millets, Mung, Pigeon-pea, Chickpea, Lentil, Khesari, Pea, Rapeseed and Mustard, Sugarcane, Tobacco, Mesta and Potato.

Ten inputs (human labour, bullock labour, machine labour, Farm Yard Manure (FYM), nitrogen, phosphate, and potassium fertilizers, irrigation, plant protection and land) are included.

Labour input is measured as the total number of male and female workers employed in agriculture at the end of each year, land is measured as gross cropped area, rental value of land is taken as the cost of land, machine labour input as the number of tractors, bullock input as the number of adult bullocks and FYM input as the number of livestock. The data on these inputs are collected by district. Cost share of each input is computed by dividing individual input cost by the total production cost for all crops at the state level. These input cost shares are superimposed on districts. Input cost share and input quantity data for each district are used for computing the input index. The farm harvest price and production of crops at district level are used to compute the output index. The TFP index is computed by dividing the output index by the input index for each of the districts.

Findings and Discussion

The input index, out put index and TFP were worked out which are presented in Table 13.1.

It may be observed from the Table 13.1 that the input index (1981-96) rose in all the district except Nawada district in South Bihar plain. The comparatively high grown in input index was observed in Darshanya district and low in Muzaffarpur district.

Out of 37 districts, 10 districts could achieve out put index growth of more than 2 per cent, however, districts of Gopalganj, West Champaran, Katihar and Aurangabadd experienced stagnation in out put growth. There were only two districts (Sitamarhi and Nawada) which experienced negative output growth.

Table 13.1 further revealed that the magnitude of TFP growth varied from -1.52 per cent in Sitamarhi district to 4.22 per cent in Saran district. Out of 37 districts, 10 districts observed stagnant-TFP growth. It is worth mentioning that about 50 per cent of districts of North Bihar experienced stagnation in TFP growth.

An analysis of these growths for two periods i.e. (1981-92 and 1990-96) revealed that there was relatively higher growth in input, output and TFP indices in 1980s as compared to 1990s. The higher growth specially in TFP implied higher contribution

TABLE 13.1
Annual Growth (per cent) in Input Use, Output, and TFP by Districts in Bihar (1981-96)

Districts	*Input*	*Output*	*TFP*
North Bihar West Plain			
Sitamarhi	0.34	-1.18	-1.52
Gopalganj	0.84	0.00	0.00
West Champaran	0.81	0.00	0.00
East Champaran	0.72	1.12	0.00
Muzaffarpur	0.00	0.00	0.00
Madhubani	1.49	1.30	0.00
Vaishali	0.51	1.36	0.85
Siwan	1.02	2.05	1.04
Samastipur	1.00	2.27	1.27
Darbhanga	1.80	4.67	2.87
Saran	1.12	5.33	4.22
North East Plain			
Saharsa	1.04	1.55	0.00
Katihar	0.52	0.00	0.00
Begusarai	1.27	2.38	1.10
Purnia	1.16	2.60	1.44
Madhepura	0.72	2.34	1.62
South Bihar Plain			
Bhojpur	0.97	1.08	0.00
Aurangabad	0.39	0.00	0.00
Gaya	1.64	2.05	0.00
Nalanda	0.93	2.38	1.44
Patna	0.14	1.71	1.56
Nawada	-3.80	-2.14	1.65
Rohtas	0.40	2.96	2.55

of technical change to output growth. The decline in TFP indices was observed in North West Alluvial plain (Zone-I) and North East alluvial plains (Zone-II) during 1990s (Table 13.2). The results present a gloomy picture of the agricultural growth in

TABLE 13.2

Annual Growth in Input Use, Output and TFP of the Crop Sector by Agro-eco Regions During 1981-90 and 1990-96 in Bihar Plains

Agro-Eco Region/ Sub Region	*Input*		*Output*		*TFP*		*Per cent Share of TFP in output growth*	
	I	*II*	*I*	*II*	*I*	*II*	*I*	*II*
North West Alluvial	1.41	0.44	2.23	1.11	0.82	0.67	36.71	60.24
North East Alluvial	1.51	0.43	2.40	-0.71	0.90	-1.14	37.35	neg.
South Alluvial Plains	1.37	-0.63	2.08	0.67	0.71	1.30	34.31	194.08

1990s. The sharp decelerating growth in the crop sector has been a major cause of concern and there is an urgent need to adequately address the issues of sustainability and technical change in the agricultural sector reforms.

Conclusion

During the green revolution era, a greater investment on Research and Development was made in irrigated agriculture. The promotion of HYV seeds fertilizer-irrigation technology had a high pay off well and rapid strides of progress have been made in food production. However, in recent years Bihar has been confrouted with diminishing returns to technological change because a large number of districts have been facing the stagnation in TFP growth. If the sustainability issue of the crop sector in Bihar is not properly addressed it may adversely affect the economic growth and household food security.

REFERENCES

Diewert, W.E. (1976), "Exact and Superlative Index Numbers", *Journal of Econometrics*, 4 : 115-145.

Diewert, W.E. (1978), "Superlative Index Numbers and Consistency in Aggregation", *Econometrica*, 46 : 883-900.

Kumar, Praduman and Mruthyunjaya (1992), "Measurement and Analysis of Total Factor Productivity Growth in Wheat", *Ind. Jr. Agric. Econ.* 47 (3): 451-458.

Kumar, Praduman and Mark W. Roserant (1994), "Productivity and Sources of Growth for Rice in India, *Economic and Political Weekly,* 29 (52) : A 182-A188.

Kumar, Praduman, P.K. Joshi, C. Johansen and M. Asokan (1998)", Sustainability of Rice-wheat Based Cropping System in India", *Economic and Political Weekly,* 33(35), September 26, A-152 to A-158.

Pingali, P.L.M., Hossain and R.V. Gerpacio (1997), Asian Rice Bowl—The Returning Crisis? *CAB International,* IRRI, Manila.

Singh, R.K.P. (2004), Agricultural Development in Bihar : Problem and Prospect *Agricultural Situations in India,* New Delhi.

CHAPTER

14

Rice Production Trend in Bihar during Last Two Decades : A Regional Analysis

D.K. SINHA, A.K. CHOUDHARY AND R.K.P. SINGH

INTRODUCTION

Rice has been the main food crop of Bihar. More than three-fourth's people of the state subsist on rice production and marketing. Bihar ranks 5th with respect to rice area and 6th in production among major states of the country but ranks 11th in rice productivity. There was almost stagnant rice productivity during seventies since per hectare productivity increased from 947 kg. in 1971 to 961 kg. in 1977-78. Rice productivity could cross 1000 kg. mark in 1980-81.

Despite the slow growth in rice production it contributes about 16 per cent to state agricultural gross domestic product and about one-fourth to income on farming households (Singh and Paris, 2003). Rice constitutes 46.46 per cent of gross cropped area and 50.62 per cent of area covered by food grain crops in Bihar. Rice is still most important crop and contributes to 44.94 per cent of total foodgrain production and generates annual human labour employment days of about 40 million man-days in Bihar.

Among different seasons rice, *Aghani* rice accounted for nearly 80 per cent of total rice area whereas *Bhadai* rice occupied as much as 16.6 per cent leaving rest as 3.4 per cent under *Garma* rice. Keeping in view the importance of rice in state economy the present analysis has been undertaken to examine the growth in area, production and productivity of different seasons rice in Bihar and an effort has also been made to assess the instability in rice production in different seasons.

Methodology

The study is based on secondary data which were obtained from various Government publications and reports. Tabular analyses were done in order to arrive at the trends in area, production and productivity of rice crop. The growth performance and instability in area, production and productivity were analysed under three study periods viz., Period I (1981-82 to 1990-91), Period II (1991-92 to 2000-01) and Period III (1981-82 to 2000-01).

The equation of exponential curve was used to measure the growth in area, production and productivity of the crop and the coefficient of variation was worked out to measure in their instability.

Rice Production Technology

Area under irrigated rice increased from 38.5 per cent in 1990-91 to 41.8 per cent in 2000-01 however the increase was more pronounced in South Bihar Plains. Area under irrigated rice increased in all the agro-climatic zones, except zone III B, mainly due to poor maintenance of Sone canal system which accounts for 50 per cent of irrigated area in this particular zone.

Breeding of improved rice varieties played a significant role in increasing rice production. Area under improved rice varieties increased from 29.6 per cent in 1980-81 to 55 per cent per cent in 2000-01, however, about 94.0 rice area is covered by improved varieties in zone IIIB. Adoption of improved varieties could not cross the level of 40 per cent in other three agro climatic zones of Bihar. In contrary to this finding it has been reported that about 70 per cent of rice seeds are either home grown or purchased/exchanged from fellow farmers (Singh and Paris 2000). However, about 15.8 per cent of *Kharif* rice area was covered by certified seeds in Bihar (NSSO, 2000). These findings clearly indicate that the farmers of Bihar are using degenerated rice seeds since there is week infrastructure for rice seed production and distribution in the state.

Chemical fertiliser is one of the critical inputs for high rice productivity. In Bihar, Farmers started using chemical fertiliser in rice production in early eighties. Per hectare use of chemical fertiliser in rice production increased from 5.52 kg. in 1980-81 to 22.42 kg. in 1990-91 which further increased to 76.5 kg. in 2000-01, however, a larger increase in fertiliser use was noticed during 1990-91 to 2000-01. Moreover, no any chemical fertiliser was used in about 5 per cent of rice area in Bihar (NSSO, 2000).

Growth Performance

In order to ascertain the growth performance of different seasons rice in Bihar, the compound growth rates of area, production and productivity of the crop grown in different agro-climatic zones of the state were worked out and analysed to get an idea about the trend in rice production in Bihar.

The overall annual compound growth rate of area, production and productivity of total rice were recorded as 0.02, 2.89 and 2.87 per cent, respectively during last two decades (1981-82 to 2000-01). It may be asserted from the above figure that the area under rice remained almost stagnant but the production and productivity of the crop got obvious impetus in its growth (Table 14.1). Further examination of data revealed that the growth rate in area under rice was found to be larger (1.36%) during decade of eighties than that of only 1.13 per cent during nineties. A similar trend was observed in case of both production and productivity. Hence, it may be said that area growth rate of rice has almost been stagnant during the period under study.

TABLE 14.1
Compound Growth Rate of Area, Production and Productivity of Rice

	Aghani	*Bhadai*	*Garma*	*Total*
Period : 1981-82 to 1990-91				
Area	0.98	3.26	6.05	1.36
Production	6.14	7.71	8.23	6.38
Productivity	5.16	4.44	2.19	5.02
Period : 1991-92 to 2000-01				
Area	0.86	1.77	5.39	1.13
Production	5.39	7.92	7.13	5.78
Productivity	4.53	6.15	1.73	4.65
Period : 1981-82 to 2000-01				
Area	-0.33	1.14	5.74	0.02
Production	2.56	3.73	9.36	2.89
Productivity	2.88	2.59	3.62	2.87

Season-wise analysis of rice crop pointed out that the area under *Aghani* rice was found to have negative growth rate (-0.33%), however, production and productivity of this season crop recorded positive growth during period under study. The reason for negative growth in area was mainly due to decline in area of rice in Zone I and Zone IIIA. The annual growth rate in area, production and productivity of *Bhadai* and *Garma* were positive and higher than *Aghani* rice during the study period.

Season-wise analysis also revealed that the annual growth rate in area, production and productivity of *Aghani* and *Garma* rice declined during nineties as compared to that of eighties except for *Bhadai* rice which consisted of higher growth rates in production and productivity during nineties. It was mainly due to the fact that the traditional ricce was cultivated in Bhadai season in eighties but modern rice varieties were introduced in the season in nineties which resulted higher production and productivity of rice in the season. The annual compound growth rate in area under *Garma* rice was recorded as comparatively higher in all three periods under study as compared to other seasons rice viz., *Aghani* and *Bhadai* in Bihar. Moreover, area under summer rice accounts for only 3.4 per cent of total rice.

Zone-wise Analysis

Analysis of growth rates of different seasons rice in four specified zones indicated that, in zone I, *Aghani* rice showed negative compound growth rates in its area during all three periods (I, II and III) under study which suggests conspicuous decline in *Aghani* rice area. In spite of decline in area, *Aghani* rice could register comparatively larger growth rates in production (6.76%) and productivity (7.13%) during nineties as compared to only 4.78 and 4.94 per cent, respectively during eighties (Table 14.2). For *Bhadai* rice, the growth rates of area and production were also found to be positive (1.93 and 7.95 %) during nineties but comparatively lower than the corresponding growth rates (4.24 and 8.36%) during eighties. Moreover the productivity growth rate has improved during nineties over the period of eighties. In case of *Garma* rice, the growth rates of productivity was estimated as negative (-0.56%), however, the growth in area (1.78 %) and production (1.21%) were found to be positive during period under study. The increase in the production of *Garma* rice might probably be due to the increase in area only.

Analysis of growth in different seasons rice in zone II indicated that growth rates of area production and productivity of *Aghani* and Bahadai rice experienced positive though larger values during nineties as compared to eighties except the productivity of *Bhadai* rice. In contrast to the above trend, *Garma* rice could register comparatively lower growth rates during nineties as compared to eighties.

It may be pointed out that in Zone IIIA, the compound growth rate of area, production and productivity of *Aghani* rice were calculated as posittive though having lower values during nineties over eighties except the area which showed comparatively high growth values during the period as above. It was further examined through the table that area and production of both *Bhadai* and *Garma* rice showed negative growth rates during nineties and so the case was observed

Table 14.2
Compound Growth Rate of Area, Production and Productivity of Rice

(1981-82 to 1990-91)

	Zone I				Zone II				Zone IIIA				Zone IIIB			
	Aghani	*Bhadai*	*Garma*	*Total*	*Aghani*	*Bhadai*	*Garma*	*Total*	*Aghani*	*Bhadai*	*Garma*	*Total*	*Aghani*	*Bhadai*	*Garma*	*Total*
(1)	(2)	(3)	(4)	(5)	(6)	(7)	(8)	(9)	(10)	(11)	(12)	(13)	(14)	(15)	(16)	(17)
Area	-0.16	4.24	-0.38	0.85	0.18	1.09	13.45	1.04	1.12	2.77	-11.77	1.06	2.13	3.27	-14.42	2.06
Production	4.78	8.36	0.35	5.62	4.54	5.49	17.63	5.68	8.29	7.96	-6.87	8.18	7.15	7.93	-15.02	7.04
Productivity	4.94	4.11	0.73	4.77	3.75	8.60	4.18	4.64	7.17	5.19	4.90	7.12	5.02	4.66	-0.60	4.98

(1991-92 to 2000-01)

	Zone I				Zone II				Zone IIIA				Zone IIIB			
	Aghani	*Bhadai*	*Garma*	*Total*	*Aghani*	*Bhadai*	*Garma*	*Total*	*Aghani*	*Bhadai*	*Garma*	*Total*	*Aghani*	*Bhadai*	*Garma*	*Total*
Area	-0.37	1.93	1.78	0.34	1.56	1.52	6.68	2.11	1.78	-16.40	-1.79	1.64	1.33	0.12	-7.14	1.32
Production	6.76	7.95	1.21	6.97	7.36	7.70	8.84	7.66	5.66	-5.75	-3.76	5.55	4.30	5.02	-6.90	4.29
Productivity	7.13	6.02	-0.56	6.63	5.80	6.18	2.16	5.55	3.89	10.65	1.96	3.91	2.96	4.89	0.24	2.97

TABLE 14.2 (Contd.)

(1981-82 to 2000-01)

	Zone I				*Zone II*				*Zone IIIA*				*Zone IIIB*			
	Aghani	*Bhadai*	*Garma*	*Total*	*Aghani*	*Bhadai*	*Garma*	*Total*	*Aghani*	*Bhadai*	*Garma*	*Total*	*Aghani*	*Bhadai*	*Garma*	*Total*
(1)	(2)	(3)	(4)	(5)	(6)	(7)	(8)	(9)	(10)	(11)	(12)	(13)	(14)	(15)	(16)	(17)
Area	-1.31	1.89	1.84	-0.44	0.34	-0.62	9.46	0.79	-0.57	-7.12	-9.42	-0.66	0.34	0.41	-12.87	0.30
Production	1.34	4.13	4.52	2.14	2.88	2.41	13.81	3.97	1.17	-3.20	-6.37	1.10	3.53	3.18	-11.57	3.48
Productivity	2.65	2.24	2.68	2.58	2.62	1.82	4.36	3.18	1.74	3.92	3.05	1.76	3.20	2.77	1.30	3.18

during overall period (1981-82 to 2000-01). Unlike the above facts, the growth rates of productivity of *Bhadai* and *Garama* rice happened to be positive though revealing larger value for *Bhadai* rice (10.65%) than *Garma* rice (1.96%) during nineties.

It may be extracted from the table that in Zone IIIB, the compound growth rates of area, production and productivity of *Aghani* rice were found to be positive though having lower growth rates during nineties over eighties. Further *Bhadai* rice could reveal similar trend except the productivity which showed marginal increase in growth during the period as mentioned above. In case of *Garma* rice, growth rates of area, production and productivity during both eighties and nineties were estimated to be negative except for productivity which showed a marginal positive value.

Instability Analysis

We tried to examine the impact of modern rice technologies on instability in area, production and productivity of rice grown in Bihar. It has been observed that the production of rice was highly instable in Bihar as compared to area and productivity as it was evident by higher coefficient of variation in production (46.6%) as compared to 5.9 per cent (area) and 19.7 per cent (Productivity). The lower co-efficient of rice area was mainly due to stagnant behaviour rice area.

Among different seasons rice, *Garma* rice showed comparatively high instability in area (33.4%) as compared to *Aghani* and *Bhadai* rice throughout the period under study (Table 14.3). But *Aghani* rice registered comparatively high instability in production during the period under study due to higher increase in its productivity as compared to *Bhadai* and *Garma* rice. *Aghani* rice could also establish more stability in productivity than that of *Bhadai* and *Garma* rice, particularly, during the period under study (1981-82 to 2000-01).

Period-wise analysis indicated that for the state as a whole, the area under total rice could get stabilised in the Period II as compared to period I as has been indicated by the declining coefficient of variation as having only 4.6 per cent during nineties and 6.5 per cent during the period of eighties. In case of production, the instability was found to be more in Period II

TABLE 14.3
Coefficient of Variation (CV) of Area, Production and Productivity of Rice

	Aghani	*Bhadai*	*Garma*	*Total*
	Period : 1981-82 to 1990-91			
Area	6.7	10.2	19.0	6.5
Production	41.2	31.4	35.0	29.1
Productivity	18.2	20.1	17.0	13.5
	Period : 1991-92 to 2000-01			
Area	4.4	6.2	16.4	4.6
Production	55.0	32.3	39.0	45.1
Productivity	17.1	19.8	9.58	13.8
	Period : 1981-82 to 2000-01			
Area	6.8	8.8	33.4	5.9
Production	72.4	49.7	42.9	46.6
Productivity	20.6	21.4	24.2	19.7

(45.1%) as compared to period I (29.1 per cent). But the instability in rice productivity was identical in both periods i.e. eighties and nineties.

So far as the *Aghani, Bhadai* and *Garma* rice are concerned, the coefficient of variation of area and yield in these seasons were found as comparatively low in period II than that of period I, indicating more stable position in area and production in period II. Contrary to this, in case of production of different seasons rice viz., *Aghani, Bhadai* and *Garma,* the coefficient of variations were calculated to be higher in period II as compared to period I, indicating thereby more instable production in period II.

Zone-wise Analysis

Perusal of Table 14.4 indicated that in zone I, the coefficients of variation of area and production of different seasons rice viz., *Aghani, Bhadai* and *Garma* were estimated to be declining in period II as compared to period I, revealing

TABLE 14.4
Coefficient of Variation (CV) of Area, Production and Productivity of Rice

(1981-82 to 1990-91)

	Zone I				*Zone II*				*Zone IIIA*				*Zone IIIB*			
	Aghani	*Bhadai*	*Garma*	*Total*	*Aghani*	*Bhadai*	*Garma*	*Total*	*Aghani*	*Bhadai*	*Garma*	*Total*	*Aghani*	*Bhadai*	*Garma*	*Total*
(1)	(2)	(3)	(4)	(5)	(6)	(7)	(8)	(9)	(10)	(11)	(12)	(13)	(14)	(15)	(16)	(17)
Area	4.7	13.2	15.5	4.5	9.8	8.9	42.6	7.4	8.0	20.3	39.0	7.9	11.2	18.1	40.0	11.0
Production	21.8	22.2	24.3	24.7	21.0	21.4	21.7	27.0	22.8	28.1	28.4	27.8	30.1	31.0	56.0	21.7
Productivity	19.5	19.6	21.8	13.6	17.3	170.4	27.3	80.9	24.7	25.8	34.5	23.5	17.8	21.9	30.5	17.3

(1991-92 to 2000-01)

	Zone I				*Zone II*				*Zone IIIA*				*Zone IIIB*			
	Aghani	*Bhadai*	*Garma*	*Total*	*Aghani*	*Bhadai*	*Garma*	*Total*	*Aghani*	*Bhadai*	*Garma*	*Total*	*Aghani*	*Bhadai*	*Garma*	*Total*
Area	4.5	6.6	12.6	3.4	7.2	8.4	19.8	7.8	8.9	52.1	37.3	8.5	6.2	41.0	35.3	6.2
Production	19.8	19.4	16.8	16.8	23.5	24.0	24.3	24.4	25.2	25.0	22.8	23.1	22.6	26.7	31.7	14.5
Productivity	23.7	20.4	6.3	13.21	21.3	22.9	11.8	14.5	18.1	49.4	13.4	19.0	13.8	24.7	29.9	15.5

(1981-82 to 2000-01)

	Zone I				*Zone II*				*Zone IIIA*				*Zone IIIB*			
	Aghani	*Bhadai*	*Garma*	*Total*	*Aghani*	*Bhadai*	*Garma*	*Total*	*Aghani*	*Bhadai*	*Garma*	*Total*	*Aghani*	*Bhadai*	*Garma*	*Total*
(1)	*(2)*	*(3)*	*(4)*	*(5)*	*(6)*	*(7)*	*(8)*	*(9)*	*(10)*	*(11)*	*(12)*	*(13)*	*(14)*	*(15)*	*(16)*	*(17)*
Area	9.6	12.2	17.5	5.62	8.4	10.7	49.0	7.9	10.4	43.3	64.3	10.4	8.9	31.6	76.3	8.8
Production	22.1	21.5	23.7	23.9	22.2	22.1	28.3	27.7	25.9	29.3	25.7	25.9	53.1	30.7	67.3	32.8
Productivity	23.2	20.8	21.5	17.2	22.0	150.1	28.8	55.1	21.1	46.2	27.7	23.6	21.1	25.8	30.5	19.5

comparatively more stability in area and production of these seasons rice in period II. But in case of productivity, *Aghani* and *Garma* rice showed comparatively more instability in period II except *Garma* rice which experienced more stability in period II. In Zone II, similar to that of Zone I, the area under all reasons rice viz., *Aghani, Bhadai* and *Garma* could establish more stability during nineties as compared to eighties but the production of these types of rice was obviously more instable during nineties. Like variation in area, the productivity of *Bhadai* and *Garma* rice could observe more stability during nineties with that of eighties except *Aghani* rice.

Further examination of the table described the fact that in both Zone III A and Zone IIIB, the area under *Bhadai* rice was highly instable during nineties as has been explained by larger magnitude of coefficient of variation having 52.1 per cent (Zone IIIA) and 41.0 per cent (Zone IIIB) during nineties as compared to only 20.3 and 18.1 per cent, respectively during eighties. The reason for this may probably be due to putting of larger area under *Bhadai* rice. The productivity of *Bhadai* rice repeated the same trend like area during the same period study. In both regions, in respect of area, production and productivity, *Garma* rice stressed comparatively more stability during period II than that of period I. It was further stated that Zone IIIB, *Aghani* rice clearly gained more stability in area, production and productivity during nineties but unlike this, Zone IIIA registered comparatively a larger instability in area and production of *Aghani* rice during nineties as compared to eighties.

Conclusions

It may be concluded that there has been positive growth in area, production and productivity of rice during the period under study but a deceleration in these growth rates has been observed during nineties. It has also been observed that the rice crop has attained more stability in its area and productivity during nineties as compared to eighties. Area under Agahani and *Bhadai* rice observed mixed trend but there has been deceleration in their growth in all the zones under study. However, productivity of these seasons crop registered growth in all the Zones under study, mainly due to adoption of modern rice production technologies. Performance of summer rice with respect to area, production and productivity has not been uniform in all the zones under study. Its performance has been unsatisfactory in Zone I and Zone IIIB, mainly due to poor maintenance of canal system in these zones.

It may further be concluded that the production and productivity of various seasons rice crop has got stabilised in Bihar during nineties because adoption level of rice production technologies seems to be getting matured during nineties.

References

Kumar, P. and Mittal, S. (2003), "Productivity and Supply of Foodgrains in India", Towards A Food Secure India-Issues and Policies (ed. Mahendra Dev, Khanna, K.P. and Ramchandran, N., Published by Institute for Human Development, New Delhi, pp. 34-58.

Shankar, T. (2003), "A Study on Land Utilisation in Bihar. A Regional Analysis", (unpublished thesis), Deptt. of Agril. Economics, RAU, Pusa, Samastipur, pp. 51-54.

Singh, R.K.P. and Paris T.R. (2003), Draft Report on Impact of Labour Migration on Rice Production System and Gender Role, IRRI-RAU sponsored Project, pp. 28-30.

———, (2000), *Sarvekshan*, Vol. XXIV (1), July-September, NSSO, Ministry of Statistics and Programme Implementation, Govt. of India, pp. 5-18/185-90.

———, Reports of the Commission for Agril. Costs and Prices, Directorate of Econ. and Statistics, Ministry of Agriculture, Govt. of India, New Delhi (Various Issues).

CHAPTER

15

Trends in Growth of Pulse Production : An Analytical Study of Tal Region of Bihar

SHAMBHU DEO MISHRA AND MD. MASOOD ALAM

BACKGROUND

India is the largest producer of pulses in the world, both in quantity and quality. The important pulses which are grown are gram, lentil, pigeon pea, green gram, black gram, pea, cow pea and horse gram. The total areas under pulse crops are around 20 per cent of the total foodgrains areas. The production has been around 14 million tonnes. Pulses are grown during both the rabi and kharif seasons. The kharif pulses, namely, arhar, moong, urad, cow pea and bean account for 44.39 per cent of the area and 38 per cent of production. The rabi pulses; namely, gram, lentil and pea, account for 54 per cent of the area and 61 per cent of the total production of the country. In terms of yield, rabi pulses are far more superior than the kharif pulses. The yield rate of rabi pulses was 691 kg./ha during the triennium ended 1995-96 as compared to 465 kg./ha in case of kharif pulses.

Pulses are grown in almost all states of the country. But Madhya Pradesh accounts for the highest area and production of pulses. The other important pulses growing states are Rajasthan, Uttar Pradesh and Maharashtra. These states have nearly 60 per cent of the total area under pulses and 68.5 per cent of the country's total pulses production. Other states are Andhra Pradesh, Bihar (about 6 per cent area and 7 per cent production), Haryana, Karnataka, Orissa, etc. Bihar ranks 6th in area and 5th in production of pulses.

India is predominantly a vegetarian country and mainly dependent for protein requirement on pulses. Pulses are the chief source of protein. The mixed diet of cereal and pulses is the common practice in Indian dietary as *dal-roti* and *dal-bhat*. It is also a good source of calcium, vitamins, etc. But e share of pulses in the overall food grains basket has declined from 16.5 per cent in 1950-51 to 7.1 per cent in 1995-96. As a result, the average protein content in the Indian diet has been going down with the decline in the consumption of pulses from 69 gms. per capita per day in 1961 to 36.5 gms. in early nineties as against the minimum required protein diet of 47 gms. as recommended by the Indian Council of Medical Research. In animal feed pulses are also used as concentrates and mixed with green fodder for maintaining a balanced diet especially for milk production. Pulses are leguminous crops having fixed atmospheric nitrogen in the soil and increase the status of soil fertility. It has been estimated that around 40 kg. nitrogen is fixed into the soil for the succeeding crop.

Adoption of new technology is now recognised as a major source of growth in agriculture. It has, however, been slow in the case of pulses production, compared to competing superior cereals, particularly, wheat, maize, paddy and other cereals. Pulses are grown under poor technology base, rainfed condition and improper infrastructural support. On account of these the yield rate of pulses is low and the growth of pulses crop-plants is also very slow. The farmer's approach in growing pulse crop is to some extent reflected by low value status, poor habitat and low level of adoption and consumption. But the attitude towards pulses cultivation is now changing. The overall scenario indicates that farmers' decisions in growing of pulses and superior cereals remain uncompromising.

However, pulse crops have assumed secondary status in the crop husbandry of the farmers despite several plus points. The per capita availability of pulses is going down day by day. This is largely due to decline in the area and production of pulse crops. It may be verified through several such studies undertaken by different institutions and persons. The findings of these studies indicate that major pulses have a declining trend in both area and productivity because of tough competition with cereals.

Pulses in Bihar

Bihar is one of the important pulse growing states in India contributing about 6.50 per cent to the country's pulses production. The area under pulse crops was reported to be 14.34 lakh hectares in 1995-96, constituting about 11.00 per cent to GCA of the state. The coverage of pulse area under irrigation was only 1.7 per cent (1993-94) which is much below the all India average of 11.2 per cent. The production has gone up to 13.50 lakh tonnes in 1995-96 over 7.08 lakh tonnes in 1969-70. This increase has indicated an increase in area and productivity of the state during the period. But the data relating to area, production and productivity of major pulses in the state during the period of 1989-96 reveal that the area under total pulses has remained nearly stagnant. However, it has shown a little bit declines from 15.30 lakh hectares to 14.34 lakh hectares in 1995-96.

Similarly the production had almost been stagnant which is evident from the data that it was nearly 13.78 lakh tonnes in 1988-89 and was 13.50 lakh tonnes in 1995-96. So far as the productivity of pulses is concerned there had been a positive growth during the period. It increased to 941 kg/ha in 1995-96 over 809 kg/ha in 1988-89. However, the increase was not stable but it recorded a full of fluctuating trend with a maximum of 956 kg/ha in 1994-95 to a minimum of 807 kg/ha in 1990-91. Thus, it may be perused that except productivity, the area and production of pulse crops in Bihar did not show any remarkable change during the period which has led to a deficient state in respect of its requirements. The total requirement of pulses in the state is estimated around 16.20 lakh tonnes, whereas, the figure touched only 13.50 lakh tonnes in 1995-96.

There are various reasons behind the above trend but it is simultaneously felt that the vast chunk of lands falling under *Tal* Area of the state is utilised for pulses production whereas the area is much more conducive and potential for rabi pulses. In Bihar, Mokama-Barahiya Tal Region prominently figures for pulses production. The region is like a saucer and extends from Fatuha (Patna district) in the west to Bhagalpur district in the east covering almost 130 kilometers in length. In rabi season, pulses are the major crops grown of this region as they occupy nearly 75 per cent of the total area.

Objectives

The broad objectives of the paper are to study the growth rate of area, production and yield of major pulses of the study area, (Mokama-Barahiya Tal Region of Bihar, to identify the constraints and to suggest the policy prescriptions.

Methodology

It is obvious that the universe of the study is Mokama-Barahiya Tal Region, falling under two separate administrative districts viz., Patna and Lakhisarai. To study the growth rate of area, production and yield of major pulses of the study area, expotential compound growth rate has been used with the help of exponential trend equation. For this, secondary data were collected from the Directorate of Statistics and Evaluation, Government of Bihar and the respective district and block agricultural offices. Further to identify the constraints the analysis is based on an empirical evidence drawn from a sample of 200 pulse growers. These sample are equally distributed in two administrative districts viz; of Patna and Lakhisarai of Tal region of Bihar. And at the last, some policy prescriptions are suggested, which have been noticed in course of field investgation.

Results and Discussion

The annual compound growth rate for gram in respect of area, production and productivity for the selected blocks, namely, Mokama, Barh, Lakhisarai and Barahiya of the Tal region have been worked out from 1991 to 2001 (Table 15.1).

TABLE 15.1
Annual Compound Growth Rates of Area, Production and Productivity of Gram under Selected Blocks of Tal Areas in Bihar (1991-2001)

Districts	*Patna*		*Lakhisarai*	
Blocks	*Mokama*	*Barh*	*Lakhisarai*	*Barahiya*
Area	-0.8003*	0.6962*	-0.0292*	0.0023*
Production	-0.6761*	0.2310 NS	-0.0334**	-0.0091**
Productivity	-0.2137 NS	0.1174 NS	-0.0041 NS	0.0065 NS

Notes : * Significant at 5 per cent level, ** Significant at 1 per cent level, NS – Non-significant.

The estimated growth for area was observed significantly declining over time in Mokama block (-0.8003 **) and Lakhisarai block (-0.0292*), whereas it increased significantly over time in Barh block (0.6952**) and Barahia block (0.0023*). The main reason for this increasing trend was high fertility status of the soil for gram under this area as confirmed by the farmers of the area concerned. The decreasing trends were observed in Mokama and Lakhisarai blocks during the same time due to the reason that this particular crop was destroyed by the unsocial elements of the area for the purpose of commercial sale at vegetative stages simultaneously due to poor law and order condition, which ultimately reduces the area of this crop in the study area.

The production growth rate for all the blocks except Barh block declined. But the sunbstantial declining trends were observed in Mokama block (-0.6761* per cent) and Lakhisarai (-0.0334* per cent). With regard to productivity of gram, a meagre decline was observed during the period in Mokama (-0.2137* per cent) and Lakhisarai (-0.0041 per cent NS), while increasing trends in respect of productivity were observed during the same period in Barh (0.1179 per cent NS) and Barahiya (0.0269 per cent NS). The increases in both production and productivity were mainly due to favourable agro-climatic conditions of the Tal area. Declining trends in both cases were observed due to damage of crops in different stages of production by the unsocial elements of the area. Complete lack of assured irrigation was one of the crucial factors for not determining the acreage of gram under the study area. Many respondent farmers reported that due to bad weather and other climatic factors at an interval of every two years, the yield of this crop became low which prompted the farmers of the sample area to shift their operated area from gram to other rabi pulse crops.

With regard to estimated annual compound growth rate of Lentil in respect of area, the Table 15.2 reveals that it has declining trends in almost all the selected blocks (except Barh block). The growth rates were observed negative for Mokama (-0.5760), Lakhisarai (-0.0378) and Barahia (-0.0349) over time. But this table also depicts that in Barh block a positive trend (0.0258) was observed during the same period. This marked decline in the area might be due to sharp decline in the acreage of the crop in the study area and had resulted in a negative growth rate as well, while Barh showed somewhat positive growth rate for the period because area of this crop rose over time. It was found that the level of irrigation was a crucial factor for decreasing acreage of the crop and non-availability of suitable inputs for this pulse crop was also noticed to be accountable for this situation.

It could be seen from the analysis of the above table that similar trend of production of this crop in all the selected blocks

Table 15.2
Block-wise Annual Compound Growth Rates of Area, Production and Productivity of Lentil in Tal areas of Bihar

Blocks	*Mokama*	*Barh*	*Lakhisarai*	*Barahia*
Area	-0.5760^{NS}	0.0258^{NS}	-0.0378**	-0.0349^{NS}
Production	-0.4449^{NS}	0.0706^{NS}	-0.0577**	-0.0530*
Productivity	-0.0231^{NS}	0.0032^{NS}	-0.0159**	-0.0216

Note : * Significant at 5 per cent level, ** Significant at 1 per cent level, NS - Non-significant.

prevailed. The production of lentil showed more declining trend as compared to area except in case of Mokama block. Barh block showed a positive trend (0.0706) which was greater than that of growth in area. In all the blocks except Barh block, marginal declining trend in productivity was observed whereas a marginal positive growth in case of Barh block during the period could be seen.

Hence, it may be concluded that production and productivity of this crop showed very meagre declining trends during the period. The production of this crop declined due to shrinkage of acreage of the crop, while the productivity of the crop showed negative trend. The probable reason for this might be irrigational facilities or other climatic factors of these areas. It was interesting to note that only Barh block showed positive trends for area, production and productivity during the period. The micro level investigation also suggests that favourable agro-climatic conditions for this crop in the block were most probably the reasons for positive trends.

The estimates of growth rates of pea crop in two blocks, namely, Mokama Barh, revealed from the Table 15.3 that the area growth rate for this crop in Mokama block showed a declining trend (-0.0379) as compound rate, whereas in Barh block, this registered a higher increasing trend (0.8220). However, the production and productivity of this crop in Mokama block also showed negative growth rates (-0.0184 and -0.0239) respectively, whereas in Barh block the trend could be seen as positive. But the rates of increase were comparatively lower in both the cases.

Constraints

Here an attempt has been made to identify the field level constraints which were being faced by the farmers in raising farm productivity. A standardised list of constraints like socio-economic, infrastructural, technological, environmental, situational and administrative have been prepared. These constraints are presented below in tabular form as perceived by the respondents.

The Table 15.4 indicates that the constraints faced by different size groups of farms differed. The table indicates that under socio-economic constraints; lack of knowledge about high

TABLE 15.3
Block-wise Annual Compound Growth Rates of Area, Production and Productivity of Pea under Tal Area in Bihar (1991-2001)

Blocks	*Mokama*	*Barh*	*Lakhisarai*	*Barahiya*
Area	-0.0379 NS	0.8220**	—	—
Production	-0.0184 NS	0.6755**	—	—
Productivity	-0.0239 NS	0.1207NS	—	—

Note: ** Significant at 1 per cent level, NS-Non-significant.

yielding varieties package the percentage response of which was highest at overall level (about 94.50%) was the main constraint. The farm size-wise analysis for it indicates that small farmers were highest in percentage (100%) and lowest being in case of medium category farms (88.50%). Besides, these constraints, 'high costs of pesticides' and 'lack of credit' reported at overall level prevailed prominently (64.0% and 62.50% respectively). Other constraints like high cost of labour was reported by the highest number of large farms (80%).

Again in case of infrastructural constraints, the table indicates that cent per cent farmers faced lack of assured irrigational facilities. Lack of sound market facilities was the another constraint as reported by the respondents at overall level (81%). The size group-wise percentage also varied between 86.0 per cent in case of small farms to 75.0 per cent for medium farms. Lack of good metallic roads was the another barrier, the percentage of which was calculated at 58.0 per cent on overall level.

The table further indicates the following technological impediments, like (i) lack of HYV seeds and disease resistance seeds, (ii) lack of soil testing facilities and, (iii) lack of agro-service centres. The percentages of the constraints at overall level were 87.0 per cent, 96.0 per cent and 85.50 per cent respectively for the above noted three constraints.

The table also reveals that the environmental constraints, like 'erratic rainfall' and 'lack of fast water discharge' were reported at overall level by 52.0 and 77.50 per cent respectively

TABLE 15.4

Constraints as Perceived by the Respondents

Constraints	*Small*	*Medium*	*Large*	*All*
A. Socio-Economic				
(a) High cost of pesticides	62.00	70.00	60.00	64.00
(b) High cost of labour	26.00	48.33	80.00	43.50
(c) Lack of credit	7.00	56.66	35.00	62.50
(d) Lack of knowledge about HYV package of pulses	100.00	88.33	90.00	94.50
B. Infrastructural				
(a) Lack of assured irrigation facilities	100.00	100.00	100.00	100.00
(b) Lack of Market	86.00	75.00	77.50	81.00
(c) Lack of good metallic road	57.00	55.00	67.50	58.50
C. Technological				
(a) Lack of HYV and disease registant seeds	93.0	85.00	75.00	87.00
(b) Lack of Soil testing facilities	100.00	91.66	92.50	96.00
(c) Lack of agro-service centres	94.00	81.66	70.00	85.50
D. Environmental and situational				
(a) Erratic rainfall	47.00	60.00	52.50	52.00
(b) Scarcity of labour during peak period	27.00	65.00	70.00	47.00
(c) Lack of fast water discharge facilities	84.00	63.33	82.50	77.50
(d) High incidence of pests and diseases	37.00	48.33	45.00	42.00
E. Administrative				
(a) Lack of involvement of experts/scientists	84.00	86.66	90.00	86.00
(b) Lack of extension backup	77.00	93.33	72.50	81.00
(c) Lack of proper training and demonstration facilities	91.00	88.33	92.50	90.50
(d) Poor law and order of the area	31.00	61.66	65.00	47.00

which strongly ensphered the pulse growers of the study area. Besides, the scarcity of labour during peak period of crop cultivation and the incidence of diseases and pests were also observed as onerous constraints perceived by the farmers, i.e., 47.0 and 42.0 per cent respectively.

The table also indicates that some administrative constraints, like lack of involvement of governmental experts and scientists also created problem in raising the pulse crops, the overall percentage of which was calculated at 86.0 per cent as reported by the growers. The percentage of these problems were found at 90 per cent and 84.0 per cent in case of large and small farms.

Lack of proper training and demonstrations in pulse crops were also major constraints perceived by the respondent farmers, the percentage of which overall level was at 90.50 per cent. Among the different categories of farms, more or less same picture was observed. Lack of extension services was also a main constraint as perceived by the growers at overall level (81%). Poor law and order situation in case of gram crop generated among the growers due to insecurity against damage by men and animals, looting of the crop at the pre mature and matured stages by the anti-social elements were also major constraints as perceived by the selected growers. These constraints were reported to have been faced by 47 per cent at overall level, but with regard to different farm-size groups, it was found highest among medium and large farms i.e., more than 60 per cent whereas in case of small farms the percentage was very less, i.e., about 30 per cent.

Thus, it may be concluded from the above analysis that constraints, like socio-economic, infrastructural, technological, environmental, situational and administrative were powerful barriers in the pulses production and these barriers hampered the profitable practices of crop cultivation in the selected areas. Therefore, it may be suggested that for remunerative production of the crops, proper measures for removing and minimising the above indicated constraints must be initiated by the governmental and non-governmental agencies.

CONCLUSION

It may, therefore, be concluded from the table that in Mokama Block growth rates of area, production and productivity of Pea declined because of a marginal shift in area under other rabi pulse crops. Similarly, production and productivity were also found declining, the reason for which has already been explained regarding both the crops of lentil and gram.

In nutshell, the growth rate analysis gesticulates us to reach the conclusion that all the selected pulse crops in the study area declined in respect of area and production except in Barh block. The productivities of the same crops showed declining trend at lower rates with regard to area and production because of several reasons as observed by the field level investigation during the period of survey and as also confirmed by the respondent farmers of the study area, which were enumerated under different causal heads, viz., socio-economic, infrastructural, technological, environmental and administrative factors. These factors were responsible for the declining trend in almost all the selected blocks except Barh block, where these problems prevailed in lower degrees in comparison to other selected blocks, the less prevalence of which were primarily responsible for increasing trends of growth for the selected pulse crops.

Suggestions

On the basis of the findings the following policy prescriptions are recommended :

1. The flow of rainwater in Tal Region is very fast. Water does not stay for long. But for good harvest, the field should remain under water for the entire season (upto September). It is, therefore, essential to check the rainwater on Mehna river at intervals so that the rain water could stay in the field. The sample farmers were found in favour of constructing Sluice Gates on Mehna river.
2. Once upon a time, "the gram of Mallick Kothi," was famous in the country—a very popular and major

pulse crop grown in the Tal region. But on account of continued attack of pests and insects on the crop, the area under gram has now been eroded. There is a popular saying in the area that "chana ka kira mazboot pahalwaan hota hai" (The insect of gram is a strong wrestler). Hence there is an urgent need to replicate the Integrated Pest Management Programme in pulses of Tal region.

3. The area under gram in the Tal region has also decreased due to crop loot, particularly gram pulse. Hence, effective steps to should be taken to improve the Law and Order situation in this area.
4. Demonstration and training facilities or backup were almost found absent in the area. Therefore, the restoration of these facilities is urgently needed so that pulse growers could be able to learn and also be encouraged to adopt the new technology.
5. There is absence of proper irrigational facilities in the area whereas during the rainy season the run-up of water is high. So if the water is harvested in pond or reservoir it will be certainly helpful to irrigate the pulse crops. In fact it has now become almost mandatory particularly when the HYV seeds and improved inputs are used.
6. Testing of soil in the region should be done at regular intervals so that proper usage of inputs could be made.
7. The infrastructural facilities, like, village roads, power, etc. should urgently be improved.

CHAPTER

16

Industrial Development in India : Reflections on Growth and Deceleration

NARENDRA PRASAD

INTRODUCTION

Industrialisation is process of transforming raw materials, with the help of capital and labour, into consumer goods, new capital goods to produce more consumer goods and social over head capital, which together with human resources can provide new services to the people. Industrialisation is generator of growth by raising income, by creating and widening employment opportunities and by raising capital formation. India launched its first plan in 1951, but this was only a collection of existing schemes. It was in the economy with the initiation of the Nehru-Mahalanobis strategy of industrial development. This strategy underlined the role of heavy industry and its development under the public sector with a view to establishing in the long run, a socialistic pattern of society. The progress of industrialisation during more than fifty years since 1951 has been a striking features of Indian economic development. The industrial growth has not been uniform since 1951. After a steady growth of about 8 per cent during the initial period from 1951 to 1965, there was a fluctuating trend since then. The cause of concern in recent years is the deceleration in the rate of growth of industrial production. It is to this question that is paper is addressed.

Pattern, Growth and Deceleration of Industrial Production in India since Independence

During the first plan no big effort was contemplated to industrialise the economy. The second plan, based on Mahalanobis model, emphasised the development of capital goods industries and basic industries. There occurred a noticeable acceleration in the annual compound growth rate of industrial production upto 1965 from 5.7 per cent in the first plan to 7.12 per cent in the second plan and further to 9.0 per cent in the third plan. The rate of growth of capital goods industries shotup from 9.8 per annum in the first plan to 12.1 per cent per annum in the second plan and again to 19.6 per cent in the third plan. The rate of growth of basic goods industries also registered a significant increase from 4.8 per annum in the first plan to 10.4 per cent in third plan. Indicates that the strong base for industrial development was laid during the period. The credit for this goes to the massive expansion of investment that took place in the public sector during the period. The public sector actual out lay on industry and minerals was 7.6 per cent in the first plan which went up to 22.1 per cent in the third plan. There was a sharp deceleration industrial growth during 1965-76 (4.1%). The period 1966 to 19786 was effectively the dark period for the Indian economy. This period encompassed a number of exogenous shocks: The devastating three year drought of 1955-68; the aftermath of increased defence expenditures resulting from the 1962 war with China and two wars with Pakistan and the oil prices shocks of 1973 etc. The annual compound growth rates in general index of industrial production went to 6.1 per cent in

1974-1979 but it came down –1.6 per cent in 1979-80. The following table depicts the annual compound growth rate of industrial production.

When we look at the index of industrial production (Table 16.1), it is seen that the best period was between 1960-65. In this period the annual average rate of growth was 9.0 per cent. There was not even a single year in this period when the growth rate was less than 8 per cent. The sharpest increase was in the capital goods industries, where the average annual rate of

TABLE 16.1
Annual Compound Growth Rates in Index Numbers of Industrial Production—1951-1980

Use based Classification	*1951 to 1955*	*1955 to 1960*	*1960 to 1965*	*1965 to 1976*	*1974 to 1979*	*1979*
(i) Basic goods	4.7	12.1	10.4	100.4	6.5 8.4	-0.5
(ii) Capital goods	9.8	13.1	19.6	2.6	5.7	-2.3
(iii) Intermediate goods	7.8	6.3	6.9	3.0	4.3	1.9
(iv) Consumer goods	4.8	4.4	4.9	3.4	5.5	-4.4
Consumer durable goods	—	—	—	6.2	6.8	5.6
Consumer non-durables goods	—	—	—	2.8	5.4	-6.1
(v) General Index	5.7	7.2	9.0	4.1	6.1	-1.6

Source : EPW, 1978 and Hand Book of Industrial Statistics, 1989.

growth was 19.6 per cent. The basic goods industries rose by 10.5 per cent during this period. The sharp downturn occurred between 1979-89, when the average growth rate of general index of industrial production turned out to be negative (-1.6 per cent) during the year. The most noticeable decline was in the capital goods industries (–2.3 %). Thus, undoubtedly the rate of growth of industrial production in 1979-80 has been much lower than what as experienced in the previous period.

In the eighties, industrial production has shown a strong increase. The index of industrial production with the base 1980-81 prices has shown a compound annual rate of growth between

Table 16.2

Rate of Growth of Industrial Production (used-based) During 1981-85 to 1990-91

	Base year 1980-81		
Use based Classification	*1981-85*	*1985-90*	*1990-91*
(i) Basic Goods	8.7	7.4	3.8
(ii) Capital Goods	6.2	14.8	17.4
(iii) Intermediate Goods	6.0	6.4	6.1
(iv) Consumer Goods	5.1	7.3	10.4
(v) (a) Durable	14.3	11.6	14.8
(b) No-Durable	3.8	6.4	9.4
General Index	6.4	8.5	8.3

Source : Complied from Hand Book of Industrial Statistics, Govt. of India, 1992.

1980-81 and 1988-89 of 7.7 per cent. The performance in the seventies when he overall industrial production grew only 4.2 per cent. The use-based classification of index of industrial production throws more light on the pattern of industrial growth. During the period 1980-81 to 188-89, basic goods industries grew at and annual rate of 8.3 per cent capital goods industries at 9.5 per cent and intermediate goods industries at 6.5 per cent. It is interesting to note that during a period of liberalised imports of capital goods, capital goods industries have shown a strong increase. They grew at 9.5 per cent per annum during the entire period of 1980-81 to 1988-89 and at 12.9% during the entire period of 1988-89. The consumer goods industries, as a whole, rose by 6.5 per cent per annum. The following table reveals the revised Index of industrial production from 1981-85 to 1990-91.

The above table shows that the rate of general index industrial growth was 6.4 per cent per annum during 1981-85, 8.5 per cent per annum during 1985-90 and 8.3 per cent annum during 1990-91. This is a marked upturn from growth rates of around 4 per cent achieved during the period of the sixties and the seventies.

But the year 1991 ushered in a new era in economic liberalisation. Labour liberalisation measures designed to affect

TABLE 16.3
Rate of Growth of Industrial Production during 1991-92 to 1999-2000

(*Per cent per annum*)

Used based Classification	*Base 1980-81= 100*			*Base 1984-94 = 100*	
	1991-92	*1992-97*	*1997-98*	*1998-99*	*1999-2000*
(i) Basic goods	6.5	6.8	6.9	1.6	5.3
(ii) Capital goods	-8.5	8.9	5.8	12.6	6.9
(iii) Intermediate goods	–2.1	8.5	8.0	6.1	8.8
(iv) Consumer goods	1.0	6.6	5.5	2.2	5.7
(a) Durables	–10.9	13.4	7.8	5.6	14.2
(b) Non-durables	4.0	4.8	4.8	1.2	3.2
General Index	0.6	7.4	6.7	9.1	6.6

Source : Handbook of Statistics, RBI 2000, Economics Survey (200-01).

the performance of the industrial sector. The following table presents the rate of growth of industrial production during 1991-92 to 1999-2000.

The above table shows that the industrial sector registered a dismal performance in 1991-2 with its rate of growth being just 0.6 per cent. The average annual rate of growth of the industrial sector in the eighth plan was 7.4 per cent annum. It slow down to 4.1 per cent in 1998-99 and again went up 6.6 per cent in 1999-2000. The worst affected sector was capital goods sector.

A brief look at the pattern and rate of growth of industrial production will provide clearly the lack of consistency in industrial growth.

The Table 16.4 presents the picture of the growth rate of industrial production upto 2001-02. In the fifties the average annual rate of growth of industrial production was 6.2 per cent. In the sixties while the first half had a very high growth rate, the second half showed a sharp decline. This deceleration in growth rate continued through the seventies. Thus over the fifteen year period 1966-80, the rate of industrial growth was at a modest

TABLE 16.4
Annual Growth Rate in the Index of Industrial Production

Period	General Index	Basic Industries	Capital Goods	Intermediate Goods	Consumer Goods
1951-55	6.7	30.9	—	5.8	3.4
1956-60	5.7	4.7	—	9.78	2.9
1961-65	9.0	10.5	19.7	7.2	5.0
1966-70	3.7	6.2	-1.4	4.00	4.0
1971-76	3.6	5.3	5.4	1.8	1.6
1976-80	4.8	5.1	5.2	—	4.9
1981-82-1985-86	7.3	8.4	7.1	6.3	6.7
1986-87-1990-91	8.4	7.4	15.8	5.5	6.6
1991-92-1995-96	6.1	6.5	6.0	6.1	6.0
1996-97-2000-01	5.7	4.2	7.7	7.1	5.5
1992-93-1996-97	7.4	6.8	8.9	8.5	6.6
1997-98-2001-02	5.1	4.1	4.7	5.8	5.5

Source : Handbook of Statistics on Indian Economy, 2001. RBI and Annual Report, 2001-01 RBI.

annual rate of 4 per cent. The growth rate picked up substantially in the decade of the eighties, when the average annual growth rate was 7.8 per cent. There was collapse of the industrial growth rate in 1991-92 and a small growth in 1992-93 (0.6% and 2.3% respectively) while the period 1992-93 to 1996-97, had an annual growth rate of 7.4 per cent, in the subsequent period the growth rate came down and the average for the next five years 1997-98 to 2001-02 was only 5.1 per cent. There is deceleration in all industries such as basic industries (4.1%) capital goods (4.7%). Intermediates goods 5.8 per cent and consumer gods 5.5 per cent during 1997-98 to 2001-02 in comparison to previous five years (1992-93-1996-97) 6.8 per cent, 8.9 per cent, 8.5 per cent and 5.6 per cent respectively. The recent slow down in industrial production has caused much concern.

Cause of Slow Down and Deceleration in the Industrial Production and its Remedies

The explanation that have been offered to explain the phenomenon of deceleration cover a wide spectrum. The deceleration in the industrial production is due to a number of structural and cyclical factors such as normal business and investment cycle, a lack of both domestic and external demand. Continuing high interest rates. Infrastructural bottlenecks in power and transport, lack of reforms in land and labour markets, internet adjustment lags resulting from industrial restructuring through merger and acquisitions, and delays in establishing appropriated institutional and regulatory framework in some key sectors.

There are many who locate the cause for deceleration in the periodic shocks that the economy had received in the form of war in 1965 and 1971, the oil crisis in 1973, and the draught in 1965 and 1966. According to them. It is these shocks which prevented the economy from gaining momentum and achieving a higher rate of industrial growth. There is another explanation offered by economics influenced largely by the Marxian analysis. These assert that the crisis in industrial growth is rooted in the path of development that India has adopted and that there is no way out unless the fundamental property relation and structure of income distribution are altered. To explain these explanations, we can grouped them into two broad categories—those that stress the supply constraints on growth and those that stress the demand constraints.

The explanation emphasing supply constraints basically argues that the growth rate of industrial production has been hampered primarily by the non-availability of critical inputs such as power, imported raw materials and agricultural raw materials. Distributed industrial relations can also a regarded as a constraint operating on the supply side. In the early phase of the development of the country, the question of demand constraint was never raised. However, in recent years, Fears have been expressed that the real constraint on industrial growth in India may be operating from demand side. Notwithstandingly, the supply and demand side constraints are the key factors responsible for the deceleration in industrial growth. In must be noted that supply availability is only a necessary but not a sufficient condition for industrial growth. In the case of demand constraints on the output of capital goods, import substitution does sound plausible as an explanations of the earlier growth and the later deceleration. But the demand constraints has a very limited role in explaining the behaviour of output of capital goods industries. The much accepted cause of the deceleration of industrial production is the decline in public investment.

So far the remedies are concerned, the new challenges posed by the fast changing world of industrial productions and industrial technology requires world of a much more dynamic governmental system which is predominantly concerned with promotion rather than regulation of industrial development. What we need today is a road map for the Indian industry. It must delineate the path, different industries must take to achieve productivity and efficiency level, comparable to the best in the world. We must have our priorities. We must know where we havé a distinct comparative advantage. The plan should address in relation to each major industry issues relating to technology up gradation, size and structure of firms and export potential. While industry- specific policies may be indicated, the focus must be on how to improve the functioning of individual enterprises to reach international standards.

To enhance the level of investment, all investment decisions should be based on future prospects, investors need to be assured of dynamism and efficiency in overall governance, for generating a general mood of optimism, it may be useful for the government to bring together in one place in the budget, the investment that will be made by the various departments and ministries. A consolidation of this can be called 'investment budget' and lastly there should be stability in the rates of taxation and tariff rates for the confidence of investors.

CHAPTER 17

Disturbing Trends in Sectoral Composition of India's National Income

REETA SINHA

As succinctly observed by National Income Committee (1951), "National Income Statistics provide a wide view of the country's entire economy, as well as of the various groups in the population who participate as producers and income receivers, and that, if available over a substantial period, they reveal clearly the basic changes in the country's economy in the past and suggest, if not fully reveal, trends for the future." This makes the study of national income and its sectoral composition important, because to quote the committee again, "If measures the volume of commodities and services turned out during a given period, counted without duplication."

The object of the present paper is to take note of the changing contours of sectoral composition of India's national income especially in post–1991 era and pinpoint the disturbing trends in the changing sectoral composition.

The growth literature, right down from Adam Smith to Noble Laureate Simon Kuznets, has charted out the precise sequence of steps an economy follows for its quest for development on the basis of ample empirical evidences. The development story begins with the primary sectory, the food sector in particular. Agriculture dominates the scene in the initial stage as survival is the basic requirement. But once the stomach is appeased, the consideration of well-being comes to the fore and industrial products enter into the orbit of demand. The surplus from agricultural sector serves to support the demand for industrial products and the story moves on to the second stage with the emergence of secondary sector, popularly known as industrial or manufacturing or commodity sector. The process of industrial production is more intricate than agriculacturing activity. Each new product is the result of a new invention and, human inguinity being limitless, there is literally no end to the maze of complexity that industrial processes might involve. Thus, as the development story moves on in the second stage, the industrial sector grows relative to agriculture through the manufacturing of ever-expanding brands of products.

As the story moves on to third and final stage of development, tertiary sector, known also as service sector, gets strengthened and agricultural sector comes down the ladder further. This sector covers a wide spectrum comprising within its fold trade, transport, storage, communications, banking, insurance, real estate and community, and personal services. Like industry, services too hold the potential for limitless diversity and the richer a nation the greater is the variation in the range of services its population enjoys.

This is the normal sectoral sequence in development quest and this pattern has the stamp of approval in growth literature. It is in this light that we will examine the emerging sectoral pattern in india's economic development. This will be examined with reference to trends in developed and developing countries.

In Table 17.1, it is clear that India has moved much ahead in respect of service sector and it is comfortably close to developed countries in this respect, but in respect of agriculture,

TABLE 17.1

Sectoral Composition : Cross–Country Data 2002

	Per Capita GDP ($)	*Agriculture share in GDP (%)*	*Industry share in GDP (%)*	*Services share in GDP (%)*
India	470	23	27	51
China	960	15	51	34
Ethiopia	100	40	12	48
Japan	34,010	1	31	68
Uganda	240	32	22	46
UK	25,510	1	26	73
US	35,400	2	23	75

Source : World Development Indicators, 2004.

things are remarkably different and India is far away from the developed countries.

The story of economic development, in terms of normal sectorial pattern, requires the share of secondary sector must grow at the cost of agriculture and only when this transformation has pushed industry to a peak, services would be poised for expansion. The expansion sector should be at the cost of a decline in the share of industry, not agriculture.

The process of development is not in evidence in India between 1980 and 2001, the share of Agriculture sector to GDP declined from 36.1 per cent to 24.7 per cent, that of industry marginally increased from 25.9 to 26.4 per cent and that of service from 36 per cent to 48.8 per cent. The Service sector can be expected to continue to show dynamism but its extent would depend on the vibrancy of Agriculture and Industry.

It is true that since Second Five Year Plan, agriculture has much headway in India and modern India has grown self sufficient in food supply, but rural economy is still repleted with unemployed labour.

The level of reval poverty continues to be very high and all evidences suggest that the incidence of rural poverty has increased in the post reform era. In fact low employment generating potential of growth in the seconday and tertiary sector has resulted in the concentration of the work force in agriculture and a persistent deterioration of relative productivity and income of workers engaged in agriculture. In 1998-99 agriculture accounted for nearly 26 per cent of GDP, but had about 60 per cent of work force engaged in it. A vast majority of unemployed labour exist in agricultural sector that industry may cheapy absorb. This calls for a realistic policy package for industrial sector but the dictates of the market and world recession stand in the way.

The continued distortions in the contours of the economy is the big challenge But a way out has to be found to bridge the gulf between different sectors of the economy unless is happens the picture of shining India on tertiary front and the suicide by farmers on agricultural front can not be reversed. The missing links between the two have to be found and unless these links are found and the gap between different sectors is bridged upon, the horizon of India's economic development shall continue to remain dim despite sparkles here and there.

CHAPTER

18

Reflections on Linkages of Real Sectors in India

DHANANJAY KUMAR

In a developing country like India where rapid economic growth has become a national goal, analysis of the sources of growth assumes special significance not only because it helps to find out what has and what has not been important in the growth which has already occurred, but also because of the obvious implications it has for the macroeconomic strategy and policies that affect the future growth—its rate as well as pattern. During the first three decades of planned economic development after independence, the main element of India's development strategy was import substitution led creating the framework of a highly regulated economy that was for all practical purposes insulated from the rest of the world. Moreover, I would also like to make an attempt to analyse the sources of growth at a less aggregated level of broad sectoral categories such as agriculture versus non-agriculture and also by the type of economic organisation. Viz., the public sector versus the private sector.

The sectoral composition of the Indian economy has undergone a structural shift over the years. The shift is perhaps best exemplified in terms of the changes in the shares of agricultural, industrial and services sector in the Gross Domestic Product (GDP). From a primarily agro-based economy during the 1970s, the Indian economy has emerged as pre dominant in the services sector during the 1990s. The shift in the composition is likely to cause substantial changes in the production and demand linkages among various sectors and in turn, could have significant ramifications for the growth and development process in the Indian economy. Experiences of the develop economies in this regard show that the growth process, in general, is highly unbalanced among sectors. Therefore, by concentrating investment on appropriate sector, the process of economic development can be accelerated.

Structural relationships among sectors in an economy are generally examined in three ways. The first and perhaps the most widely used one is based on input-output (I-O) tables, which provide valuable insights into the interdependence of various sectors. However, since preparations of these tables involve voluminous data collection, they are generally not available on an annual basis. Tables for different time periods could reveal the broad trends in structural shifts, results based on them are generally static and generally relate to the reference period. The second technique is purely statistical and involves rigorous causality tests in the growth of various sectors. In both these approaches, empirical results are generally focused on identifying the 'key' or 'causal' sectors. The third approach involves econometric models encompassing various sectors in an economy not only for identifying the key sectors, but also for generating dynamic forecasts and policy simulations.

In the Indian context, all the above techniques have been extensively used by various researchers. Among the different approaches, the I-O approach has been used by Dhawan and

Saxena (1992), statistical causality tests have been conducted by Chowdhury and Chowdhury (1995) and econometric models have been specified and estimated by a plethora of researchers [Ahluwalia and Rangarajan, 1986; Pani, 1984; Storm, 1997; Palanivel and Klein, 1999]. The above studies broadly highlight that the sectoral composition of growth has important implications in the Indian context.

In view of the economic reforms that started during the late 1980s and accelerated during the 1990s, the issue has acquired a new dimension. The economic reforms have led to substantial increase in the degree of openness in the Indian economy. However, after witnessing remarkably high and stable growth during the 1990s, the Indian economy at present is showing symptoms of recession. Though exact factors responsible for the downturn in the growth performance are yet to be identified, the general perception is that deceleration in the domestic and external demands are the major factors responsible for this retardatin. Against this backdrop, this paper attempts to analyse some of these issues by re-examining the sectoral links under alternative framework. The paper analyses the broad trends in the structural shift using an aggregated 3 x 3 I-O table consisting of agriculture, industry and services for different years.

Impact of Sectoral Linkages in India

Prior to examining the impact of sectoral linkages in the Indian economy, it would be useful to review the changes in the sectoral composition of the gross domestic product, in terms of share of agricuture, industry and services sector. Sectoral shares, at 1993-94 prices, are given in Table 18.1.

From Table 18.1, it can be seen that over the three decades (from 1970-71 to 2000-01), there is a major shift away from the agriculture towards services sector and industrial sector. Agriculture sector, which accounted for about 46 per cent of the total GDPR in 1970-71, contributed only 24 per cent by 2000-01. On the other side, during the same period the share of services sector was consistently increasing and reached 54 per cent in 2000-01 from 38 per cent in 1970-71. Over this period, share of industry increased to 22 per cent in 2000-01 from 16 per cent in

TABLE 18.1
Sectoral Composition of GDP at 1993-94 Prices

	Share in GDP (%)			
Sector	*1970-71*	*1980-81*	*1990-91*	*2000-01*
Agriculture	46.34	39.71	32.20	24.00
Industry	15.58	17.62	21.70	21.80
Services	38.07	42.66	46.09	54.20

Source: Computed from different CMIE Reports.

19970-71. It may be interesting to note that these shifts have been gradual, at least till 1990-91. During the 1990s, however, there was a sharp rise by about 8 percentage points in the share of services sector and almost a similar fall in the agricultural sector, with very little change in the share of the industrial sector. We can analyse it with the help of two tables.

Table 19.2 provides average per annum growth rate in respect of different sectors of the economy.

TABLE 18.2
Sectoral Growth Rates of GDP at 1993-94 Prices

Sector	*1980-81 over 1970-71*	*1990-91 over 1980-81*	*2000-01 over 1990-91*
Agriculture	1.49	3.42	2.68
Industry	4.35	7.84	5.82
Services	4.25	6.43	7.46
Overall GDP	3.07	5.61	5.75

Source : Computed from different CMIE Reports.

The sectoral growth pattern reflects that the performance of all the sectors was reasonably good during the 1980s, contributing to a GDPR growth of 5.6 per cent. In the 1990s, though GDPR growth was higher than the 1980s, it was driven mostly by the services sector. Industrial growth rate has been relatively high

TABLE 18.3
Growth of GSDP in Major States in the 1980s and 1990s (Annual average in per cent)

State	*1983-87/ 88*	*1987/88- 93/94*	*1993/94- 99/2000*	*1983- 93/94*	*1983- 99/2000*
Andhra Pradesh	2.63	4.91	5.28	5.21	2.27
Assam	3.03	4.15	1.95	3.83	3.20
Bihar	4.25	2.56	4.60	3.43	3.45
Delhi	10.25	7.31	9.55	9.25	7.01
Goa	4.33	8.22	10.44	7.93	8.06
Gujarat	0.20	7.33	7.16	5.69	7.03
Haryana	4.82	10.48	5.67	8.73	8.00
Himachal Pradesh	6.10	5.49	7.00	5.54	6.16
Karnataka	5.20	6.58	8.05	6.52	6.77
Kerala	4.57	7.49	5.14	6.65	6.48
Madhya Pradesh	4.26	6.56	4.93	6.45	6.10
Maharashtra	4.82	8.73	6.11	7.72	7.45
Orissa	3.31	2.80	3.53	3.95	3.44
Punjab	5.57	4.49	4.99	4.87	4.73
Rajasthan	1.78	7.87	8.43	7.37	7.49
Tamil Nadu	6.03	6.90	6.47	6.75	6.77
Uttar Pradesh	4.79	4.68	5.40	5.58	5.02
West Bengal	4.72	6.01	7.22	5.46	6.26
All-India	4.26	5.31	6.60	5.37	5.79

Source : 1. Raw data obtained from CSO.

during 1980s when agricultural growth was also relatively high at 3.42 per cent. Similarly, low growth rate in the industrial sector in the 1970s was also accompanied with low growth in agricultural sector, pointing to a close linkage between the sectors. Growth rate in services sector was only 4.25 per cent during 1970s, which increased substantially to 6.43 per cent during the 1980s and accelerated towards 7.5 per cent in the 1990s.

Growth of State Domestic Product in Pre-and Post-Reform Era

In this study examine the growth performance at both the all-India and state levels and by broad sectors, namely the primary, secondary and tertiary sectors. The analysis is done here for 18 major states. Jammu & Kashmir is excluded because of Political disturbance during the 1990s.

The all-India average growth rate for the period 1983-1993/94 stood at 5.6 per cent achieved for the 1980s, and the growth accelerated to 6.6 per cent during the period 1993/94-1999/2000. It may be seen that except for few states, viz. Assam, Bihar, Orissa and Punjab, all the other major states had recorded over 5 per cent growth during the 1983-1993/94, against the all-India growth rate of 5.37 per cent per annum. Delhi, Goa, Karnataka, Kerala, Maharashtra, Madhya Pradesh, Haryana, Tamil Nadu and Rajasthan have progressed rapidly during the 1980s with over 6 per cent per annum growth, with Delhi, Haryana, Goa, Maharashtra and Rajasthan recording the highest rate of above 7 per cent. In general, there was a comparatively balanced regional growth during the 1980s, even though the disparity widened across the states. However, the 1990s (essentially the period involving 1993/94-1999/00) belong to the relatively small and industrialised states. Highly industrialised states like Gujarat, Delhi, Goa and Rajasthan, grew at over 8 and nearly 7 per cent per annum respectively. Assam, Orissa and Bihar Continue to lag behind the all-India average. Unlike the aggregate GSDP, the sectoral growth of GSDP displays enormous fluctuations between sectors and intra-sector.

Vision of Sectoral Growth in India

Visions of sectoral growth commensurate with the overall vision of 8.5 per cent growth rate involve growth rates of 5 per cent for agriculture, 9 per cent for industry and 9.5 per cent to 10 per cent for services. In relation to the average growth rates observed during the last 15 years, the growth rates envisaged in the above vision of India's GDP growth over the next two decades imply an acceleration in the growth rates by 1.8 percentage points in agriculture, 2.5 percentage points in industry, 2 percentage points in services and 2.55 percentage points for the economy as a whole. A significant part of the higher growth of total factor input would be contributed by a faster growth of capital input resulting from an increase in the domestic saving rate from the current level of 23.5 per cent to around 28.5 per cent by 2025. While the decline in the growth rate of population envisaged in the demographic vision would lead to some reduction in the growth of labour input measured in terms of man-years especially after 2015, such a decline is likely to be more than off-set by a significant improvement in the quality of labour resulting from major changes in the skill composition of working force. Thus, the vision of 8.5 per cent GDP growth over the next two decades requires acceleration in TFP growth by 1.9 percentage points.

Conclusion

The accelerating growth of the Indian economy is presently under global discussion. To devise an appropriate strategy for accelerating the growth rate, the paper examined the linkage of growth among the agriculture, industry and services sector in the economy. Despite the substantial increase in the share of the services sector in GDPR, suggested that the agricultural sector still plays an important role in determining the overall growth rate of the economy through its linkages to the other sectors. While in the 1960s the linkage was primarily through the production channel, during the 1990s, it translates primarily through the demand channel. A small dynamic econometric model was developed to explain the interactions of different components of aggregate demand. The results and the policy simulations based on the model were, in general, consistent with the findings based on I-O table.

The study bears several important policy implications in designing an appropriate growth strategy. It highlights that the sustainability of a relatively high GDPR growth in recent years driven by growth of the services sector alone would be difficult to maintain over a long run-would be adversely affected by demand constraints and its performance would then depend upon the uncertainty in demand from the rest of the world through exports. Also, as production of services requires inputs from others sectors, there could be supply constraints due to slowdown in the growth of productive capacity in the rest of the economy.

Empirical results of the study thus highlight the need for a proper balancing of the 'inward looking' (emphasis on agriculture) and 'outward looking' (enhancing the scope of exports) strategy. The paper suggests that this two-pronged strategy could generate adequate demand leading to a sustainable high growth trajectory in the Indian economy. The important conclusion, which emerges from this study and which need to be re-emphasised is that though in the study period, the share of agriculture in GDPR has declined, its contribution in terms of generating demand for the other sectors of the economy, especially the industrial sector, has become more pronounced as reflected through the I-O table 1993-94. Even now, the agricultural sector accounting for approximately one-fourth of GDPR, supports approximately two-third of the population in the country. Thus, the policy measures, which could form part of the agenda of the second-generation reforms, should be focused on stimulating demand in the agricultural sector in rural areas by way of deepening economic activities.

References

Ahluwalia I.J. and C. Rangarajan (1986), 'Agriculture and Industry: A Study of Linkage the Indian Experience, Mimeo, *World Economic Congress of International Association*, December.

Chowdhury, K. and M.B. Chowdhury (1995), 'Sectoral Linkages and Economic Growth in Asia: Evidence from Granger Causality Test', *The Indian Economic Journal*, 42, pp. 59-75.

Dhawan, S. and K.K. Saxena, (1992), 'Sectoral Linkages and Key Sectors of the Indian Economy', *Indian Economic Review*, 37, pp. 195-210.

Palanivel, T. and L. Klein (1999), 'An Econometric Model for India with Emphasis on the Monetary Sector', The Developing Economies (XXXVII).

Storm, S. (1997), 'Domestic Constraint on Export-Led Growth: A Case-Study of India', *Journal of Development Economics*, 52, pp. 83-119.

B.B. Bhattacharya and S. Sakthivel (2003), 'Economic Reforms and Jobless Growth in India in the 1990s', *Published in The Indian Journal of Labour Economic*, Vol. 46, No. 4.

Pani, P.K. (1948), 'A Macro Model of Indian Economy with Special Reference to Output, Demand and Prices (1969-70 to 1981-82)', Reserve Bank of India, Occasional Papers, 5, pp. 113-239.

CHAPTER

19

Growth of Agriculture in the Post-Liberalisation Era

MD. TARIQUE

I. INTRODUCTION

India, which followed the socialistic pattern of development and built a vast but controlled and regulated economic system, had to follow the trends in the world trade. Though late, the National Policy of Economic Reforms and Liberalisation was announced in 1991-92. In fact, limited reforms and liberalisation had already been initiated during 80s. After signing the WTO agreement, India is bound to go for full-scale economic reforms and liberalisation of trade and commerce. Initially, economic reforms and liberalisation covered the industrial and service sectors. After the Agreement on Agriculture (AoA) under the WTO regime, we started reforms and liberalisation in the agriculture sector. From 1st April 2001, as per the AoA, all Quantitative Restrictions (QRs) have been removed.

Starting with General Agreement on Trade and Tariff (GATT) in 1947, the developed world excluding the communist block, emphasised liberal trade practices and integration of the world economy. Though the process of Liberalisation, Privatisation and Globalisation (LPG) began in sixties, it got accelerated during seventies and eighties when a majority of the developing countries joined the process. The trade liberalisation covered mainly industrial and service sectors while agriculture remained one of the most protected sectors all over the world. It was trade war between the USA and European Community in agriculture, which forced them to bring agriculture under the Uruguay Round of GATT. The signing of the Uruguay Round of GATT by all member-countries under the WTO regime in 1994 provided a legal framework for LPG.

The Agreement which paved way for the establishment of the World Trade Organisation (WTO) in place of General Agreement on Tariff and Trade (GATT) broadened the scope of operations by bringing in services, intellectual property rights and several other trade-related issues into its fold. Each country, small or big or rich or poor, has one vote. Although economically stronger nations will have a larger say in its functioning, at least theoretically, it is a democratic organization. There is also a dispute settlement body, which dispenses justice in trade disputes between countries. The most significant change between the GATT regime and WTO regime is that while it was optional to join any particular agreement emanating from a particular round of talks of GATT, a member-country has to be a party to all the 29 agreements negotiated in the Uruguay Round or else it has to leave the organization.

With the liberalisation of trade in agriculture and removal of QRs, the Indian agriculture is now exposed to the competitive environment in the global market under the WTO regime. The opportunities opened up in the new environment could be rewarding as well as threatening to farmers. In fact, the questions related to the effectiveness of AoA under the WTO regime to Indian farmers, the efficiency of Indian agriculture to face the challenges of competition in the global market, impact of Trade Related Intellectual Property Rights (TRIPs) and patenting on the accessibility to advanced farm technologies, particularly high quality seeds and plant material and other related matters are hotly debated these days. Before examining these questions it is prudent to have a look on the Agreement on Agriculture (AoA) under the WTO regime. It is in this backdrop that the present piece of writing tries to uncover the impact of trade liberalisation on Indian agriculture. The entire article is split into six sections. The first section goes to the introductory portion. The second portion analyses the agricultural performance in the post-liberalisation era. The parameters undertaken are agricultural Production, Yield and Area under cultivation. The third part compares the agricultural performance against the Tenth Five Year Plan targets. In the fourth part a comparative analysis of the pre-reform period with the post-reform period has been made. The fifth part deals with the potentialities and weaknesses of the Indian agriculture with respect to other leading economies. The sixth and the last segment goes for the concluding observations.

II. ANALYSING AGRICULTURAL PERFORMANCE IN THE POST-LIBERALISATION ERA

1. Analysing Agricultural Production

If we look at the production index of foodgrains and non-foodgrains in the post-liberalisation era we find a modest compound growth rate of 1.8 percent in the case of foodgrains, 1.6 percent for non-foodgrains; showing a marginally higher rate of growth for foodgrains. One of the reasons for the lower rate of growth has been the drought in the year 2002 as a result of which the overall agricultural growth rate was negative at –7 percent in the year 2002-03. The coefficient of variation for both foodgrains as well as non-foodgrains is similar which shows no major divergence in the production of two major categories of agricultural products. However, wheat confirms a high C.V. value (14.92) reflecting a larger degree of fluctuation in the production as against a lower value for rice (5.09). Further, the average production of rice spanning over a period of fourteen years (1991-92 to 2004-05) is also higher than that of wheat. This has resulted in frequent import of wheat by Government to meet the buffer stock requirement. The average production of foodgrains is higher than the mean non-foodgrains production over the same period. These facts are clear from the Table 19.1 and the corresponding Figure.

TABLE 19.1

Production Index (Base Triennium Ending 1993-94=100)

Year	*Rice*	*Wheat*	*Foodgrains*	*Non-Foodgrains*	*All Commodities*
1991-92	95.99	111.78	99	110	104
1992-93	93.63	114.82	104	114	109
1993-94	172.7	103.9	135.1	110.7	123
1994-95	175.9	114.2	141	118.8	130.1
1995-96	165.5	107.8	131.4	122	126.8
1996-97	175.7	120.4	145.1	130.3	137.8
1997-98	177.5	115.2	140.9	176.8	120.6
1998-99	185.1	123.8	150	131.9	141.1
1999-2000	192.9	132.6	152.9	123.8	138.5
2000-01	182.7	121	141.9	118.2	130.2
2001-02	200.7	126.3	155.3	124.6	140.1
2002-03	154.5	114.2	132.2	110.8	121.6
2003-04	189.9	125.2	153.9	128.1	141.2
2004-05	183.5	125	148.6	132.8	140.8
Mean	167.59	118.3	137.95	125.2	128.91
Standard Deviation	32.88	7.93	17.27	16.82	12.15
Co-efficient of Variation	5.09	14.92	7.99	7.45	10.61

Source : Handbook of Statistics on the Indian Economy, RBI, 2005-06. Ministry of Agriculture, Government of India.

If we take a quick look at the absolute production levels of the key components of the items viz. rice, wheat, pulses, cereals and foodgrains (Table 19.2) we see that the average production of rice, wheat, pulses, cereals and foodgrains are 82.63, 66.83, 13.12, 181.11 and 194.23 million tonnes respectively during the period 1991-92 to 2005-06. Further the coefficient of variation is also high in case of wheat (8.84) than rice (7.93) giving higher fluctuation in the production. The lowest value of C.V. is

Fig. 19.1
Comparing Production Index
(Base Triennium Ending 1993-94=100)

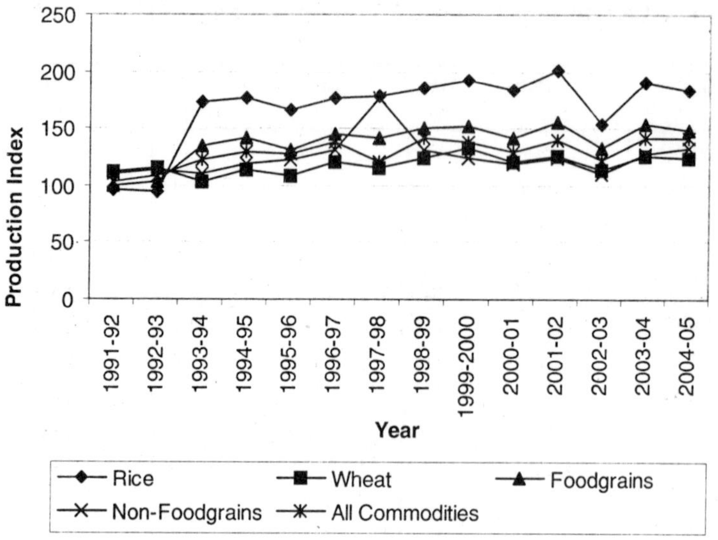

Table 19.2
Production in Million Tonnes

Year	*Rice*	*Wheat*	*Pulses*	*Total Cereals*	*Total Foodgrains*
(1)	*(2)*	*(3)*	*(4)*	*(5)*	*(6)*
1991-92	74.68	55.69	12.02	156.36	168.38
1992-93	72.86	57.21	12.82	166.66	179.48
1993-94	80.3	59.84	13.3	170.95	184.26
1994-95	81.81	65.77	14.04	177.46	191.5
1995-96	76.98	62.1	12.31	168.11	180.42
1996-97	81.74	69.35	14.26	185.19	199.44
1997-98	82.53	66.35	12.98	179.29	192.26
1998-99	86.08	71.29	14.91	188.7	203.61
1999-00	89.68	76.37	13.41	196.39	209.8

(Contd.)

TABLE 19.2 (Contd.)

(1)	*(2)*	*(3)*	*(4)*	*(5)*	*(6)*
2000-01	84.98	69.68	11.07	185.74	196.81
2001-02	93.34	72.77	13.37	199.48	212.85
2002-03	71.82	65.76	11.13	163.65	174.77
2003-04	88.53	72.15	14.91	198.28	213.19
2004-05	83.13	68.64	13.13	185.28	198.36
2005-06AE	91.04	69.48	13.11	195.19	208.3
Arithmetic Mean	82.63	66.83	13.118	181.115	194.229
Standard Deviation	6.55	5.91	1.16	13.61	14.27
Coefficient of Variation	7.93	8.84	8.84	7.51	7.35

Source : Handbook of Statistics on the Indian Economy, RBI, 2005-06.
Ministry of Agriculture, Government of India.

FIG. 19.2

Comparing Production (Million tonnes)

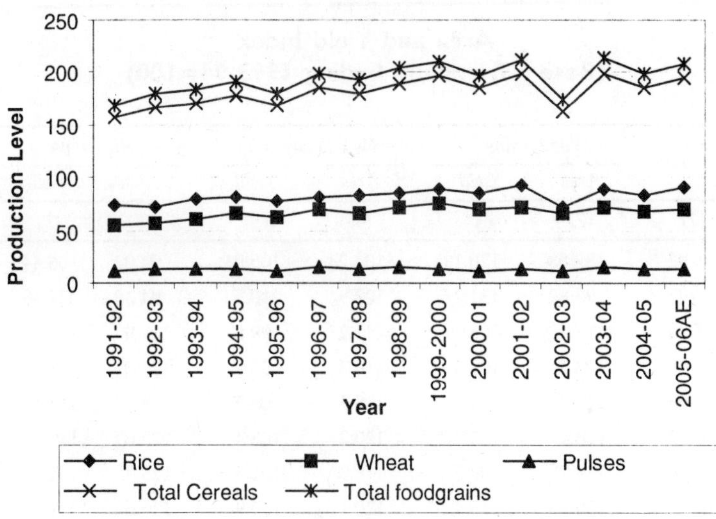

obtained for foodgrains (7.35) showing stability in the production. The highest variability in production is being found in the case of wheat and pulses with a value of 8.84. The corresponding Figure 19.2 clearly shows lesser fluctuations giving lower degree of variabilities in the production of given crops.

2. Analysing Agricultural Area under Cultivation

An analysis of the area sown index number for the foodgrains and non-foodgrains in the post-liberalisation era gives a slight growth rate of 0.16 per cent whereas the non-food grains has shown a negative growth rate of –0.38 per cent during the period 1991-92 to 2004-05. However, the growth rate in the area index for non-foodgrains during the period 1991-92 to 1998-99 showed a modest growth rate of 1.1 per cent. The average area sown during the period is higher for foodgrains as compared to the non-foodgrains. Simultaneously, the coefficient of variation is also high (11.05) for foodgrains as against a lower value for non-foodgrains (5.63). This is clear from the Table 19.3 and the corresponding figure.

TABLE 19.3
Area and Yield Index
(Base : Triennium Ending 1993-94=100)

Year	*Foodgrains*		*Non-Foodgrains*		*All Crops*	
	Area	*Yield*	*Area*	*Yield*	*Area*	*Yield*
(1)	*(2)*	*(3)*	*(4)*	*(5)*	*(6)*	*(7)*
1991-92	89.88	126.19	104.23	105.01	94.02	106.44
1992-93	90.82	131.27	102.9	110.53	94.39	111.48
1993-94	127.4	106	111.2	99.5	121.9	101
1994-95	128.8	109.5	114.3	103.9	123.8	105
1995-96	125.4	104.8	118.3	103.2	123	103.1
1996-97	128.4	113	120.2	108.4	125.6	109.7
1997-98	128.7	109.5	118.8	101.5	125.3	104.4
1998-99	130	115.4	120.1	109.9	126.6	111.4
1999-00	127.8	119.6	117.5	105.4	124.3	111.4
2000-01	125.7	112.9	114.3	103.4	121.8	106.9

(Contd.)

TABLE 19.3 (Contd.)

(1)	(2)	(3)	(4)	(5)	(6)	(7)
2001-02	127.5	121.8	114.9	108.4	122.7	114.3
2002-03	118.2	111.8	102.4	108.2	113.1	107.6
2003-04	123.7	124.4	107.4	119.1	118.4	119.3
2004-05	124.8	119.1	116.1	114.4	121.8	115.6
Arithmetic Mean	121.22	116.09	113.05	107.20	118.34	109.12
Standard Deviation	13.40	7.89	6.37	5.24	10.76	5.15
Coefficient of Variation	11.05	6.79	5.63	4.89	9.09	4.72

Source : Same as Table 19.2.

FIG. 19.3

Comparing Area and Yield Index

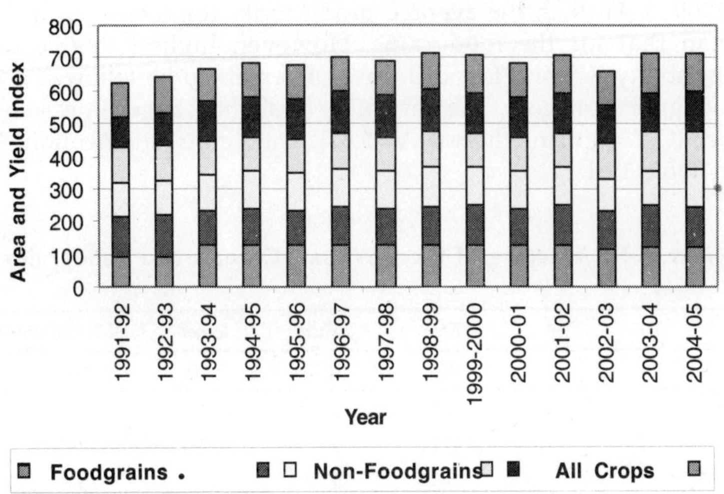

The major shift has been in the production of oilseeds, which was seen as having far reaching policy implications. But this was temporary and in recent years the import of oilseeds has increased considerably. This is mainly due to high cost of cultivation and lower international prices of oilseeds.

Analysing Agricultural Yield

While analysing the agricultural yield we find a very dismal figure in its growth in the post-liberalisation era. The compound growth rates for the foodgrains, non-foodgrains and all crops in the period 1991-92 to 2000-05 were only 1.53, 1.41 and 1.49 per cents per annum respectively as against the figures of 2.77, 3.08 and 2.89 per cents per annum respectively during the period 1951-52 to 1990-91. Though the mean yield for the period for foodgrains (116.09) is higher than the non-foodgrains (107.20), the yield growth has shown more fluctuations for foodgrains (C.V. is 6.79) than non-foodgrains (C.V. is 4.89). However, the average yield for all crops has increased with highest degree of consistency (C.V. is 4.72). These facts are clear from the Table 19.3 and the corresponding Figure.

If we look at the yield figures in terms of Kg./hectares as shown in Table 19.4 and the corresponding figure, highest mean value is obtained for wheat (2584.71) to be followed by rice (1900.5). Further, the average productivity for cereals is more than that for the foodgrains. However, highest degree of variability is being found in case of cereals to be followed by foodgrains category. The variability is slightly larger in case of rice (C.V.=6) than wheat (C.V.=5.81). The figures are mentioned in Table 19.4.

TABLE 19.4

Yield in Kg./Hectare of Rice, Wheat, Cereals and Foodgrains

Year	*Rice*	*Wheat*	*Cereals*	*Total Foodgrains*
(1)	*(2)*	*(3)*	*(4)*	*(5)*
1991-92	1751	2394	1574	1382
1992-93	1744	2327	1654	1457
1993-94	1888	2380	1701	1501
1994-95	1911	2559	1760	1546
1995-96	1797	2483	1703	1491
1996-97	1882	2679	1831	1614
1997-98	1900	2485.	1776	1552

(Contd.)

TABLE 19.4 (Contd.)

(1)	*(2)*	*(3)*	*(4)*	*(5)*
1998-99	1921	2590	1856	1627
1999-00	1986	2778	1926	1704
2000-01	1901	2708	1844	1626
2001-02	2079	2762	1980	1734
2002-03	1744	2610	1753	1535
2003-04	2077	2713	1987	1731
2004-05	2026	2718	1930	1703
Mean	1900.5	2584.71	1805.36	1585.93
Standard Deviation	114.07	150.23	124.58	109.01
Coefficient of Variation	6	5.81	6.9	6.87

Source : Handbook of Statistics on the Indian Economy, RBI, 2005-06. Ministry of Agriculture, Government of India.

FIG. 19.4
Comparing Yield Performance

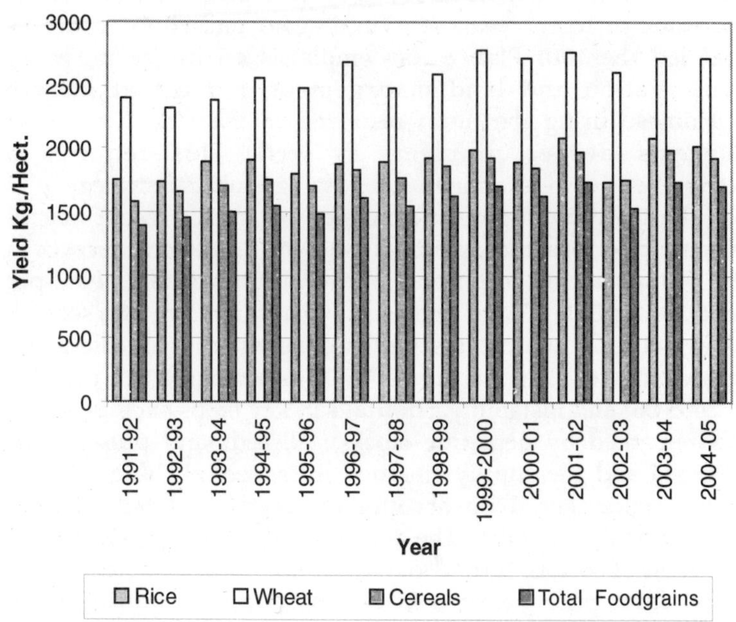

III. COMPARING THE PERFORMANCE AGAINST TENTH FIVE YEAR PLAN TARGETS

Though Tenth Five-Year Plan had targeted Gross Domestic Product (GDP) growth in agriculture and allied sectors at 4 per cent per annum, aiming to reverse a sharp deceleration in the second half of the 1990s from 3.2 per cent per annum in the period 1980-81 to 1995-96 to 1.9 per cent per annum during 1996-97 to 2001-02, this has not been achieved. Drought conditions caused agriculture GDP to fall by seven per cent in the first year of the 10th plan (2002-03) and, despite a smarter rebound by 9.6 per cent in the second year (2003-04), growth in the first two years of the plan averaged only 0.9 per cent per annum. With the monsoon weak in 2004, agricultural growth in 2004-05 will be modest at best, being placed at 1.1 per cent according to advance GDP estimates. On this basis, GDP growth in agriculture and allied sectors during the first three years of the 10th plan averages only 1 per cent per annum. The 10th plan target of 4 per cent growth is therefore, far from being realised. In fact, per capita agricultural GDP shows no significant upward trend after 1996-97, only fluctuations. The erratic monsoon in recent years has once again underlined concerns that led the 10th Plan to lay emphasis on irrigation, water conservation and land management, but actual growth outcomes during the ninth plan and in the 10th Pan so far suggests deeper problems as well. This requires a comprehensive re-examination of the agricultural strategy.

Further, the optimism generated by India's recent macro-economic performance which has shown 10.2 per cent growth in the manufacturing sector and an overall growth rate of 9.2 per cent during 2006-07, has been somewhat marred by the setback to agriculture which has suffered substantial deceleration (growth rate of 2.7 per cent in 2006-07 as compared to 6 per cent in 2005-06) and instability. Shortfalls in key crops such as wheat (accompanied by depleting stocks), oilseeds and pulses have emerged and the supply situation in respect of these crops is further endangered on account of weather-related adverse international conditions. The decline in the global production of wheat in 2006 has turned out to be the largest in ten years. Apart from poor harvests in key producing countries, their carry over stocks are declining and cereal acreage is losing out to the fast growing demand for bio-fuel production. Alongside, in the domestic economy, infrastructural bottlenecks are tightening. Managing the supply situation is emerging as a formidable challenge. In the current scenario, limitations on the supply response to the momentum of growth are showing up as excess demand pressures.

Growth of input use in agriculture also decelerated after 1996-97, to about 2% per annum from over 2.5 per cent during 1980-97. The second mainly after 1997-98 when, reversing an earlier trend, output prices began to fall relative to input prices.

Part of the deceleration in agricultural growth can, therefore, be attributed to lower profitability leading to slower increase in input use. But, in addition, growth of input productivity (defined as difference between output and input growth) fell from about 1 per cent per annum prior to negligible thereafter.

The 10th plan foodgrains target was modest. It aimed to meet a requirement of 230 million tonnes in 2006-07, estimated on the basis of nutritional norms and about the same in per capita terms as actual production of 212.9 million tonnes in 2001-02. Nonetheless, actual performance is well below this. Drought caused foodgrains output to fall to 174.2 million tonnes in 2002-03, and the subsequent recovery to 212.1 million tonnes in 2003-04 remained below the level of 2001-02. The second advance estimate for 2004-05 places kharif production at only 102.9 million tonnes, about 9% lower than in 2003-04. Although rabi is expected to be much better, overall foodgrains production in 2004-05 is unlikely to cross the 2001-02 level. In 2002-03, the first year of the Tenth Plan, monsoon failure caused production to decline further to 15.1 million tonnes. There was a rebound to record 25.1 million tonnes in 2003-04, but growth continues to be negligible. In the current year, 2004-05, there has again been a marginal fall in output.

This poor performance is more worrying in view of the fact that the underlying trend of rice and wheat production was already less than population growth by the end of the Ninth Plan. Yield growth decelerated throughout the 1990s to only about 1 per cent per annum from 3 per cent during the 1980s, indicating a potentially serious exhaustion of technological progress. The huge stocks that emerged at end of the 1990s have so far masked this. But, since large exports at below domestic prices and subsequent poor monsoons have now reduced stocks to almost normal, a significant production effort is necessary to meet requirement. For this, it will be essential to tap potential of the Eastern region, in part by ensuring adequate price support and removing distortions that have recently depressed prices in this region because of sale from stocks built-up from traditional surplus areas through high Minimum Support Prices (MSP).

Unlike rice and wheat, yield growth of coarse cereals was maintained at about 2 per cent per annum through the 1990s, mainly because of good performance in maize. However, except maize, area shifted from coarse cereals to other crops and, as a result, there was no growth in total coarse cereals output. Pulses yields continued to stagnate although these crops have been under a Technology Mission since early 1990s, and the area under cultivation has also shrunk. Despite some promising new varieties and proven benefits from micronutrients and sprinkler irrigation, there is as yet no breakthrough at the farm level. Although the MSP of pulses have been increased recently to encourage technology adoption, it is the view of the Commission for Agricultural Costs and Prices (CACP) that a sharp increase in imports has blunted this effort.

Oilseeds have been under a Technology Mission since 1986 and there was substantial expansion of area, yield and production till the mid-1990s. But in the absence of technological breakthrough and because of pressure from cheaper imports, the Ninth Plan period saw stagnation in yield and decline in area, taking production down from 24.4 million tones in 1996-97 to 20.7 million tonnes in 2001-02. In 2002-03, the first year of the Tenth Plan, monsoon failure caused production to decline further to 15.1 million tonnes. There was a rebound to a record 25.1 million tonnes in 2003-04, but growth continues to be negligible. In the current year, 2004-05, there has again been a marginal fall in output.

Imports of edible oils were less than 10 per cent of domestic production till 1994-95, but have since increased sharply so that import volumes are now at par with domestic production. Rising domestic demand, trade liberalisation and a sharp fall in world edible oils prices in the late 1990s contributed to this rise in imports. Domestic prices of edible oils/oilseeds remained low and were disincentives to domestic producers. India is already among the largest markets for global edible oils trade, and productivity improvements are required for domestic oilseeds production to remain competitive. This calls for a fresh look at the working of the Technology Mission on Oilseeds and Pulses (TMOP), which appears to be failing in its objectives.

Cotton production had also fared poorly during the Ninth Plan. Yields declined due to a combination of lower prices and increased pest incidence following rapid price induced area expansion in the previous decade. Output fell from 14.2 million bales in 1996-97 to 10 million bales in 2001-02. Drought caused production to fall further in 2002-03, to 8.7 million bales, the lowest since 1987-88. Although this recovered to 13.8 million bales in 2003-04, production remained lower than reached in 1996-97. The second advance estimate for 2004-05 however shows substantial increase to 17.1 million bales. Nonetheless, India's cotton economy continues to suffer from well-known problems causing low yield and poor quality. It is also well known that, if these problems are addressed, very large gains are possible with end of the Multi-Fibre Agreement. In view of this, a Technology Mission on Cotton (TMC) was launched in February 2000 and approval given for cultivation of Bt varieties. With limited results from these efforts thus far, mills are importing larger quantities of quality cotton. There is an urgent need to re-look the TMC and, in particular, to involve the textile industry more closely on cotton technology.

Sugarcane production increased at about 1.5 per cent per annum during the Ninth Plan, from 278 million tonnes in 1996-97 to 297 million tonnes in 2001-02. But this was entirely on account of area expansion, with yield growth decelerating to almost nil from about 2 per cent per annum in the previous decade. In the Tenth Plan period, production fell to 282 million tonnes in 2002-03 and again, more sharply, to 236 million tonnes in 2003-04. The second advance estimates for 2004-05 indicate further marginal decline. Recovery of sugar from sugarcane has also not increased much during the last decade. This twin failure on yield and recovery points to weakness on the part of industry to leverage research and extension, make available good planting material, propagate better agronomic practices and improve crushing efficiency. Although Indian cane yields are relatively high and cost of cane production relatively low by world standards, Indian sugar was unable to compete in the world market when world prices crashed in 1998. This is despite the fact that levy obligations on mills were reduced sharply and licensing eased. Very large sugar stocks built up as production expanded much more than domestic demand in response to liberalisation of industry and excessive State Advised Prices. The main concern now is whether the large subsequent downturn indicates a return to the high amplitude cane cycles that were moderated during the 1980s and 1990s or whether industry will emerge more efficient out of the downturn. Issues such as use of ethanol in automobile fuel and of profitable cogeneration of electricity are important in this context.

To summarise, almost every sector experienced lower growth after 1996-97 than in the previous decade and a half. The magnitude of deceleration was such that although 2003-04 was a year of excellent monsoon and record production, per capita output in that year was less than 1996-97 in every crop sector except horticulture. Underlying this was productivity deceleration across all sectors, implying lower cost reduction through technological progress than earlier. The deceleration coincided with a downturn in world prices, and this impacted domestic farm prices more than in earlier decades because of greater openness. The consequence was that farm incomes became more variable and decelerated more than output in many cases.

IV. AGRICULTURAL PRODUCTION : A COMPARATIVE ANALYSIS WITH THE PRE-REFORM ERA

The annual compound growth rate in area, production and yield of major crops during the 1980s and 1990s is given in Table 19.5. A comparison of agriculture performance in the Nineties *versus* Eighties shows that there was a decelerating trend in the yield of almost every crop in the Nineties. The only silver lining was a trend towards greater diversification of agriculture during this decade. Amongst foodgrains, wheat has maintained high annual growth, though some deceleration is noticed in the 1990s because of productivity levels having plateau in Punjab and Haryana. Rice and Wheat production taken together, recorded an annual growth of 2.27 per cent in the 1990s compared to 3.59 per cent in the 1980s. Pulse and coarse cereals have recorded little or no growth in the 1980s and in the 1990s. Some area expansion observed under non-food crops in the 1990s is attributable mainly to the growth in the area under cotton and sugarcane, perhaps at the cost of shrinkage in area under coarse cereals. However, the growth in yield of non-food crops in the 1990s has been lower than that in the 1980s.

A look at the Table 19.5 clearly shows that there has been a deceleration in the production and yield of almost every crop during 1990s as compared to 1980s. Then the question arises that why should we go for the process of liberalisation and globalisation in the agriculture sector?

TABLE 19.5

Annual Compound Growth of Crop Area, Production and Productivity

(Percent)

Crop	*1980-81 to 1989-90*			*1990-91 to 2000-01*		
	Area	*Production*	*Yield*	*Area*	*Production*	*Yield*
Rice and Wheat	0.43	3.59	3.15	0.84	2.27	1.42
Rice	0.41	3.62	3.19	0.63	1.79	1.16
Wheat	0.47	3.57	3.10	1.21	3.04	1.81
Coarse Cereal	-1.34	0.40	1.62	-1.84	0.06	1.65
Pulses	-0.09	1.52	1.61	-1.20	-0.58	0.27
Total Foodgrains	-0.23	2.85	2.74	-0.20	1.66	1.34
Non-Food Crops	1.12	3.77	2.31	0.84	1.86	0.59
Oilseeds	-1.51	5.20	2.43	0.44	0.66	0.61
Sugar Cane	1.44	2.70	1.24	1.72	2.62	0.89
Cotton	-1.25	2.80	4.10	2.21	0.92	-1.26
All Crops	0.10	3.19	2.56	0.08	1.73	1.02

Source : *Economic Survey*, 2001-02.

Globalisation in the context of agriculture can be best discussed in the context of three components:

(a) Improvement of productive efficiency by ensuring the convergence of potential and realized output,
(b) Increase in agricultural exports and value added activities using agricultural produce, and finally,
(c) Improved access to domestic and international markets that are either tightly regulated or are overly protected.

These components are linked in various ways. For example, productive efficiency would enhance value added activities in agriculture through agro-processing and exports of agricultural and agro-based products. These activities in turn would increase income and employment in the industrial processing sector. Thus globalising agriculture has the potential to transform subsistence agriculture to commercialized agriculture and to improve the living conditions of the rural community. However, economic reforms within India are necessary to pave the path to successful globalisation. The stated objective of the new economic policy is to raise the economy's growth rate from the current 5.5 per cent achieved over 15 years to about 7 or 8 per cent per year. Ahluwalia (1996)[2] explains that this indirectly requires an improvement in agricultural growth from between 2 and 3 per cent in the past to about 4 per cent per year. Although initially, with respect to agriculture, there was no major policy reform package in the 1990s, it was however anticipated that the opening-up of the agricultural sector to foreign trade, the move to a market determined exchange rate and reduction of protection for industry would, over time, benefit the agricultural sector.

(a) Productivity Gains from Globalisation and Economic Reforms

In the wake of India's efforts towards globalisation and economic reforms, the expected benefits of Total Factor Productivity (TFP)[3] growth can be represented using the production frontier. The production frontier traces out the maximum output obtainable from the use of inputs. In the Figure 19.5, F_1 and F_2 are the production possibility frontiers in time 1 and 2 respectively. Opportunities from globalisation and economic reforms can lead to:

(a) Shift from A to B due to technical efficiency.
(b) Shift from B to C on existing frontier due to input growth.
(c) Upward shift from C to D due to technological progress.

FIG. 19.5

Total Factor Productivity Gains from Globalisation and Economic Reforms

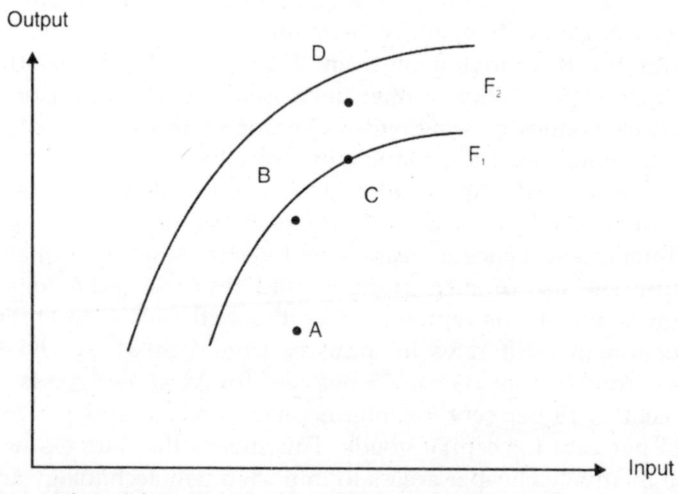

Source : Adapted from Mahadevan and Kalirajan (1999).

Each of the below mentioned shifts, which constitute various sources of TFP growth, can be linked with trade gains. The movement from A to B led by technical efficiency allows increases in output when inputs and technology are used to their fullest potential to obtain the greatest yield. Given that India has been involved in agricultural production for so long, there would be learning-by-doing gains that can help boost production given the expected increase in demand as India opens up. The increased production would enable a better utilization of inputs, especially that of advanced capital technology. The reduction in the tariff rate for agricultural products from 113 per cent in 1990-91 to 26 per cent in 1997-98 is also expected to motivate local producers into rethinking their production techniques and efficiently utilizing the inputs and technology to keep costs of production down in order to remain competitive. The optimum or efficient use of land and water resources would then allow agriculture to respond to the demand for other products such as horticulture and livestock which is expected to increase following a rising trend in the per capita incomes of both rural and urban groups. The move from an overvalued exchange rate to that of a market determined rate would also make agricultural exports cheaper and hence boost exports. The new trading opportunities would necessitate an increased use in the quantity of inputs to boost output and this allows for the movement from B to C along the existing production possibility frontier. Increased exports would bring about economies of scale and as Verdoon's law states, output growth would lead to productivity growth.

The scale of output under increased exports would justify the huge fixed costs underlying technologically advanced equipment and hence increase incentives to adopt high quality inputs. The use of such inputs would result in technological progress and this is represented by the shift from C to D. The reduction in tariff rates in industry from 1990-91 to 1997-98 range from 153 per cent to 25 per cent for consumer goods, 77 per cent to 18 per cent for intermediate goods and 97 per cent to 24 per cent for capital goods. This means that farmers now have relatively cheaper access to imported new technology and better capital equipment as well as the option of adopting better farming techniques and this should lead to technological progress. In particular, the development of agro-processing as an instrument for agricultural and rural modernisation will bring benefits, given its capital-intensive and technology-intensive nature. Lower duty rates on plastics and metals also lower costs of packaging. These forms of cost efficiency should allow competitive pricing of products. In addition, external competition can be expected to motivate local producers into the production of improved quality intermediate inputs for agriculture.

The importance of technology in agricultural development was first demonstrated in the 1970s with impressive growth in yields following the introduction of new wheat and rice varieties. But this technology was limited to areas of assured irrigation, as the new seeds also required heavy inputs of fertilizers and pesticides for optimal results. However, the potential for further extending this technology is not yet exhausted, as there is scope for expanding irrigation further and improving the quality of irrigation in many areas. For further technological progress, genetic engineering and the biotechnology revolution provides a prospect of developing new varieties that can flourish with less dependence on water and chemical inputs. Such reduced dependence upon chemical fertilizers and pesticides is also desirable because of environmental considerations, which are an increasing concern. It must however be acknowledged that the link between trade liberalisation and productivity growth is two-way as they both feed on each other. The above discussion has shown how productivity gains can be obtained from openness but to benefit from openness via increased demand for exports, agricultural products need to be priced competitively. In other words, productivity growth is necessary to lower the costs of production.

(b) Increase in Agricultural Exports and Value-added Activity

The expected increase in exports due to liberalisation simply did not occur. India's share in world exports was 0.6 per cent in 1997; India has to aim for at least 4 per cent by 2005 in order to meet the growing import demands for capital goods, raw materials and crude oil as well as to meet her external financial commitments.[4] For the last decade or so, India's share in world exports of agriculture has been between 2 per cent and 3 per cent. Furthermore, as Table 19.3 shows, India is not as competitive as the other countries and calculations show that India's crop yields have increased at a slower rate over the 1990s.

In addition, the agricultural sector's output growth decreased from 3.19 per cent during 1980s to 1.73 percent during 1990s. Kalirajan and others (2001) explain that two important reasons for the slowdown are that there was no major breakthrough in developing new high-yielding varieties during the 1990s and there was a decline in the environmental quality of land, which reduced the marginal productivity of the modern inputs. What could this mean in terms of the effectiveness of the policies of reduced protection to industry, a market determined exchange rate and the opening of the agricultural sector to foreign trade?

First, although the reduction to protection of industry is substantial, there is reason to believe that the reduction was not necessarily sufficient to benefit the agricultural sector whose tariffs were also drastically reduced. Hence, the expected shift in resources to agriculture did not occur. Second, is the apparent ineffectiveness of the market-determined exchange rate in boosting exports? This is however not surprising as the exchange rate may not be a key factor determining agricultural exports demand for India. In general, unlike manufacturing industries, agriculture did not benefit much from these two policies because the share of imported inputs in the value of agricultural production is small. It is likely that a change in the mindset and attitude of farmers has yet to take place and there are delays or hesitation in embracing India's openness. Third, in opening-up the agricultural sector to foreign trade, India has taken major steps towards trade liberalisation since 1991, partly on its own initiative and partly from its commitments to WTO. But why have the benefits from trade liberalisation been slow to come?

One reason is that prospects for growth in agricultural exports depend partly on domestic policies and partly on the removal of protectionist policies pursued by developed countries such as Japan and members of the European Union (EU). An OECD report (1998)[5] estimated that the producer equivalent subsidy in the OECD countries increased by US $ 9.3 billion from 1988 to 1993 and this subsidy as a percentage of the value of production in 1997 was 9 per cent in Australia, 20 per cent in Canada, 47 per cent in EU and 70 per cent in Japan. These protectionist practices do not seem likely to come to an early end. An UNCTAD report (1999)[6] noted that 29 member countries of the OECD spent an average of US $ 350 billion a year in agricultural support during 1996-98. Schumacher (2000)[7] further reports that the EU provides product-specific trade distorting domestic support to at least 50 different agricultural products. The implication of these reports is that food exports from India may not show a large increase given the international environment and the still-existing restrictions on exports in the major importing markets based on the self-sufficiency argument and food security. Other macro-economic factors, such as the recession in developed countries in 1996-98 as well as the 1997 South-East Asian financial crisis have clouded the possibilities of increasing Indian exports.

(c) Access to Domestic and International Markets

Another problem faced by Indian agricultural exporters is the protectionist measures in the form of non-trade barriers that developed countries use to restrict market access. This is by tightening requirements of quality, testing and labelling, and anti-dumping and countervailing measures. For example, in May 1997, the EU banned marine products from India citing unhygienic processing conditions. The extra costs of meeting the standards required in export markets as well as costs associated with changes in the production mix and transactions associated with exports may well be discouraging Indian exporters.

One existing problem of India's agricultural protection is the use of input subsidies. The general argument favouring this has been that it is necessary to encourage the use of particular inputs for production for various benefits. For India, Gulati and Sharma (1995)[8] show that the input subsidy in percent of GDP increased from 2.13 in the triennium ending 1982-83 to 2.73 in the triennium ending 1992-93. The total food subsidies were at a staggering level of Rs. 252 billions, 5.31 per cent of Central Government expenditure. But the benefits of these subsidies have accrued to only certain classes of farmers in some regions cultivating irrigated crops. Furthermore, highly subsidized prices of inputs such as irrigation water and electricity for pump sets have encouraged cultivation of water-intensive crops, over-use of water, ground water depletion/salinity and water logging in many areas. Subsidy for nitrogen fertilizer on the other hand has resulted in nitrogen phosphorous potassium imbalance and acted as a disincentive for use of the environmentally friendly organic manure. As a result, the linkage between food crops and non-food crops, which include fodder, has been reduced. These adverse consequences are a drain on the fiscal burden of central and state Governments. Thus, if not properly monitored, input subsidies can be counter-productive and, in this context, protection to lower costs of production should be done selectively in the course of liberalisation.

In fact, Agenda 21 of the United Nations Conference on Environment and Development in 1992 stressed that there is a need for integration of environmental considerations in the pricing of natural and other resources in such a way that prices reflect social costs. Such a pricing policy will not only lead to a more efficient use of scarce resources but also result in subsidy reductions and improvements in environmental quality. The money saved from the reduction of subsidies can be spent in the development of rural infrastructures, agricultural research, farmers' education and other forms of support for agriculture.

Although India missed the opportunity to open up two decades ago, its attempts to do so now must be regarded as better late than never. Others such as Desai (1999)[9] observe that, "the logic of the global economy as well as India's interests dictate that India becomes proactive in its liberalisation policies. India must liberalise not because it has no choice but because it is the best choice". His lament that India has adopted a 'victim mentality' when it really needs to adopt a 'winner mentality' has become less of a concern as over time, India has shown commitment to stay on the bandwagon of globalisation. Having realised that globalisation is a necessary but not a sufficient condition for high growth production; India has undertaken economic reforms, both internal and external. However, it must be ensured that these reforms are synchronised so that the pace of both reforms is set right in order to work hand in hand to promote agricultural productivity growth.

V. COMPARING INDIAN AGRICULTURE POTENTIALS INTERNATIONALLY

On the basis of above-mentioned facts we find that all is not well with regard to the performance of the Indian agriculture in the post-liberalization and WTO era. The reasons are various bottlenecks faced by the Indian agriculture.

However, if we compare the growth rates of various indices as mentioned in Table 19.6, we find a silver lining in the tunnel as the growth rates of these indices in India are higher than the growth rates in other leading economies.

A comparative study of some of the other countries in the world with that of India clearly explain how much India lags behind with respect to the variables like crop production index, food production index, livestock production index, cereal yield and agricultural productivity in both pre and post-liberalisation era (Table 19.6). India is even behind civil war devastated country, Sri Lanka in terms of crop production index, cereal yield and agricultural productivity in both pre and post liberalisation era. The agricultural productivity in Sri Lanka in 1979-81 was 2.38 times, and even in 2000-02 it is 1.8 times higher than India. In terms of food and livestock production index though Sri Lanka was in a better position in 1979-81, India has improved with a higher value in the post-liberalisation era in 2000-02. China was below India in terms of crop production index, food production index and livestock production index in the pre-reform era, but after making a spectacular performance in the post-liberalisation era, it is not only far ahead of India but also even in a better position than many developed countries in terms of these indices. The crop production index during the mentioned period has increased at a compound rate per annum in China by 4.08 percent, in Australia by 3.11 percent, in India by 2.7 percent, more than the increase in world average by 2.45 percent. An impressive compound growth rate is seen for food production index (livestock production index) with the figures of 3.19 per cent (4.2%) in India against 5.46 per cent (7.96%) in China, 2.01 per cent (1.4%) in Australia, 1.24 per cent (1.39%) in U.S., almost zero (–0.25%) in U.K., and 2.5 per cent (1.71%) as world average. The cereal yield (kg./hectare) was just 25 per cent of Japan in the pre-liberalisation era but increased to 40.65 per cent in the post-liberalisation era. The value is 35 per cent of U.K. value, highest in the table in the post liberalisation era. However, the compound growth rate in productivity shows a dismal figure. It is just 1.92 percent per annum in India as against 4.8 per cent in Canada and 4.67 per cent in United States.

On the basis of above analysis we find that India has done well in terms of the growth rates of various indices (except

TABLE 19.6
Agricultural Output and Productivity

Country	Crop Production Index[11]		Food Production Index[12]		Livestock Production Index[13]		Cereal Yield[14]		Agricultural Productivity[15]	
	1989-91=100						Kilogram per hectare		Agriculture value added per worker 1995 $	
	1979-81	2000-02	1979-81	2000-02	1979-81	2000-02	1979-81	2000-02	1979-81	2000-02
(1)	(2)	(3)	(4)	(5)	(6)	(7)	(8)	(9)	(10)	(11)
Australia	79.9	152.2	91.3	138.8	85.6	116.1	1,321	1,758	20,872	36,327
Canada	77.6	106.7	79.7	123.5	88.3	142.2	2,173	2,521	16,002	43,064
China	67.1	155.6	60.8	185.9	45.4	226.7	3,027	4,845	161	338
India	70.9	124.2	68.2	131.8	62.6	149.8	1,324	2,390	269	401
Japan	108.3	87.1	94.1	91.6	85.1	93.2	5,252	5,879	17,378	33,077
Sri Lanka	99.3	114.8	98.1	117.2	92.0	147.7	2,462	3,520	642	725
U.K.	80.1	97.2	92.2	92.4	98.1	93.1	4,792	6,841	20,326	32,918
U.S.	98.6	118.3	94.5	122.5	89.0	123.6	4,151	5,830	20,672	53,907
World	79.1	131.5	78.8	133.1	79.6	136.4	1,605	2,233	—	—

Source : World Development Indicators. 2004.

productivity index), the country lags far behind if given a look at the absolute figures. Some of the reasons for these lower absolute values and a dismal compound rate of increase in the overall productivity level are:

- The arable land in India in 1999-01 is just 0.16 hectare/capita as against the values of 2.58 in Australia and 1.48 in Canada.
- The irrigated land, as percentage of cropland is just 32.2 per cent in India as compared to 54.7 per cent in Japan and 40.7 per cent in Australia during 1999-01.
- The fertilizer consumption (hundreds of grams per hectare of arable land) is merely 1074 in India in comparison to the values of 3162 for Japan and 2170 for European Union.

If we compare the use of agricultural machinery in terms of the availability of tractors per 100 square Kms. of arable land it is merely 94 in India against the figures of 4601 in Japan and 984 in European Union.[10]

VI. CONCLUSION

In conclusion we can say that India has a large and diverse agricultural sector. Its contribution to total GDP was 52.5 per cent in the early 1950s, which has come down to 19.6 per cent of GDP in 2003. Arable land area is the second largest in the world (after the United States), and irrigated crop area is the largest in the world. In the last five decades, the Government's objectives in agricultural policy and the instruments used to realize the objectives have changed from time to time, depending on both internal and external factors.

The compound growth rate in the agricultural sector in the post-liberalisation era can be summarized in the Table 19.7.

The data for growth rates in area, production and yield shows overall dismal figures for Indian economy in the post-liberalisation era. Rice and pulses have shown negative growth rates in terms of area sown. Though the figure for wheat is positive, data for all the commodities taken together gives a negative trend. In terms of production and yield, oilseeds have

TABLE 19.7
Growth Rates in Area, Production and Yield (1990-91 to 2003-04)

	Area	*Production*	*Yield*
Foodgrains	-0.22	1.35	1.30
Wheat	0.75	2.08	1.78
Rice	-0.06	1.19	1.26
Pulses	-0.08	0.51	0.71
Non-Foodgrains	-0.06	1.67	1.03
Oilseeds	0.53	2.05	1.59
Sugarcane	0.62	-0.17	-0.28
All Commodities	-0.18	1.47	1.21

given good results but this has been mainly due to groundnut (3.2% increase in yield) whereas the yield of rapeseed and mustard increased just by 1.2 per cent and production by just 0.84 per cent. Oilseeds have been under a Technology Mission since 1986 and there was substantial expansion of area, yield and production till the mid-1990s. But in the absence of technological breakthrough and because of pressure from cheaper imports, the Ninth Plan period saw stagnation in yield and decline in area, taking production down from 24.4 million tonnes in 1996-97 to 20.7 million tonnes in 2001-02.

An analysis of the annual compound growth rate in area, production and yield of major crops during the 1980s and 1990s shows that there was a decelerating trend in the yield of almost every crop in the Nineties. The only silver lining was a trend towards greater diversification of agriculture during this decade. In such situation the basic question that arises in ones mind is why should India go for liberalisation and globalisation? The answer to this lies in three facts—improvement of productive efficiency by ensuring the convergence of potential and realised output, increase in agricultural exports and value-added activities using agricultural produce, and finally, improved access to domestic and international markets that are either tightly regulated or are overly protected. The inflexible attitude adopted by India since independence strength the logic that although we missed the opportunity to open up two decades ago, our attempts to do so now must be regarded as better late than never. India must liberalise not because it has no choice but because it is the best choice. A common apprehension that India has adopted a 'victim mentality' when it really needs to adopt a 'winner mentality' has become less of a concern as over time, India has shown commitment to stay on the bandwagon of globalisation. Having realised that globalisation is a necessary but not a sufficient condition for high growth in production; India has undertaken economic reforms, both internal and external. However, it must be ensured that these reforms are synchronised so that the pace of both reforms is set right in order to work hand in hand to promote agricultural productivity growth and definitely India will be a net gainer in the long-run. Therefore, India must liberalise not because it has no choice but because it is the best choice. India has successfully set sail on the waters of globalisation and economic reforms and even in the wake of economic and political instability, she has to carefully steer her course in order to reap the benefits of increased productivity growth in the agricultural sector.

Notes and References

1. Ahluwalia, M.S. (1996), "New Economic Policy and Agriculture: Some Reflections", *Indian Journal of Agricultural Economics*, Vol. 51, No. 3, pp. 412-26.
2. TFP growth is productivity growth related to the use of all inputs in production and is given by the residual of output growth not accounted for by input growth.
3. Kalirajan, K.P., G. Mythili and U. Sankar, eds. (2001), *Accelerating Growth Through Globalisation of Indian Agriculture*, Macmillan, India.
4. OECD (1998), *Agricultural Policies in OECD Countries* (Paris).
5. UNCTAD (1999), *Trade and Development Report*, Geneva.
6. Schumacher, Jr., A. (2000), "International Agricultural Trade At A Crossroads", *Economic Perspectives, An Electronic Journal of the US Department of* State, March 2000.
7. Gulati, A., and A.N. Sharma (1995), "Subsidy Syndrome in Indian Agriculture", *Economic and Political Weekly*, 30 September 1995.
8. Desai, M., (1999), "What should be India's economic priorities in a globalized world?", Indian Council for Research on International Economic Relations, New Delhi.
9. The analysis is based on the data obtained from World Development Indicators, 2004.

10. Shows agricultural production for each period relative to the base period 1989-91. It includes all crops except fodder crops. The regional and income group aggregates for the FAO's production indexes are calculated from the underlying values in International Dollars, normalized to the base period 1989-91. The data in this table are three years average.
11. Covers food crops that are considered edible and that contain nutrients. Coffee and tea are excluded because, although edible, they have no nutritive value.
12. Includes meat and milk from all sources, dairy products such as chese, eggs, honey, raw silk, wool and hides and skins.
13. Measured in kilogram per hectare of harvested land, includes wheat, rice, maize, barley, oats, rye, millet, sorghum, buckwheat, and mixed grains. Production data on cereals refer to crops harvested for dry grain only. Cereal crops harvested for hay or harvested green for food, feed, or silage, and those used for grazing, are excluded.
14. Refers to the ratio of agricultural value-added, measured in constant 1995 U.S. dollars, to the number of workers in agriculture.

Index